MICHAEL SIMKINS has appeared in more than 100 plays and musicals, from the National Theatre and the RSC to the fringe and the West End. He's made countless TV appearances, usually as policemen or unsuspecting husbands, as well as turns on the silver screen in such films as Mike Leigh's *Topsy-Turvy* and *The Iron Lady*. His memoir about breaking into the acting profession, *What's My Motivation?*, has become required reading among drama graduates anxious to discover what the business is really like. He is also the author of *Fatty Batter*, *Detour de France* and *The Last Flannelled Fool*. He lives with his actress wife, Julia Deakin, in London.

Also by Michael Simkins:

What's My Motivation?

Fatty Batter

Detour de France

The Last Flannelled Fool

THE RULES OF ACTING

MICHAEL SIMKINS

EBURY
PRESS

1 3 5 7 9 10 8 6 4 2

This edition published 2014
First published in 2013 by Ebury Press, an imprint of Ebury Publishing
A Random House Group company

The Random House Group Limited Reg. No. 954009

Addresses for companies within the Random House Group can be found at
www.randomhouse.co.uk

A CIP catalogue record for this book is available from the British Library

The Random House Group Limited supports the Forest Stewardship
Council® (FSC®), the leading international forest-certification organisation.
Our books carrying the FSC label are printed on FSC®-certified paper.
FSC is the only forest-certification scheme supported by the leading
environmental organisations, including Greenpeace. Our paper
procurement policy can be found at www.randomhouse.co.uk/environment

Designed and set by seagulls.net

Printed and bound by CPI Group (UK) Ltd, Croydon, CR0 4YY

ISBN 9780091951290

To buy books by your favourite authors and register for offers visit
www.randomhouse.co.uk

For Alan Ayckbourn

Simply the best...

The Seven Ages of Man
(by William Shakespeare)

All the world's a stage, and all the men and women merely players;
They have their exits and their entrances;
And one man in his life plays many parts,
His acts being seven ages.

The Five Ages of an Actor
(as identified by the author)

Who is Michael Simkins?
Who is this Michael Simkins?
Get me Michael Simkins!
Get me a young Michael Simkins!
Who was Michael Simkins?

CONTENTS

SO YOU WANT TO ACT?

Be careful what you wish for.

A friend of mine who's been in the business for some years recently went up for a movie set in Peru during the Spanish Inquisition, and filming in La Paz, to play the role of a corrupt cardinal.

So the screenplay is emailed to him via his agent at his home in Wantage on the Friday evening. My friend learns the sides of his one big scene in preparation for the interview on Monday morning, but decides not to wade through the entire script. After all, it's the weekend, it's a subsidiary role, his daughter has her fourth birthday party on Saturday and his in-laws are staying.

In any case, apart from the fact that he's appearing in a play each evening, merely to print out the entire 170-page text would take up most of an entire ink cartridge, which, at current Hewlett-Packard prices, is the best part of £30. Nevertheless he learns the main speech and duly travels up to town first thing on Monday for the interview.

My friend nails it in one take. Afterwards the director asks him to take a seat.

'That was wonderful,' he says. 'Tell me, what do you think of the screenplay?'

My friend, of course, hasn't read the screenplay.

'It's terrific,' he says. But remember, it's a movie, he needs the money, and it's filming in La Paz. You might do the same.

'You like it?' the director replies.

'Marvellous. Couldn't put it down.'

'What about the ending?'

My friend, of course, hasn't read the ending.

'Great,' he says.

'So you're OK with nudity?' asks the director.

My friend can't say, 'What nudity?' because he's already claimed to have read the script. But the play in which he's currently appearing requires him, albeit briefly, to enter the stage dressed only in a codpiece; so on the basis that this is unlikely to be much worse, my friend says he's all right with it.

'Well in that case, the job's yours,' says the director, extending his hand. 'The office will be on to your agent this afternoon to do the deal. Sound good?'

'Great' says my friend. Thank you.'

'Not at all,' continues the director, 'and in any case the nudity won't be so bad. The way I hope to shoot the scene means you'll be able to wear a modesty cloth. And the pig we're using is very tame. It lives near you: in Banbury in fact. It's fully trained, fetches a ball and suchlike.'

'Then again,' he continues, 'we've no idea how it's going to react when it's sodomised by an actor.'

By the time my friend has returned home the deal has been struck. Even if he'd entertained second thoughts about accepting it in the light of this fresh information, he daren't express them to his agent, as she would then be cast in an equally bad light for sending along time-wasters. So he has to do it.

It turns out the scenes, all interiors, aren't shooting in La Paz. Instead, they're being shot in an impromptu film studio fashioned from a disused car plant near Stevenage.

Three weeks later he turns up for the scene with the pig. The good news is that the filming will be done through a lot of smoke, guttering candles and the light of a single magnesium flare high above, so in order to forestall possible complications they've managed to create a lifelike latex model of the rear end of the pig, which my friend will be able to work with so as to save any potential aggravation for the master and mid-shots.

That's the good news.

The bad news is that the director doesn't think he's going to be able to shoot round a modesty cloth. Would my friend be happy just to wear a 'cock sock'?

A cock sock, it's explained, is a small flesh-coloured linen pouch that fits nearly over the penis and testes and is held in place by simple elastic round the base of the shaft and scrotum. It will still ensure that when the real pig is brought in for the money shot, my friend's genitals will not be actually touching the pig's anus or balls. He announces this piece of news to my friend as if telling him he's won the lottery.

My friend notes the word balls.

It transpires the pig is male: a giant Gloucester Old Spot answering to the name of Boris: which means that my friend can now add gay sodomy as well as bestiality to his inventory of specialist skills when he next advertises in *Spotlight*.

An hour later, my friend finds himself on set, surrounded by candles and the hissing magnesium flare, and kneeling behind a latex facsimile of Boris, wearing only his newly-fitted cock sock.

The director explains the action. The Cardinal has now been drugged, and actually wakes to find his genitals have been glued to the back end of the pig by his enemies.

Obviously my friend's genitals will not actually be glued to the pig, so the trick will be for my friend to appear to be struggling to detach himself from the pig while in actual fact ensuring that the model doesn't come away from his loins and thus spoil the conceit.

After the third attempt my friend is ready to cry. He's wearing only a cock sock, is simulating bestiality with a latex model of a male pig, the temperature in the studio is sub-arctic, and tiny flecks of ash from the magnesium flare above are settling on his back and burning his skin.

After lunch they bring in the real pig, under the control of his owner and official pig wrangler, a woman called Genevieve.

She explains they've constructed a tiny wooden trough for Boris, which they're going to fill with fermented apples, his favourite delicacy and one that will ensure he'll remain entirely preoccupied throughout the simulated sodomy/bestiality.

Genevieve assures my friend that Boris is unlikely to bite if working his way through a basket of apples. 'But I should be careful if he starts to reverse out of the stall' she adds, 'he's twelve stone in weight and all that force is channeled through the trotters, which makes them like stilettos. If he steps on your feet he'll crush your bones to pulp…'

They only have time for three or four possible takes, the reason being that Boris will be crunching his way through a veritable orchard, and the fermenting alcohol will ultimately act as something of a stimulant, like cider, at which point he will become disorientated and fractious.

Just when you think it couldn't get any worse, it doesn't. Apart from one terrifying moment when Boris upsets the basket of apples and leaps over it in an attempt to consume the scattered remnants, he is in fact a model of propriety. Indeed, my friend assures me that the only glance he gave behind him during the whole process had a sort of world weary 'just another working day – are you safely in yet' expression, of the sort that wouldn't have disgraced the most seasoned porn star.

Best of all, my friend was able to complete the scene without inadvertently becoming aroused, either through stress, the sheer cold, or anything else. Or at least that's what he told his wife and children on his return to Wantage. The producers later presented him with a framed photograph of the sordid act, one that he's currently wondering whether to display in his bathroom.

This is exactly the sort of incident that could only happen in the acting game. One moment you're dreaming of giving your Hamlet at the RSC or taking over the role of James Bond, and the next you're naked and nestling your genitals against a Gloucester Old Spot.

Still, if you've learnt nothing else, you've already learnt three important lessons for any actor.

1. Always read the script.
2. Never try to blag your way in an interview.
3. Don't try your luck in the profession unless you're prepared to earn your rent by having sex with a pig.

And in case you were wondering, it's not yet on general release.

PART ONE

Who is Michael Simkins?

MICHAEL SIMKINS

WINNER OF TWO R.A.D.A
AWARDS 1978

32, North Road
Brighton
Sussex
0273-603756

Height 6 feet 1 inches   Blue Eyes

The actor Lloyd Owen told me a story of an incident that occurred when he was a teenager.

Lloyd grew up in a theatrical family. His dad, Glyn Owen, was one of the stalwarts of British theatre and television throughout the 1960s and 70s and had a career about as unpredictable and varied as you could ever want. The son of a railway guard in Bolton, he started out in the Black & White Minstrels before graduating through straight theatre (notably at The Royal Court opposite O'Toole and Finney) and a regular part in the ATV medical series *Emergency Ward 10*, to playing Jack Rolfe, the headstrong boat builder in BBC's Sunday night flagship drama series, *Howard's Way*. The character of Rolfe was a savvy, no-nonsense hard drinking rough diamond – which, according to Lloydie, pretty much summed up the old man perfectly.

Sometime in the mid-1980s Glyn was appearing in the West End and one day announced he was taking his stage-struck son out between the matinée and evening performance. Lloyd sensed even at the time that this was a rite of passage moment, the occasion when your dad decides to relate to you as a man rather than as a mere offspring.

The destination turned out to be a small actors' drinking club in a basement near Leicester Square called the Kismet,

Club (also known as the Iron Lung), beneath what is now a big Prêt A Manger, but which back in the 70s used to be a Renault car showroom.

The club was one of several small, smoky dives that once proliferated throughout theatreland (the most famous being the legendary Gerry's Club on Shaftesbury Avenue) that catered for actors and actresses who required a refuge in which to shelter from the harsh realities of the profession, a place in which they could drink away the cares of another afternoon while waiting for the phone to ring in a convivial atmosphere and surrounded by fellow pros who would understand their particular form of ennui.

As Lloyd followed his dad down the wrought iron circular staircase leading to the basement, Glyn stopped and turned to face him.

'Son,' he said, as he pressed the entrance buzzer. 'Remember the smell of this place. It's the sweet smell of failure…'

The club that Lloydie visited, and most of its like, has long gone now, and the area of Soho between Gerrard Street and Oxford Street, which was once the acting profession's second home has changed in nature. It's somehow fitting that what was once Glyn Owen's old drinking den should now be beneath a gleaming Prêt. For where once the social currency of theatreland was smoky basements and cheap perfume, nowadays Prêt is where you'd be most likely to find the modern actor – perched crisply on a high stool in a designer sweater going through lines before an imminent audition or checking his Blackberry for messages from his agent.

Gin-and-its have been replaced by skinny macchiatos, twenty Players by granola bars, and beer-sodden oak tables by halogen-strafed counter tops. Even the more commonplace gathering places – the traditional greasy spoon – have virtually disappeared. Venerable old establishments such as the Bon Bouche café at the top of Carnaby Street, Di Marco's on the Strand, and the legendary Piccadilly Restaurant in Denman Street, once populated by actors filling up on shepherd's pie and sugary tea, have been swept aside in the endless desire for noodles, designer coffee and organic beansprouts.

The business and those who populate it has undoubtedly lost much of its tawdry romance in recent years. The bar of the National Theatre is no longer open to cast members during showtime (a number of second half performances best summed up as 'tired and emotional' have seen to that). And where once actors sat around in pubs nursing a pint and reading discarded newspapers, now they're far more likely to work as receptionists, yoga teachers, or performing role-play workshops for big business. It's less easy to float through your career on a current of occasional interviews and the odd foray into regional rep than when I started out. Modern living is a serious business requiring extensive funds. Topers and drifters no longer have a long shelf life.

Yet much about the business remains the same. Acting, so memorably described by Sir Ralph Richardson as a means of 'keeping a large group of people from coughing', is still basically about standing on the outside of society, looking in and pulling faces. We may have savings accounts, foreign holidays and pension plans (or at least we did till the Eurozone went belly up), but it still remains at heart a deliciously rackety old profession.

This book won't tell you how to act. Nobody can do that – not even a drama school (if they claim to, ask them for your money back and report them to your local trading standards office). But just as a decent drama school will help you make the most of your natural talent, this book may help you avoid some of the practical traps that lie in wait for the unwary.

I went to RADA in the spring of 1976, one of an intake of 21 students who had, rightly or wrongly, been adjudged to be the *crème de la crème* of the thousands of applicants. Three years later, with us all about to leave and embark on our careers, one popular and trusted teacher informed us that of the 21, half would have given up within five years, the majority within five more, and that by the turn of the century there'd barely be a man left standing.

If you want to know the accuracy of his prediction, you'll have to skip to the end. But my advice (as you'd expect) is to read the book first. After all, if you are only interested in odds, percentages and probabilities you shouldn't be pursuing a career on the stage in any case (though I can recommend a good accountancy course).

Good luck. Who knows, I might even bump into you in the Leicester Square Pret some day. If I do, please put down your iPhone, tell Harvey Weinstein you'll call him back, and offer to stand me a muffin.

WHAT IS ACTING?

One of the many traditions at RADA, the Royal Academy of Dramatic Art, where I trained, used to be the custom of inviting a guest speaker to address the entire academy at the end of the summer term. Once a year, usually in the last week of July, students, stage management and the entire teaching staff, would gather in the Vanbrugh Theatre in Bloomsbury for a couple of hours while a colossus of the business pontificated on their life and times; after which there'd be a brief Q&A.

Among the speakers I was lucky enough to see during my three summers there, was Janet Suzman, and on another occasion when Laurence Olivier was slated to appear but cried off at the last minute, Kenneth Williams, star of countless chat shows and *Carry On* films.

The occasion that stays with me, though, was the appearance of Ralph Richardson. Richardson was one of the three genuine titans of the business, (along with Gielgud and Olivier himself) – a mercurial and unquantifiable actor, whose presence dominated British drama throughout the second half of the 20th century and whose intangible artistry was so bewilderingly his own that whatever he did, he was utterly unique.

Look at him on YouTube if you get a chance. You'll see what I mean; and you sure as hell won't see anyone else like him. Whether in film or on stage, he seems, in everything he does, to be wandering through the part, as though he's just blundered in off the street and can only just recall the lines. Thus each and every role is fashioned until it seems a seamless part of his psyche – so much so that you can't imagine anyone else ever playing it. With the possible exceptions of Michael Gambon and Jim Broadbent I've never seen anyone whose craft remains so compelling and yet so elusive.

At the age of 75, Richardson was then a familiar sight in central London, still roaring around on an old BMW motorcycle, the ends of his waterproof coat flapping in the wind, a pipe clamped firmly in his mouth, and with his trademark burnished brown shoes resting on the pedals.

Such was his standing in the business that at every first night of a new play at the National Theatre a firework would be let off in his honour, a ceremony known as 'Ralph's Rocket' – or at least it was until a combination of IRA bomb scares and the dead hand of 'health and safety' did for it.

Richardson didn't disappoint. This particular afternoon he ambled on as if he'd found himself unexpectedly addressing a speech day at some minor public school. For some minutes he hardly spoke: instead, we watched spellbound while he fumbled around, adjusted his seat, poured himself a glass of water, and rummaged for his spectacles.

Was he senile, or was this some supreme demonstration of the actor's artistry? As always with Richardson, it was impossible to tell. Although he eventually settled and began talking about the business in a distracted fashion, I recall little of consequence of his talk, yet it remains one of the most mesmerising interludes I've ever witnessed on a stage.

At the end there was an opportunity to ask questions. The final slot was given to a member of staff, in this case the inimitable 'Toschka' Fedro, an elderly Polish dancer who taught Restoration movement and who was the most exotic of many blooms on the RADA payroll.

Her own life could nearly match Richardson's for incident. She'd once been a famous ballerina and a favourite of the impresario Max Reinhardt, and rumour had it she'd received a medal from the NKVD (the Communist Secret Police) as a hero of the Soviet Union. Now she spent her declining days rasping out instructions of how to perform rudimentary pliés to great teenage lunks like me in a thick European cackle, part Great Garbo and part Anne Widdecombe.

She staggered to her feet, her two spindly legs encased in nylon slacks, while the rest of the audience slumped low into their seats. Fedro was in her own way a genius, yet her perpetual lament on the attitude of young actors and their lack of curiosity about the world around them was not something we needed to hear again; especially today when we were having so much fun. Yet long experience had taught that this would inevitably be the thrust of her query, one that would surely be endorsed by an actor of Richardson's standing.

'Meesthuuurrr Rrrreechehdsshun,' she rasped. (I'll drop the phonetics from now on but you get the drift.) 'Do you not agree young actors these days are notoriously ignorant of the world in which they live? Do you not think that those who train for the profession are held back by a lack of curiosity, both in the world around them and events that have shaped their lives, and especially in the rich tradition of drama and dramatists whose views they purport to represent?' ('*rrruuppprrreeshhuunntttt*'.)

Richardson looked up into the flies, as if addressing an ethereal voice on some celestial two-way radio with dodgy reception. For some moments he fumbled with his fob watch, adjusted his tie, and then went through each and every pocket of his immaculate suit, as he searched for a large spotted handkerchief with which to wipe his nose. After an impossibly long pause, he spoke.

'Madam,' he replied dreamily to an imaginary figure above him, 'nothing could be further from the truth. Actors need to know nothing about history, world affairs, or the workings of government. All they need to do is to be able to dream. If you can dream, you can act. That's all it is – a sort of real-life dreaming. Knowing about life won't make the slightest difference if you can't do that – and if you can, little else matters.'

The roar of approval from all but the confounded Toschka could have been heard on Tottenham Court Road. I didn't dare look round, but I vividly imagined the clunk of aging springs as she slumped back, confounded, into her chair. When Richardson eventually left it was to a standing ovation. My last sight of him was climbing onto his motorcycle, parked on the kerb in Gower Street, before roaring off into the traffic.

That's at least how I remember the occasion, although it's possible I might have dreamt it. But I knew, there and then, that no other possible occupation would do for me. Who wants to work for a living when you can dream instead?

Richardson is a particularly joyous example of the sort of person for whom acting provides a haven from having to take life too seriously. The profession is for everyone who's prepared to give it a go and can manage to cling to the rock face. No exams, no yearly reviews, no financial targets or balance sheets hanging over you every time you clock in to work. You don't need to do much more than write your name (in fact you don't even have to do that – there are any number of dyslexics in the business). And like rock climbing, all it requires is that you have a strong stomach, a head for heights, and an ability to resist the temptation to look down.

Even now, half a century after John Osborne blew apart forever the notion of acting as being the art of correctly clasping a cigarette holder, the profession still has a certain raffish association. 'Tell your readers we're all a load of gippos,' one well-know performer shouted to me across the street when he heard I was writing this book. Estuary English may have replaced RP as the default dialect, but nonetheless the popular perception is still one of a career in which its denizens are a bit racy, a bit fly, likely to wear outrageous headscarves, embrace ordinary civilians at inopportune moments, refer to everyone as 'darling' (mainly to cover the fact they can't remember your name) and who are spontaneous and excessive in every aspect of their lives except when it's their turn to buy a round. We're fair game because we've chosen to put ourselves ever so slightly outside the social norm.

SO YOU WANT TO BE AN ACTOR?

It's a good question to ask yourself before you read any further. Because once you've dived in, it's not easy to haul yourself back out onto the bank again. Acting may well lead to fame, fortune, and a sense of a life well lived: but it may equally result in penury, disappointment, and cirrhosis of the liver. The natural optimism, sanguinity and will-to-win against all odds that all actors require has a life-force of its own, and will sweep any other considerations from your mind.

There are many reasons why you might want to act – to escape a stultifying home environment, to travel, to get laid, to become famous, or merely because it's a bit like dreaming. But before you do so you'd be well advised to consider your intentions for a moment.

Here are four reasons *not* to become an actor.

1. To please your parents

This may seem an odd one to start with, given the perception of parents throwing their hands up in horror at the very thought of their little darling going off in pursuit of fame and fortune. But for everyone who's defied parental advice, there are many others who did it because they wanted to please their parents, both keen am. drammers, who by dint of circumstance had never had the opportunity to pursue a career on the stage themselves.

One of the country's finest actors, who grew up in a small seaside town in North Yorkshire, recently told me of an incident which occurred to him. His parents had always considered that to be a real actor, you had to appear on *Coronation Street*. In their small, tight-knit and highly parochial corner of Britain, nothing else mattered: not the RSC, not sitcoms, certainly not your name in lights on Shaftesbury Avenue. In fact they wouldn't have known where Shaftesbury Avenue was or what to do with it had they found it.

No, if you were to confirm your status in Saltburn you had to be propping up the bar of the Rovers Return. And despite a robust and successful career over two decades, he thus always felt he'd failed them.

Then he got a guest spot in *Corrie* – a 12-week storyline – heavily featured as a casual chancer who tries to cheat one of the regulars out a large sum of money by feigning a romantic attachment. So excited was he at the prospect of proving himself in the eyes of the two people whose benediction he most craved, that he drove up to his parents' house on the night of his first episode, just to watch it with them.

And you know what happened? They both fell asleep. By the time he burst through the door of the Rovers they were snoring loudly, and only came to after the final credits had rolled. My mate watched himself in silence with tears coursing down his face. He later concluded that they simply couldn't process the collision between the world they viewed on the screen and the fact that their only son had become part of it. Neither he nor they ever referred to the programme again.

2. To Become Famous

Look, once upon a time, becoming an actor was the best way to show off, get a fan base and secure your own booth on *Celebrity Squares*. But there's no need nowadays. There are so many quicker and less brutal ways to achieve fame and fortune. Go on *X Factor*; download a clip onto YouTube of you teaching your pet dog to say 'sausages'. Scale Nelson's Column clad only in a mankini. Make a video in which you prance around on an imaginary horse shouting 'Gangnam Style!'

In this insatiable, celebrity-obsessed world in which we all exist, the media is looking for something – anything – with which to fill their news columns or daytime schedules, and as long as you can swing a punch you'll be up and running – at least until the next self-obsessed crackpot comes along and steals your thunder. There's simply no need to endure three years at drama school.

3. Because you love am dram

Look, I love am dram. I grew up doing it. Plays, musicals, operettas; as a teenager I longed for those precious evenings, twice a week, when I could leave work and hurry off to my local church hall to immerse myself in the giddy world of theatricals.

But doing it for a living is very different from doing it for a hobby. People – especially professionals – are fond of pronouncing the essential difference between amateurs and professionals to be one of talent. They (we) all too often fall into the lazy trap of deriding amateur productions, with their stiff-limbed portrayals and characters gathered glassily around tatty sofas.

But they're missing the point. The only absolute difference between them and us is that professionals are prepared to put up with the terrible uncertainty of it all. I've known some wonderful amateurs and some terrible pros. Amateurs simply won't risk it full time.

4. Because you've failed your exams and it looks like it might be a laugh

This is the worst reason of all to give acting a go.

Some years ago a friend of my wife's asked me if I could give her teenage son some coaching for an imminent tilt at a drama school. The audition was the following week but she'd really like the chance for someone in the business to have a look at her boy and see if he could be improved. Intrigued, I readily agreed to give him a couple of hours one morning to go over his pieces and see if I could sharpen them up. We agreed to meet at 10 am.

By 10.40 he still hadn't arrived. I called his mum, who apologised that he'd overslept but who assured me he was on his way. At about 10.50 there was a knock on the door and a desultory apology. We went into the lounge and I asked him to do one of his pieces, which, if memory serves me, was a monologue from Jez Butterworth's play *Mojo*. Good choice.

It soon became apparent that the boy had hardly looked at the thing, let alone worked on it. He couldn't get through more than a couple of phrases at a time without having to refer to the script, yet when I gently pointed out that the audition was only two days away and this was not the best preparation for a life in a notoriously competitive and overcrowded profession, he burst into tears.

The back-story turned out to be much as I'd predicted. He'd failed his GCSEs, decided that acting might be a laugh, and had applied for a three-year drama diploma at some God-forsaken metropolitan college in Manchester. And truth to tell, they took him anyway. The moment he finished the course he went to work as an estate agent, and in fairness, seems very happy with his lot.

And why you shouldn't listen to anyone's voice but your own...

Here's a story that will either confirm or confound the last few thousand words.

In 2001, I was installed in a big West End musical, pumping out show after show for 12 long months. One evening I was in the wings, waiting, as I did every evening at this time, for the wig mistress to check my hair when an unfamiliar face shimmied up beside me and starting teasing my hair.

She was about 5' 4", with short jet black spiky hair, a ton of eye shadow and an East End accent so thick it would have Barbara Windsor purring with pleasure. She was, she explained, standing in for the regular and would be looking after me for the next fortnight.

Bit-by-bit I learnt something about her. She'd been born in Dagenham, she'd trained as a hairdresser, and it was now her full-time occupation. Thus I was somewhat taken aback when she announced one night she'd got an audition for *EastEnders*. She'd recently completed a part-time course at what I recognised immediately as a drama school in the hinterlands of King's Cross.

Being a gracious sort of bloke, I made all the right noises about wishing her luck, yet inside it was impossible not to feel sympathy. 'Good on her,' I recall thinking, 'But does she really imagine she can just walk into the profession and become a household name overnight?'

She turned out to be Jessie Wallace, one of the most natural, gifted and dynamic soap opera actresses of her generation, and a woman whose alter ego as Kat has become something of a gold standard for the genre.

So what do I know?

Something has fundamentally altered in the last 30 years. I was lucky. Back in 1976, acting was a decidedly dicey career. Those friends of mine who went into proper jobs – banking, insurance, high finance, teaching and the like – always averred that they envied me my courage and audacity, and would loved to have given acting a go themselves, but were put off by fear of penury and not knowing where their next pay cheque might come from. 'It's just too uncertain,' they'd say.

But guess what?

Now we're all in the same boat. Every profession has become like the acting game – shedding jobs, amalgamating overnight with other companies, restructuring pay grades, forcing through voluntary redundancies or going out of business altogether. Even those who've survived have done so by lurching from job to job, gig to gig, short-term contract to short-term contract, having to accept less money, longer hours and with no idea how long each job will last before they're forced to retrain or reapply for their old jobs.

To which I reply, 'Welcome to my world.'

TO BE OR NOT TO BE

I once attended an end-of-term drama awards ceremony at an exclusive secondary school in Surrey, one with a formidable reputation for preparing gifted young teenagers from wealthy bohemian families for admission to drama schools and a career in the media. Among the panel of judges this particular night were two icons of 1970s popular entertainment, Terry Scott and James Ellis, both of whom were invited up at the end of the evening to say a few words.

Scott, you may recall, was a colossus of 1970s telly sitcom, achieving national status in both *Hugh and I* and later *Terry and June* (as well cementing his place in the pantheon of showbiz greats with the novelty song, 'My Bruvver').

Ellis, by contrast, was a serious actor of prodigious talent, one whose versatility and passion was perhaps never fully recognised due to his becoming associated with the character of Bert Lynch in *Z Cars*.

Scott's dictum was simple and feelingly expressed. 'Find something you're good at and stick to it,' he said. 'Specialise. That's the secret of how to stay in the business. Once you've found a niche, polish it, hone it, and make it work to your advantage. You'll do so much better.' So impassioned was he that tears welled up in his eyes as he spoke, and as he returned to his chair there was a slight *frisson* among the audience that his words seemed something of a valediction. Which they were – Scott was suffering from cancer at the time and died not long afterwards.

He was followed by Ellis, who, in contrast with Scott's pressed slacks and Pringle sweaters, looked the epitome of the gnarled old pro.

'Whatever you do,' he began, stabbing a finger in the general direction of the audience, 'try everything. Try any part that's offered, however unlikely it might seem or however terrible you are in it. Fall on your arse. Don't specialise. It'll kill you. The moment you become an actor the business will try and pigeonhole you, until in the end you're playing nothing but the same thing day in day out.'

'Stuff that,' he continued angrily. 'For if you let it, it'll hollow you out from the inside till there's nothing left.'

Two actors, both vastly successful, both with diametrically-opposed views.

That, as they say, is showbiz.

SAFETY NET

One of the questions I get asked most frequently by those contemplating a career in showbiz is, 'Should I get some academic qualifications first?' This, at least, is simple enough to answer, as I can merely quote the playwright David Mamet.

In his book on acting, *True and False*, he wrote, 'If you want to be in theatre, go into the theatre. If you want to have made a valiant effort to go into the theatre before you go into real estate or law school or marry wealth, then perhaps you should stay in school.'

Not surprisingly (given it's Mamet), I couldn't have put it better myself. Though I'll try. The fact is, you don't learn how to leap on a motorbike over a row of twenty-four double-decker buses by first studying quantity surveying. It's the same with acting. Get stuck in. In a profession such as this, if you're worrying about plan 'B', then plan 'A' is already toast.

WHICH ROUTE TO TAKE?

It was American TV personality Alton Brown who said, 'A journey of a thousand miles begins with a cash advance.'

During the summer of 2012, I found myself one Sunday afternoon walking through an area of London with which I was unfamiliar. Eventually I stumbled across a tatty side street in which was located a small independent drama school I'd not heard of before.

Yet perhaps it's hardly surprising: for there are about 1400 official establishments in the UK offering courses with the word 'drama' in them; ranging from high-end academies with venerable histories, embossed notepaper and stupefying lists of famous thespian alumni, through to one-man outfits in West Bromwich offering to take your teenage daughter and turn her into the next Adele in return for a couple of Thursdays each month. In nearly all of them, the prospectus/website will mention the mission statement 'to prepare the aspiring student for a life in professional theatre': because after all, that is what people who flock to such places ultimately dream about. And narrative always wins out over statistics.

But if a life as a professional actor is the aim, all but a handful are unfit for the purpose. This place in West London for instance, had on its website a list of past graduates who've successfully passed through and who are now active in the business. Yet even the ones who are cited as proof of purchase seemed to be merely clinging on at the very fringes of the profession: the odd pub show here, a guest in an episode of *Casualty* there, but beyond that distinctly lean pickings, and certainly a poor return for an annual investment of nearly 10k.

The truth is, all but very few of the 1400 places alluded to as offering training in 'drama' can be discarded. If you're really serious about giving the profession a crack, there are only a handful of ways of entering and keeping in the business.

LET'S DO THE SHOW RIGHT HERE

Starting at the bottom and working your way up is the oldest, and most romantic way of breaking into acting, and is the preferred method of many of our best loved thesps from years gone by. 'I applied at the stage door, asked for a job, and to my joy, after several minutes of anxious waiting the general manager arrived, thrust a broom into my hand and told me to start sweeping the stage. Six months later I was playing Juliet.'

This sort of stuff is the lifeblood of theatrical legend, tapping into the grand old charm of the theatre with its images of individuals plucked from the street to become overnight sensations. And perhaps it's no coincidence that this peripatetic approach has produced some of the country's most transcendent actors and actresses: including Ralph Richardson, who got into the business by paying a local theatre manager ten shillings to teach him how to act. Ditto Margaret Rutherford, who survived a childhood in which her father murdered her grandfather and whose mother subsequently hanged herself from a tree, similarly inveigled her way into the business by hanging around theatres until someone offered her a cup of tea.

Great stuff, but sadly this sort of scenario nowadays rarely obtains. For a start, most theatres don't have a stage door, and those that do require a swipe card or complicated passcode to get through. Even if you can get in, you'll find the stage door cubicle unmanned, or at best, occupied by a keeper who has probably less knowledge of what's going on inside the building than you do.

And when they do put you through to the admin department, most of the staff will be in a human resources meeting or enjoying a weeklong conference as part of an Arts Council-funded course in community outreach programmes.

There are exceptions of course. Take Nick Frost for instance. One of our most naturally talented comedy actors, he specialises in playing amiable blunderers caught up in events beyond his control (as witnessed by a whole string of successes such as *Hot Fuzz*, *Shaun of the Dead*, *The Boat That Rocked* and many other projects).

Yet his career began entirely by chance when he happened to form a friendship with a bloke called Simon Pegg in the

Cricklewood branch of Chiquito, where they were both working as waiters. Now, a decade and a half on, Frost is one of the best-known faces on both sides of the Atlantic. But he's the exception that proves the rule; for every aspiring actor who started at Chiquito's and who is now acting, there are many thousands more who are still waiting tables at Chiquito's.

GO TO OXFORD OR CAMBRIDGE

The playwright Alan Ayckbourn wrote the line, 'Some people are born with a silver spoon in their mouths. Others have an entire canteen of cutlery.' And should you be lucky enough to gain admission to these centres of gilded excellence, chances are you'll be handed a one-way ticket to fame and fortune along with your mortarboard and ceremonial scroll.

Cambridge, in particular, is responsible for launching the careers of just about everyone who's anyone in showbiz. Those that aren't actually performing are film producers, comedy writers or running the BBC. Which only really leaves those in government and the upper echelons of the secret service.

Oxbridge graduates are, in truth, a different breed from the rest of us, and one that still manages (without in any way wishing to) to fill us with a vague sense of inferiority. We may like to pretend we're all one big happy family when we're wolfing down egg and chips at the local caff during rehearsals, but the fact is that most of those who've been to Oxbridge have brains the size of Bletchley Park, and have to expend most of their colossal brainpower in slowing their thought processes down in order to allow the rest of us to keep up.

Effortlessly confident, mentally adroit, they seem to breeze along in the profession as if transported on an invisible current of invincibility. And that's because they don't suffer from the one terrible handicap that is the lot of most jobbing thesps – namely, lack of self-belief. So if you're lucky enough to get a place at one of these venerable old institutions, take it with both hands, get stuck into the Footlights, and wait for the call.

ARE YOU SITTING COMFORTABLY?

A friend of mine rang me recently to ask if I could give some counselling to his 17-year-old daughter, who, having done a bit of acting in her mid-teens, was thinking of trying for drama school.

'What are her other options?' I asked.

'Well. She's just finished filming a movie in Tennessee, and is due to fly to China next month to make a teen pic about a group of kids stranded on a desert island – a sort of *Fame* meets *Lord of the Flies*. And then there's a new adaptation of *Little Women* she's slated to do the year after next. She has her heart set on a career in the business. Not being an actor myself I don't know how to advise her. She so wants to be an actress.'

'She already is one,' I snarled back. 'Why on earth does she want to wall herself up at drama school for three years if she's already got movie projects stacked up from arsehole to breakfast time? If she doesn't want to do them I'll take them off her hands – I'll happily wear a bonnet or a cutaway bikini if it means I don't have to do *A Murder Is Announced* at Sonning next summer.'

My friend may not have appreciated my Anglo-Saxon language, but my sentiments were clear. It's hard enough to get started in the business as it is: so if you've already got a head start, cling to it like buggery. You don't need three years in drama school if you're already in the profession.

I realise that for every child actor such as Daniel Radcliffe there are always ten Macaulay Culkins, and the ability to look cute aged six while eating Heinz baked beans or chasing a Labrador with a toilet roll in its mouth is no guarantee you'll be any good once your hormones kick in. But if you've got real ability and already have a foothold in the biz, play it for all you've got.

Some years ago, I played a defence council in a big storyline in the Channel 4 soap opera, *Brookside*, in which a young boy (and a regular in the series) was in the dock on a charge of attempted murder. The storyline was especially piquant given the resonances of the James Bulger case, and it was vital we pitched it with truth and accuracy.

The young lad playing the accused was called Raymond Quinn. Despite the enormous pressure and long hours (trial scenes are always particularly exhausting to film) he seemed so relaxed that while the rest of us pored over our scripts in between takes, he busied himself by playing with his toy cars on the parapet of the dock.

But when he came to his big scene, in which he was subjected to a gruelling and lengthy examination, he blew the adults off the screen. So powerful was his performance that it was genuinely upsetting to behold. It's no surprise that 15 years later, Ray's a regular face in the West End and on TV. Even aged 12 we could all see he was the real deal. No training necessary.

A FUNNY THING HAPPENED ON THE WAY TO THE RSC

In Trevor Griffiths' seminal 1975 play about aspiring stand-ups, *Comedians*, one of the hapless candidates breaks off from his forlorn attempts in front of a stony Saturday nightclub audience to mutter, 'There's something running down my leg, I hope it's sweat...'

Stand-up has always been a conduit by which to get into mainstream acting: and with the genre more popular (and sexy) than ever, the trickle is threatening to become a flood. Lenny Henry has recently been collecting awards by the bucketful, Rob Brydon is a virtual fixture and fitting on TV dramas and the West End; while of the new generation, Miles Jupp is currently largeing it with great success at the National Theatre.

One moment you're getting rolled-up crisp packets chucked at you in some basement dive, the next you've got your own six-part comedy drama on Channel 4. You only need to be seen by the right person and it all suddenly clicks.

Yet those who've done stand-up and lived to tell the tale assure me it's no easy option. For the majority of practitioners there's little to look forward to except nightly humiliation and solitary despair. But if enduring grimy pubs, fetid dressing rooms and a drink problem by the age of 30 is your idea of a good time, then go for it. I'll be the first to get to my feet when you collect your Olivier award. In the meantime, keep an eye out for Alan Carr's John Gabriel Borkman and Sarah Millican's Hedda Gabler at a theatre near you soon.

Of course, if none of the above categories describe you, there's only one practical option, and the one on which I'm most qualified to speculate. I speak, of course, of drama school.

DRAMA SCHOOL

Decent, properly-funded drama schools may not be able to teach you to act, but what they can do is to make you think you can, which is the next best thing. In art as in life, confidence is more than half the battle in a profession that thrives on self-assurance and withers under nerves.

You may start out not knowing your exit from your entrance, but you'll leave it with an expectation of being employed. That's what's drama school does. It changes your mindset.

There are currently 22 drama schools in England and Wales which are recognised by the government as fit and proper places in which to train, and which are consequently eligible for official funding. Getting into one of these is already a huge step towards realising your dream.

If you're successful and are offered a place at one on the list, you'll automatically be eligible for a loan to cover your course fees, an amount you'll have to repay over the next 50 years. But no matter – that can be dealt with when you're up and running. The first problem is to be accepted by the school. The financial ruination likely to result from your actions is dealt with in a later section of the book (*please see appendix 17: bankruptcy*).

It's all very different from when I started out. Back in 1976 further education was free at point of delivery and, although drama school tuition was officially classed as 'discretionary', your local authority would cough up with barely a murmur. Life was simpler back then.

In my case, this curious way of arranging matters did ensure one particularly piquant ceremony: having already been given the blessing of the world's most celebrated drama school, I then had to subsequently perform my audition pieces again, this time for a civil servant from East Sussex County Council. The meeting took place in an office in Lewes on a Thursday morning in January 1976, during which the official responsible for such matters sat no more than three feet away from me across a formica desk, while I performed my two speeches to the sound of clacking typewriters from adjacent rooms and traffic rumbling past the windows.

We were so close that, had I wanted to, I could have leaned across and kissed him. Maybe that's what he was afraid of. At the end of my second speech he coughed nervously, thanked me for coming, and showed me the door as fast as he could. The result was not only three years funding, but £1000 per annum living expenses, plus free travel on British Railways in case I needed to get home to Brighton at the weekends to have my mum wash my dance support belt.

It's all changed. And although all 22 accredited schools and colleges are recognised and funded, there are actually only five or six which can claim to offer a serious path towards realising your dream. If you want to have a serious chance of achieving an Oscar, a mansion on Wilshire Boulevard and a serious coke habit, there are a mere handful of major players.

Which one is best is a matter of speculation. Most graduates of RADA will tell you their alma mater is the elite, and as an ex-graduate myself I feel so fortunate to have trained there that on the odd occasions I'm shopping in Hampstead I will, if passing his gravestone in the local churchyard, doff my trilby hat to Sir Herbert Beerbohm Tree, founder of the academy.

Of course I don't. When did you last see an actor wear a trilby?

There are others who can also claim pre-eminence. The Central School of Speech and Drama in Swiss Cottage has an equally enviable reputation for turning out serious contenders and, like RADA, has its own purpose-built theatre in which to showcase its wares – an important consideration.

The Guildhall School of Music and Drama has a similarly prodigious reputation for both drama and music and, thanks to the redevelopment of its premises in the 1980s as part of the Barbican complex, brand new state of the art facilities. LAMDA (The London Academy of Music & Dramatic Art) is another place with an impressive back catalogue and a burgeoning reputation. Then there's the Bristol Old Vic Theatre School, which has a similar track record as well as links to the prestigious Bristol Old Vic Company.

Some people swear by The Drama Centre, Mountview Academy of Theatre Arts, or East 15. But if you can't get into the favoured few, you're basically on your own. Not only will you have to fund your studies yourself, but also you'll have little to show for it at the end except for some happy memories.

Let's number-crunch for a moment.

Each of the top couple of dozen drama schools will be disgorging between 20 and 40 highly-qualified and talented students every year into a profession which is already grossly overcrowded. That's an average of 720 graduates each and every year.

Even if the casting directors, producers and leading theatrical agents could get to see all of the students in that time (and they can't) they'll only have places on their books for a fraction of that number. Which means they're likely to concentrate their fire on the establishments most likely to produce the next Sheridan

Smith or Eddie Redmayne. That means RADA, Central, and one or two others. But beyond that?

Let's suppose for a moment that you've sent off for the prospectus, coughed up your £50 for your three minutes of fame, and have got yourself an interview.

This is where the fun begins.

GETTING IN

'Talent is as common as horseshit in a stable. The cultivation of it is extremely rare...' So said Eric Morris, acting coach, Hollywood guru and a man who is described on his website as 'one of the most exciting drama teachers in the history of American performance'; which shows he also knows a thing or two about the importance of self-publicity.

The drama school audition is to aspiring actors what Becher's Brook is to the racehorses in the Grand National. Successfully negotiate it and before you lays open pasture, cheering crowds, national acclaim, a slap on the rump from potential employers, and hopefully years of fame and fortune along with a regular slot on *A Question Of Sport*. But fail to get over and all you've got to look forward to is a wait of 12 months before you can have another tilt, or worse, a posse of men in white coats and gumboots approaching you with service revolvers.

You'll also need a lot of luck. When I auditioned for RADA back in 1976 there were just over 1000 applicants for the 21 available places on the two-and-a-half year course. By 1991 when I went back to direct there for a spell, the number of available places had crept up to around 30, yet it was more than cancelled out by the number of applicants per annum having risen to 3000. Now, a further two decades on, the number of applicants has nearly doubled.

The various drama schools each have their own method of winnowing the wheat from the chaff, but basically you can expect to be invited for an initial audition, where you'll have to perform two pre-prepared audition speeches, one modern and one classical, each of three or four minutes long; after which (if you're fortunate enough to get the thumbs-up), a couple of recalls (including a one-to-one session with the head honcho) and a communal workshop lasting several hours. You might also have to sing a song. If you get through to an offer with less than four separate trips you can count yourself either lucky or a genius.

Your drama school audition is the single most important interview you're ever likely to have. So if you do nothing else in your miserable life, you must maximize your chances of getting noticed.

Fifteen minutes of fame

Shakespeare wrote 37 plays, containing 884,647 words: so for your classical speech you've got plenty to choose from. Whichever of the myriad speeches or soliloquies you select, the most important thing is that you like it yourself. Does it feel comfortable? Do you feel you can identify with the character speaking the lines? If not, go back to your Collected Works and keep trawling. There's a speech out there somewhere with your name on it.

In some drama schools you don't have to choose the old Bill at all but can go for one of the other contemporaneous playwrights, most of who are supposed to have written Shakespeare's plays in any case. But be warned – there's a reason we cross ourselves and doff our cap whenever we mention the Bard. He's the *grand fromage* of playwrights, and although it might seem attractive to mess about with some Marlowe or Webster, they won't offer you the same degree of raw genius with which to work. Most of Shakespeare's contemporaries only wrote plays as a hobby in between their day jobs, such as spying on the French, bedding the king's mistress or discovering tobacco. Shakespeare by contrast was a proper playwright.

You're far better off keeping to the master than trying to hew a speech out of some trundling Jacobean shocker such as *The Metamorphosis of Pigmalion's Image.*

And your modern?

There's so much good stuff around it's hard to know where to begin. Harold Pinter, Sara Kane, Caryl Churchill – the list of modern authors writing fabulous stuff for young actors is almost endless. If you're struggling for inspiration, there are lots of books of good contemporary speeches, all accessible online, or in person if you're near enough to French's Theatre Bookshop in Bloomsbury, where you can spend many happy hours scanning them in person (the rather flinty shop staff may not thank you for it, but as long as you purchase a 50 pence postcard depicting Ken Dodd in pantomime at the London Palladium before you leave, they can't really complain).

It's always a good idea to choose a piece that you like because you saw it performed somewhere. It also means you'll be able to talk cogently about it if the audition panel ask you why you chose it. Extra marks. And whatever else you do, have another, third speech up your sleeve just in case they ask for an extra one. Make sure it's every bit as good as your two front-line offerings. It may just make all the difference between success and failure. And if you're worried about forgetting your lines, it's always an idea to choose a piece by Pinter, as a lengthy pause in the middle of a sentence will be judged to be part of your interpretation.

And your song?

Look, it's not about the voice – they're not looking to see if you're a new Pavarotti or Callas, but to see what emotions are released by your having to handle the process of warbling in public. Whether or not you sing 'Nessun Dorma' or 'The Birdy Song' isn't the point – both are perfectly acceptable choices – but the mere act of singing in public will reveal a great deal about you, even if you end up making a noise like a seal being harpooned on the ice floes of Newfoundland. If nothing else, it will show you're prepared to make a total tit of yourself without flinching. Which is just as well, as you'll be doing much the same thing for the next three years.

The interview

So you're sitting in the corridor awaiting your turn, armed and dangerous and bristling with your two speeches plus a back-up and a song, then the door swings open, and the second-term student earning some extra cash by doing some extra-curricular flunkying opens the door and beckons you in. You enter, and before you, slumped behind a table looking as if they haven't slept for a week, are four or five individuals of different ages and sexes, on whose advancement you are now entirely dependent. What else can you have done to give yourself the best possible chance of making a splash?

Learn Your Lines

This maxim is going to be repeated so often that you'll be asking for your money back. Can't help that. Everything about your moment in the spotlight will be heightened, strange, and calculated to throw you off your stride. If you don't have the lines nailed down with the mental equivalent of Jewson's Sticks like Shit, this is when you'll forget them. Anything and everything will conspire to put you off – the ringing of somebody's mobile phone (make sure it's not yours), the profusion of dandruff on the shoulder of one of the panel, or even the braying laughter of somebody walking past the door to the audition room.

That's not to say auditioning is a memory test. Quite the opposite. If you do 'dry' (see how I'm already gently sliding in a bit of actor's lingo here just to make you feel at home) it won't be the end of the world, but it'll feel like it – and in my experience if you dry once under pressure, there's a good chance the jitters will set in, and you'll do it again until the lines are sloshing around in your head like runny egg. Learn the lines. I can't put it more starkly than that.

Actually I can. Learn the fucking lines.

Know who you are

It's not just greenhorn students who have an unrealistic knowledge of their strengths and weaknesses.

One of the saddest vignettes I ever encountered was of an elderly actress who specialised in elderly dowagers and below-stairs cooks. I recall her gently declaring to nobody in particular, 'Of course, the part I really want to play before I die is Cleopatra,' before adding wistfully, 'But I suppose I'm a bit old now.' It was the phrase 'I suppose' that broke my heart. The fact was, she already looked less like Elizabeth Taylor and more like Shaw Taylor.

So choose a part that suits you. There's no point having a go at Falstaff if you weigh 8 stone 5 pounds dripping wet. And don't plump for a generic character that doesn't have their own personality but is merely a mouthpiece for the author (I'm thinking here of The Chorus in *Henry V*). They rarely work in isolated circumstances such as these.

Don't over-prepare

This may sound counter-intuitive, but it's an important tip. One of the laments of audition panels is that so many applicants turn up with pieces that have been manicured to buggery. Every scintilla of the performance has been rehearsed and polished until all the life has been squeezed out of it. The panel doesn't want to see you act – they want to see if you can act. Two very different things. Make sure your offering is fresh, healthy, and a tad unwashed.

A good maxim for life as well in fact.

Never perform a piece by someone who might be on the panel

Seems unlikely? I know of at least one incident when an auditionee chose a speech that turned out to have been written by one of the individuals scrutinising them. The applicant fluffed, dried, and worst of all, paraphrased most of the original lines (after which the playwright in question had to be restrained from clambering over the desktop to throttle him).

Cobblers

Whatever you do, resist the temptation to cobble together speeches from fragmentary bits of dialogue. It's probably OK to splice together two long chunks, but any more than that and the offering will come over as fractured and clunky.

Don't just do something, sit there

'Stop, look, listen' is always good advice, whether you're trying to traverse an unmanned railway level crossing or auditioning for drama school. Most applicants are so wired and nervous when they finally enter the audition room that they're impervious to anything short of a nuclear detonation. They don't stand where they're supposed to, perform the entire speech upstage towards the far corner, rather than where the audition panel can actually see them, or begin gabbling away before the panel has even settled back. Take your time, gather your thoughts, and let the people whose job it is to help you, help you.

Dress appropriately

If you're performing a classical piece, don't turn up in skin-tight hot pants and tights embossed with 'fuck me' sideways down the side of each leg. And while nobody is suggesting you turn up in a corset and bustle, at least dress in something that will help you to inhabit the role, rather than making your job even more difficult. In other words, don't wear shorts and flip-flops if you're giving your Titania.

Study your quarry

It's amazing how many students don't understand what they're talking about. One male student recently who was playing a scene from a play about gay seduction came to the line, 'I put my hand on his packet,' only to reveal a carton of cigarettes, one of which he removed and mimed smoking. While such howlers won't necessarily debar you, they won't impress.

Shock horror

Don't take your clothes off or manhandle the audition panel. This may seem stating the bleeding obvious, but one actor I know who was performing a speech from Hamlet managed to justify an entire full frontal strip show during his 32-line speech, while another I once auditioned, who was performing a speech about a woman recollecting her experience of being grilled in a police interview, managed to perform a startlingly convincing facsimile of masturbating with one hand. Not that I was complaining, but it meant I didn't listen to a bloody word of what she was saying. Panellists aren't prudes, but we're here to watch you act, and shock tactics don't help you or us.

Props

Props are naff. One girl who arrived to perform a soliloquy from *Cleopatra* turned up with a veritable trunkful, including a small dagger with a tin foil blade, a rubber asp and a tiny glass phial that broke during her speech and gashed her hand.

I come to bury Caesar?

What I'm talking about here is the curse of modern living, the upward inflection, and its various bastardised cousins of modern linguistics. In an early episode of a wartime drama in which I was appearing, I recall a scene in which the commanding officer (me) had to interrogate a young barmaid who was acting as a fifth columnist.

Her defiant response to my questioning was a simple and defiant, 'Heil Hitler!', yet she managed to deliver it with a 21st century post-Cool-Britannia innit-upward inflection (e.g.: 'Heil Hitler?') One could almost hear Churchill turning in his grave. And I know you'll all be writing in to remind me that Winston himself was no stranger to an upward inflection, but he's allowed – it was a different sort of upward inflection – and in any case he won the bloody war for us.

Keep your guard up

After your pieces, the audition panel will probably want to have a chat with you. It's an important part of the interview, one that can reveal a lot. So keep your wits about you. You're not out of the room yet.

What they want to know is: are you reasonably well balanced? Will you fit in? Are you going to start trashing the joint if you get a poor run of parts? Most important of all, they'll be looking to see if you have any real interest in drama. Why are you interested in acting? Have you seen anything recently? Who are your favourite actors and actresses (please don't answer Judi Dench, it's the last resort of the bluffer).

The post-speech chat really matters. Engage in it, offer them some real conversational traction and you'll do your chances of being recalled a power of good.

And finally

Oh, I nearly forgot one thing. Don't, whatever you do, choose Launce's speech from *Two Gentlemen of Verona*, the one where he talks to an imaginary dog called Crab. This was put to me most explicitly by one audition stalwart, who told me they see hundreds of them and that the speech simply doesn't punch its weight, even if you turn up with a real dog. His actual words were, 'It's about as funny as a children's ward.' That still leaves you with over 884,000 words to choose from. So best avoid.

And finally, finally

William Goldman famously said, 'In showbiz, nobody knows anything.'

I didn't tell my acquaintance at the time, but in fact Launce's speech from *The Two Gentlemen of Verona* was exactly the speech I chose back for my own audition. So above all, go with your gut instinct. If you feel at ease with what you're doing, the chances are they will too.

OUR ANSWER IS... MAYBE

What is the connection between RADA and the following list of famous actors? Gary Oldman, Anthony Sher, Ewan McGregor, Joan Sims, Ralph Spall and Joanna Lumley?

RADA didn't let them in. They did however all get into other drama schools, and got along very nicely as a result. So if you fail, it doesn't necessarily mean you can't act. Some of the best in the business have had to try four or five times before they got in.

Sooner or later, if you're any good, and are prepared to keep going back for more, you'll eventually get a phone call, at the end of which you'll hear three little words. Hopefully it'll be the first of many such occasions on which they're uttered; yet however long you remain in the business, they're always the sweetest sound in the world.

'It's an offer.'

PART TWO

Who is This Michael Simkins?

MICHAEL SIMKINS

CROUCH ASSOCIATES
01-734 2167
59 Frith Street, W1

Height 6 feet 1 inch   Blue Eyes

The best piece of advice about the business I ever heard was one related to me by an actress who'd trained at the Italia Conti School of Acting in the 1950s. At the start of each new academic year, the elderly woman who ran the place would announce to each new intake that there were only two things you needed to know about the profession. 'It's not fair and don't be late.'

My time at RADA began at 10 am on Monday 7 May 1976. I was 20 minutes early.

My diary entry for the day recorded the event with the sort of adolescent gaucheness that could only be the trademark of someone who wore a tie, considered *On the Buses* to be the acme of comic sophistication, and who still believed teenage rebellion to be crossing the road without looking, right, then left, then right again.

'First day of many. Lots of movement and speech (and stiff joints), but I'm in one piece so all could be worse. Back at 7.' With hindsight I'm only relieved I didn't add 'had custard for lunch.'

In contrast to these bland recollections chronicled in my journal, my first dozen or so weeks were actually a baptism of fire. I was thrust alongside 20 other successful candidates from all corners of Britain and beyond, each of whom initially regarded me as something out of the pages of *Just William*.

The demographic was typical of the sort you'll still find today. They included a student from South Africa, two from Scotland and four from the United States, and ranged from a public schoolgirl through to a brilliantined hunk who'd spent his recent years playing Baccarat with Lord Lucan in smoky Belgravia casinos.

There was a boy from Glossop whose dad was a coal miner, a Turkish Cypriot from Lewisham, and a Guinness-drinking Irishman who spent his time smoking joints or dozing in the students' common room. At least three individuals had yet to break their duck sexually (including myself), and several more seemed to have already drunk deeply in this department with whatever type and species came to hand. Our only interconnecting theme was a desire to act and a sense of disbelief at our good fortune.

As well as basic training in movement and voice, various other disciplines were built into the seven-term course, each designed to complement and broaden our skills base. Besides Restoration movement with the aforementioned Toschka Fedro, we had stage combat conducted by a venerable old cove with pince-nez and a pair of sagging jogging bottoms, and a weekly lesson in radio technique conducted by the grandly named Charles Lefeaux, a spry old gentlemen with a goatee beard who always dressed in immaculate tweed suits.

There were classes in tumbling, make up and improv, while speech and diction were in the hands of Elizabeth Pursey, who conducted lessons alongside a pet Poodle called Pierre who threatened to take the fingers off anyone who tried to pet him. The only skill not adequately represented back then was in TV technique (in fact I can only recall a single class, most of which was taken up with the teacher trying to work out how to adjust the camera tripod. You won't find that nowadays.)

At first it was a strange and bewildering environment, and my sense of inferiority was only heightened whenever I spent time in the student common room. A cramped and insanitary haven on the third floor, furnished with flea-infested sofas and carpet tiles that stuck to your feet when you walked, it was inhabited mainly by final term students, each of whom seemed impossibly sophisticated. Actors such as Kevin McNally and Anton Lesser sprawled there, smoking roll-ups as they read Chekhov or played backgammon, while the women, usually clad in eye-boggling leotards and smelling of scent and sweat, sat discussing agents or current boyfriends as they massaged their toes. The idea that in a few short terms I might be doing much the same thing seemed not only impossible but also faintly obscene.

RADA has been thoroughly redeveloped in the intervening years, and it's difficult now to get any sense of the rackety old charm that was once its trademark. Nevertheless, there's much about the coursework that remains the same, and as with all drama schools, it soon seems a lot less forbidding once you've found your bearings.

At any drama school worth the name, as your course advances the emphasis will inevitably shift from training to productions, until in the last couple of terms you'll be either rehearsing, performing, or marketing yourself so as to catch the eye of prospective employers.

One way or another, you certainly won't have time to read books like this, or anything much else. But whereas you arrived as a twit, you'll leave as an actor.

THE HAPPIEST DAYS
OF YOUR LIFE

Should your experience at drama school mirror my own, you'll find all this endless movement, voice, speech, stage fighting and TV technique will ultimately coalesce into one amorphous mental mosaic, the precise details of which you'll later have trouble recollecting. Your abiding memory will be one of being constantly knackered, totally skint, and in a permanent state of mild sexual frustration. All perfect training for the world beyond, of course.

What you will remember, however, will be the actual productions.

The plays, musicals and other assorted events that litter your path throughout the course form the milestones by which you – and the teaching staff – measure your progress. At first they'll be barely performances at all, little more than rehearsed readings in fact, usually involving a single performance in a bare room, with minimal props, no scenery or costume, and only attended by tutors and fellow students. As the course progresses they'll become more opulent affairs, culminating in full-scale projects that wouldn't disgrace your average repertory theatre.

The allocating of roles for these occasions will often seem haphazard, not to say capricious. There'll be some in your term who seem to bounce effortlessly from one starring role to another, while others (including possibly you) will feel as if you've already been tacitly consigned to the 'cameo' department, playing old crones and one-scene servants for what seems like an eternity.

Don't despair. It's rarely personal. Casting for thirty-odd students each and every term is an imperfect science, and in any case, some of the allocation has to be necessarily audacious to ensure the requisite roles are filled: although nothing you're likely to encounter will match my own time, which saw one student 'black up' to give his Othello, and an Afro-Caribbean girl in my term 'white up' to play an elderly dowager (remember, this was back in the 1970s).

But whatever the play and your contribution to it, each occasion will sear itself in your memory. In my case it began half way through my first term with a scratch staging of Peter Shaffer's *Black Comedy*, performed for one afternoon only in a room at the back of the building.

You may recall the summer of 1976 was one of the hottest on record. Hyde Park looked like the Atacama Desert, railway tracks buckled in the heat, Denis Howell was appointed minister for drought, and ice cream was fetching higher prices than cocaine.

The afternoon of our performance was so scorching that within minutes of commencing my portrayal, my purple C&A nylon shirt bought specially for the occasion had become transparent and about four shades darker; such was the cascade of sweat coursing down my forehead and into my eyes that I was unable to keep them open. Luckily Shaffer's play concerns a load of people blundering about in the dark after an unexpected power cut, so the fact I was blundering around anyway was hardly noticed.

By the second term we'd progressed to a tiny studio space in the bowels of the building, for a short run of Arnold Wesker's 1966 social drama *Their Very Own And Golden City*, in which I was giving my gnarled old Durham draftsman. With precious little else to hang on to I smeared my performance with an all-purpose northern dialect, and my hair with the residue from the bottom of an unshaken bottle of Milk of Magnesia to simulate white hair (an old thesps' trick I'd read about). It didn't save my blushes but at least kept my acid reflux at bay.

One of the truest maxims of acting is that it's always easier to play a lead than it is a walk-on: and it was midway through the fourth term, in a production of Moliere's *Tartuffe*, that I finally got the chance to play a lead, that of the cuckolded husband, Orgon.

Until now I'd been fending off an increasing sense of being a bit of a dead loss: but something must have gone in because during the first public performance, I made an instinctive decision to run two of my character's lines together, rather than break them up as suggested by the text; even as I spoke them I knew I was going to get a laugh. It was the first time I'd garnered a decent reaction since I'd entered the place fifteen months before, and while it would be exaggerating to say I never looked back, from that point on the training started to come together.

SHOWCASES

However much you shine in the productions, nowadays it will be the graduates' showcase event that will most affect your prospects.

Showcases, along with Pot Noodles and Peter Andre, could only be an invention of the late 20th century. Initially the province of only RADA, nowadays all major drama schools have embraced this simple means of displaying all the available talent in a single hit. The theatrical equivalent of speed dating, they offer a quick-fire mezze of all departing students strutting their stuff in one glorious ninety-minute confection: ideal for time-stressed potential employers, who can attend a performance simply by taking an extended lunch break.

These occasions are a heady cocktail of Opportunity Knocks, Miss World, and I'm A Celebrity Get Me Out Of Here. The performances are usually packed to the rafters with producers, agents and casting directors, each trying to sniff out the next big thing before their rivals do.

Once the presentation is over it's customary for the cast and audience to meet in the bar for a glass of wine and an informal chat. It may be advertised as a 'social', but in fact it's anything but. There's business to be struck here, at least for those who've caught the collective eye of their sponsors.

For the remainder it can be slow torture. In my case I stood on the fringe of the room along with a knot of other no-hopers and also-rans, knocking back glasses of cheap white wine and fistfuls of Hula Hoops, while at the other end of the bar the two or three gilded angels whose talent had been noted were bombarded by calling cards and invitations to 'pop into the office.'

If I'm overstating the misery of such occasions, it's not by much. Showcases are horrid, frightening, sphincter-tightening occasions at which it's all too easy to feel like a total loser. However, stay strong. The profession is a marathon, not a sprint, and one day you'll look back and laugh and wonder why you allowed yourself to get so depressed by it all.

That is, if you haven't hanged yourself from the nearest lighting gantry in the meantime.

And in one sense they're extremely useful: for however long you stay in the business, and whatever vicissitudes it throws at you, nothing will ever match the horror of the showcase. If you can survive that, you can survive anything. When the French philosopher Albert Camus wrote, 'Shall I kill myself, or have a cup of coffee?', I can only presume he'd just performed a speech from *Present Laughter* to a theatre full of disinterested employers while carrying half a jar of antacid preparation on his head.

EVERYBODY OUT!

After two-and-a-half years, I left RADA on a sultry summer's evening in 1978. Having completed our final performance in the Vanbrugh Theatre, we cleared our lockers, zipped our suitcases, and gathered in the bar for a last, lachrymose farewell to the teaching staff and our classmates. Within the hour we were to scatter to all corners of England, plus Ireland, Scotland, the United States, and South Africa. In all but a few cases, I wasn't to see them again for nearly three decades.

My own destination was perhaps the most prosaic of any – a train back to my parents' home in Brighton. I had no job, no agent, no interviews, and no prospects (though I did have some soup and a round of cheese sandwiches thoughtfully left for me by my mum on a Pyrex plate before she went to bed.)

The following morning, I woke up back in my old room: and unless something happened soon, I knew it would be all too easy to simply drift back to where I'd been three years previously – working in a toy shop, doing a little gentle am dram to keep my hand in, and eating too many crisps. Unless I got my act together my years at the world's most celebrated drama school would soon seem like a distant dream.

My diary entry sums up my feelings with a raw terror I can still smell whenever I open the page: 'The idea of starting life tomorrow as a jobbing actor is petrifying.'

I'd obviously learned more than I thought.

It was Michael Caine who famously said, 'I'm a skilled professional actor. Whether or not I've got any talent is beside the point.'

For most actors, fulfilling Michael Caine's criteria means working in theatre, TV or the movies. This is what you did your training for, this is what kept you going, this is what has fuelled your dreams – playing to packed houses in the West End or at the RSC, starring as the new sidekick in *Lewis,* or perhaps even popping across to Hollywood to try your luck as a movie star.

All these are each dealt with at some length in subsequent sections of this book. But first, you need to get a toehold in the profession: anything that can get you started and begin chipping away at that £30,000 overdraft you'll have racked up. And you've got at best about 18 months in which to do it before you're trampled underfoot by those following in your wake.

If you delay, you could find yourself going straight from *Who is Michael Simkins?* to *Who was Michael Simkins?* without any of the intervening stopovers. And I wouldn't wish that on my worst enemy.

Let's have a look at the various options open to you: any of which might make the crucial difference between survival and doom.

FRIENDS AND NEIGHBOURS

So the multi-Oscar-winning director John Huston dies and goes to heaven. As he draws near the pearly gates, Saint Peter approaches him. 'Mr. Huston,' he says, we're so glad to see you. God's making a movie, and he's been hanging on for you to arrive as he wants you to direct it.'

'Out of the question,' replies Huston. 'I'm old, tired and dead. I don't want to do any more movies.'

'But Mr. Huston,' continues St Peter, 'Wait until you hear who's he got lined up! The screenplay is by William Shakespeare, the soundtrack's penned by Mozart, the set designs are by Michelangelo, the costumes by Salvador Dali, and Busby Berkeley has agreed to do the choreography.'

'Wow!' says Huston. 'That sounds terrific. Reckon even I can't turn that down. I'll do it. By the way, who's playing the lead?'

'Ah,' says St Peter. 'Well the thing is, God has a girlfriend called Debbie...'

More than any business, showbiz is not about what you know, but who you know. Woody Allen said that 90% of success is turning up, but he omitted to mention the crucial fact that you need to know where to turn up, and who to mention sent you.

Luck, inside knowledge, and knowing the people who matter are the most important commodities. Talent helps, but if you're in the right place at the right time, it's the mere icing on the cake. That's why so many good actors never get off the starting blocks and so many bad actors end up as movie stars.

The Roman philosopher and dramatist Seneca (5 BC–65 AD) once classified luck as being, 'the intersection between preparation and opportunity'. So what to do? Should you write begging letters? How important is it to get an agent? What about joining Equity? Is it presumptuous to get an accountant when your savings currently stand at minus £30,000? How are your teeth? Do you have a presentable interview suit? And some decent photos?

And what's on offer out there? Should you try to get a job in regional theatre? Or a commercial tour? A play on the fringe? And while you're about it, panto season is approaching, the one time when nearly anyone with two arms and a head can get paid employment (just as long they're prepared to do *Mother Goose* at Slough). And if none of this floats your boat, perhaps you could get some radio drama? Maybe even an advert?

And what should you do to keep body and soul together while you're waiting? Telesales? Role-play? Waiting tables? Or should you just sit back, sign on, and wait for the offers to come rolling in?

Hopefully all this will be clarified in the next few pages.

But first of all, your Debbie needs some God.

AGENTS

Of all of Harry Venning's wonderful Hamlet cartoons (featured each week in the trade paper *The Stage*, and satirising the life of a jobbing actor in the shape of an itinerant luvvie pig), my favourite has to be the eponymous porcine hero turning up at his agent's office.

'Quiet at the moment!!!' he yells. 'You always say it's quiet at the moment! Can't you agents ever say anything else?'

The agent looks at him with barely-concealed disgust. 'Well, I could say you are a mediocre actor of unexceptional appearance, and finding you work is like looking for an off-licence in Tehran. Would you prefer I say that?'

Hamlet considers for a moment. 'So why do you think things are quiet at the moment?' he eventually asks.

Agents can reach the parts of the business you can't access by yourself. They know where the jobs are to be found. They're on first-name terms with the casting directors. They hang around in theatre foyers with the movers and shakers. They go on holiday with important producers. They have a season ticket to the Groucho. And even if they can't actually get you work, they can get you through the door. For which of course, should you be successful, they'll take a hefty wedge out of your weekly wage for their trouble.

Actors like to advertise agents as grasping parasites who rake off between 10% and 15% of our hard-won earnings. Agents by contrast, are equally disposed to classify us as grasping parasites that rake off between 85 and 90% of theirs. In other words, our occupations are symbiotic. They can't survive without us, but it's no longer really possible for us to exist without them. So we're tied together like competitors in a three-legged race, hobbling towards a mutual goal, trying as best we can to synchronise our lurching efforts in the hope that we can cross the finishing tape together.

Although their job spec is to get you interviews, they're so much more: your business manager, negotiator, advocate, publicist, counsellor, nursemaid, and in the case of one I know, reserve dog walker. Consequently the best ones will combine the diplomatic skills of Ban Ki-moon and the determination of Lance Armstrong with the single-mindedness of Pol Pot and the persuasiveness of Joanna Lumley.

They are not, however, your friend. Confuse the two and you're in trouble.

Never knowingly undersold

You need an agent. If I'd been writing this even ten years ago, my advice might have been very different. Back then it was perfectly possible to start out on a career without one, or rather, by using the GPO as an agent manqué. As long as you could afford writing materials and stamps you could bombard theatres and TV channels with begging letters, secure in the knowledge that sooner or later, something would stick.

When I started out for instance, I couldn't get an agent to look at me. But it didn't matter, as a letter to a small provincial repertory company in Kent caught the director's eye, which led to a contract. No matter that it was 'Play as Cast' with a special Equity low wage of £47 per week. I was away.

Some weeks into the gig and having by now been given the role of Sarah the cook in the pantomime, I sent a letter to a top London agent who at the time represented Glenda Jackson. It was a desperate shot in the dark, yet as a result of my request (and entirely unbeknown to me) he travelled personally all the way down on the train through a fierce winter snowstorm to see a matinée.

Never mind that he only stayed till the interval before battling back through the blizzard to his customary berth at the Garrick

Club. To paraphrase his sentiments, 'Any 21-year-old who's damned fool enough to attempt a panto dame deserves a break.'

Nonetheless I could once have survived quite happily without representation for many years; but that was then. Nowadays so much of the business of finding actors for parts is done through emails and automated casting breakdowns that trying to get by without an agent is the theatrical equivalent of trying to pay your utility bills by carrier pigeon.

That's not to say that any agent is better than no agent. A duff one is the worst of all worlds, as you'll sit on your increasingly fat arse at home in the mistaken belief they're lining up interviews, while they sit on their increasingly fat arse waiting for you to get a job so they can rake off their cut.

The trick is to get with the right one for you.

Taste the difference...

Who was it who said, 'I love Sainsbury's. They keep all the riff-raff out of Waitrose'?

Like supermarkets, there are several tiers of agents on offer, each with different price structures, ranges of products and prices. At the top – the equivalent of Harrods' Food Hall if you like – are the personal managers, who represent a mere handful of clients, each one so exclusive they won't even travel in the same car as their chauffeur.

A step down are the Waitroses, the big international agencies, all chrome and floor to ceiling windows, usually with offices in central London guarded by a concierge in the lobby. The agents themselves dwell high on the fifth floor in sequestered splendour, surrounded by an entire army of minions, while they spend their precious time flying to Broadway, attending preview screenings of *Downton Abbey* or wrangling with the producers of *I'm A Celebrity get Me Out Of Here* about the quantity of camels' eyeballs their client might have to expect to eat in the event of signing up to the forthcoming series.

Below that is the next tier – the so-called boutique agencies (Sainsbury's), the ones with a client list numbering 70 or 80, ranging from promising beginners to well-regarded titans of the business who nevertheless are not quite famous enough to stop the traffic. These agents are in some ways the best – too big to fail but small enough to care.

Lower down still (Tescos) are the ones that represent a whole fleet of stalwarts who form the ballast of any theatre or TV project. Some will be Taste The Difference, others, own-brand, but they generally fly off the shelves and rarely exceed their sell-by date. Then via Morrisons, Budgens and Asda, until you get to the one-man bands usually run by divorced women operating out of their spare bedrooms in East Sheen. Their clientele are the artistic equivalent of bulk consignments of pickled gherkins in brine or factory-dented tins of Angel Delight.

We're talking Lidl.

Finally there are the co-ops – an apt title, as, like their commercial doppelgänger, they're small friendly outlets, run for the mutual benefit of the client list and not quite like any of their competitors. These run on different principles, saving costly overheads and expensive salaries by employing their out-of-work clients to man the phones. The snag is that actors are not always at their best when using technology or propelling anyone's interests except their own.

If you go with a co-op, you'll be expected to put in at least a day a week (unpaid) in the office, and your casting suggestions will be the subject of fortnightly scrutiny by all the other clients, some of whom may not agree with your view of their strengths and weaknesses ('Why do I keep getting put up for *Embarrassing Fat Bodies*?). But at least it guarantees you the odd interview, even if you only suggest yourself.

The exclusive agents have first dibs on the major films and TV projects. They get the scripts first, are coveted by the producers for a few highly bankable stars, and may be able to persuade the producers to take on a few of their 'B'-listers as a sweetener for securing the services of their main client. The problem is that they'll be so busy sorting out Daniel Craig's private jet that they may have little time to devote to getting you seen for Salisbury Playhouse.

Each agency down the food chain then feasts on the remaining carcass of the project before it's passed on to the next tier, until it finally arrives at the divorcees in East Sheen, who often have little more left on which to pick than the giblets.

But let's assume you've targeted two or three likely possibilities. The next problem is persuading them to see you for an interview.

Fresh for you every day...

The best way of getting noticed is a personal recommendation. Agents have to wade through between 30 and 40 requests per week, and anything that suggests you come with a personal stamp of confidence will get you noticed above the general clamour, even if it's only a recommendation from your elder brother's old girlfriend from uni who now puts the numbers up on *Countdown*. Otherwise your carefully crafted letter, plus the expensive 10 by 8 photograph and SAE you've enclosed along with it will end up on the dreaded 'slush pile', which is about as likely to succeed as it sounds.

Check the letter is properly spelt, the accompanying mug shot is classy rather than something taken in your local post office photo-booth and finally, if the agency is long-standing, ensure that the head of the firm you're personally addressing is still alive.

Why pay more?

So you've been invited in to 'have a chat'. Whether you're successful depends on that ethereal quality called 'chemistry', and sadly that's something you can't legislate for. However, there are a few do's and don'ts which, if followed, will improve, albeit minimally, your chances of success.

Agents want to know two things. Can they make money from you, and are you going to be a pain in the rectum? So avoid being too cheesy or sycophantic (phrases such as, 'It's been my life's obsession to be represented by you' will soon have them fumbling for the panic button). Remember your place. They're auditioning you, not the other way round (one agent I spoke to assured me there were a surprising number of meetings where the actor being considered opened with, 'So, what made you want to be an agent?)

Make them laugh. Don't blag or brag. And be prepared for unexpected setbacks. One agent I went to see many years ago barely allowed me to blurt out more than my name before putting his hands over his ears and commanding me to leave the room. 'Your voice is too loud,' he said, 'Stop shouting. No wonder you can't get a telly career. You need a hearing specialist rather than a new agent.'

Mind you, I still reckon he was going deaf.

If you're jettisoning your old agent in order to go with them, don't, *however tempting it might seem*, start slagging off the incumbent. 'Nobody likes a squealer.' It's a maxim as true in theatrical agents as it is in Alcatraz.

Every little helps...

So an agent has offered you a berth. Curiously, in this highly litigious modern world, you'll rarely see a contract. Your partnership is still essentially a gentlemen's agreement, one that can be terminated by either party at any time. Your agent will take 10% of your weekly wage if you're in theatre, moving up to 12.5% for TV and 15% for movies. If they have the slightest shred of common decency they won't charge you anything for fringe or low-paid work.

The first few weeks after joining are a time of great excitement. You may even be canvassed as to which area of the business you want to focus on, conversations that will go something like:

'So, darling, how do you see your career panning out?'

'Well, having only done panto at Stafford Town Hall and a fringe show in the Cock & Bottle on Westbourne Grove I really think it would be helpful if I could get into major international feature films...'

'Good idea. Yes, I can see the sense in that. It's nice to have a client with a clear direction for what he wants to do; it makes things so much easier for us. I'll tell the girls in the office, and we'll get onto it straightaway.'

This is all very fortifying, but such sentiments are so much hot air. Never mind the fine words, unless you're Ben Whishaw or Gemma Arterton, your agent is simply going to try and get you placed, even if it's driving lorries for Billy Smart's circus.

As one agent put it to me recently, 'Unless you're hot, strategies are pointless.'

Nevertheless your new liaison should kick off with a flurry of appointments. This is the honeymoon period; don't expect it to last. Your agent is merely trying to demonstrate just how capable they are, and how hard they will be working for you.

Once it's settled down, things will tail off a bit. You may even find yourself talking not to the person who hired you, but one of their assistants, usually a girl called Hayley. The temptation always, especially when things are slack, is to call your agent to rattle their cage and demand some tummy tickling. It's human nature, but try to resist the temptation. They're working away, and don't need reminding of your existence. And in any case, whenever you call you'll be haunted by a vague sense that it's not a convenient moment.

Either they'll be just off to lunch, just back from lunch, just off to the gym, just back from the gym, leaving for a first night, or already occupied with a much more important call. So don't be dismayed if your breezy attempts at chit-chat receive no more than a long agonised silence followed by a glassy-voiced, 'Really darling, that's interesting'. If it seems as if they're not listening, they're not listening.

Or rather, they're only half-listening. They'll be simultaneously waving to their assistant to put the much more important call on hold while they deal with your enquiry, signalling to the taxi driver in the street outside to assure them they're on their way, or simultaneously scrutinising an email that's just come in alerting them that a much more prized client currently shooting a movie has just been arrested for wandering naked round the hotel lobby at 3 am.

It's nothing personal. Their distracted air is a healthy sign. Any agent who's got time enough on their hands to hear what you had for breakfast or what you made of last night's episode of *The Killing* is on the skids. It means nobody's calling them. It means you're with the wrong agent.

In any case, they already know why you're ringing. You're calling for one of two reasons. 'Why is it so quiet at the moment?' or, 'Have you heard whether I got the job I went up for?'

The answer to the first – 'Why is it so quiet at the moment?' – is contained in the aforementioned Hamlet cartoon. And the second – 'Have you heard anything?' – is, of course, 'No.' If it were 'Yes', they would already have rung you. What do you think they are, sadists?

The one thing all agents fear is having you turning up unannounced at their office. Can you imagine the furore if you suddenly descended on your bank manager, slumped down on their sofa and began making free with the chocolate digestives? That's why an increasing number of top agents no longer have offices in central London but in hinterlands such as Hammersmith and Barons Court. It's not that the rents are cheaper, it's just that it's more difficult for actors to drop in on the flimsy pretext that they were passing by.

How are you darling?

If, on the other hand, your agent calls you, there are only two reasons (three, if they're calling to dump you, but for advice on dealing with that please see appendix 33, *Contacting the Samaritans*). Either they've got you an interview, or they're calling with the result of one.

Any call from your agent about the result of a pending job interview will always begin with the same sentence as soon as you pick up the phone.

'How are you darling?' they'll ask.

Far from the exasperating nicety it seems, this brief enquiry is actually part of an important and time-honoured ritual. The way in which they trot out this preliminary query will already tell you whether it's going to be good news or bad. It's the theatrical equivalent of the airline pilot telling you to fasten your seatbelt. Learning to read the vocal runes of these simple words gives you a precious second or two in which to prepare for the inevitable, which might be a perfect touchdown at JFK or, more likely, a belly flop into the middle of the Pacific.

If the initial, 'How are you darling?' is said with a slight upward inflection, it means you've got the gig. Agents love breaking good news, as it confirms their own status and in any case, they're genuinely thrilled to see you happy. By keeping you hanging on that tiny moment more before breaking the news, it makes their subsequent orgasm even more exquisite for both parties.

Scenario One
'How are you darling?' (upward inflection).
'I'm good, thanks.'
'Well, you're about to feel a whole lot better. It's an offer!'

Cue laughter, tears, fanfares, and general merry-making. This is the best part of any job – hearing those three lovely words, 'It's an offer!' Nothing you'll subsequently experience in the gig itself comes even close. In the case of one big TV series I secured, my agent even put me onto two-way speakerphone so the entire office staff could share in my cries of joy and reciprocate with communal applause down the line. It was followed by a bottle of champagne delivered the next morning wrapped in enough raffia paper to furnish any number of school nativity displays.

Scenario Two

'How are you darling?' (downward inflection).
'I'm good, thanks.'
'Good. But I'm ringing with some disappointing news I'm afraid. It didn't go your way.'

Didn't go your way is a euphemism for, 'You blew it.' Agents have any number of euphemisms to inform you that you blew it. 'It hasn't gone your way', 'It's gone in a different direction', 'It's a matter of chemistry', or in the case of one excuse offered to me recently, 'They didn't think your performance was quite the right temperature…'

What they mean is, 'You blew it.'

If the news is bad, try to hold it in. 'Thanks for telling me', will more than suffice. It may not be much fun to hear, but it's not much fun for them to say either. Your agent will try to patch you up as best they can (variants include, 'Well, if it's any consolation they're idiots'/'They must be mad' /'They must be out of their minds' and finally, 'Something better will come along soon.)' Don't press for further details. You need to go off and do your crying in the rain, and in any case they're being waved at by their assistant to break the next piece of bad news to another client who's gnawing their own arm off in worry.

The fact is, you blew it.

And while agents will do their best for you, remember that they're working simultaneously for several separate interest groups, each of whom have priorities that are mutually exclusive.

That's not to say they don't feel your pain. It's just that they can't afford to cheese off exactly the people whose patronage they're relying on and whom they've spent many years courting. So before you start barking, 'Unless you make this call I'm off', think twice. You may not get the answer you were expecting.

Do not make friends with your agent

That's not to say you can't enjoy the good times together – the awards ceremonies, the first nights, the freebies. On the contrary, celebrate your mutual success. You've both earned it. But don't get into bed together, either physically or metaphorically: for as surely as the paparazzi follows Jedward, there'll come a time when you'll want to sleep with someone else. And when it does you don't want the spectre of a shared New Year in a Landmark Trust property or that promise they made to be godparent at your child's christening next spring to be hanging over you.

Changing your agent

The old saying that changing your agent is like, 'Swapping deckchairs on the Titanic' may be a hoary old truism, but the fact is, actors only ever look after number one. We have to. If your career is marooned on the hard shoulder with the bonnet open, you'll need to change your agent anyway. But even if you suddenly strike celebrity gold, it won't be long before that part of your brain that ultimately dominates proceedings – namely, your ego – starts to drip poison in your ear.

'See? You're doing well, just as I always knew you would,' it whispers in honeyed tones, 'I always knew you were something special. Now you're getting noticed this may be your one and only chance to break through. Don't let this opportunity slip through your fingers. There'll be somebody out there who can really help you make it to the top. Don't hang about with this schmuck – go find them. You may not get another chance.'

And before you know it your greasy little fingers will be tapping away on the keyboard, framing letters of enquiry to those agents who represent the actor you really want to be. 'Dear so and so, I am currently considering changing my agent and was wondering if, in the light of my current prominent profile on TV, it would be possible to come in to have a chat...'

And suddenly there you are, sitting in someone's office, swapping *bon mots*, telling them how highly regarded they are, expressing your frustration that you're not being seen for the parts you want to, and before the cock has crowed three times you'll be inventing all sorts of spurious excuses why this is where you really need to be.

Thus agents are in an impossible position; damned if they do and damned if they don't. Whatever efforts they make on your behalf, they're ultimately signing their own death warrant.

Leaving your agent

The only thing you need to know about leaving your agent is that they already know it's going to happen. Don't ask me how. It's just one of the dark arts they specialise in. They know you, probably better than you do yourself, so the slightest derivation from your normal tone will already have set alarm bells ringing. And if you suddenly call them to say you 'need to come in to talk…'

The first time I left an agent was to take my leave of the one who took me on after my sojourn in Canterbury panto. Having already secured a replacement, I phoned to tell them I needed to come in and talk. As far as I recall, this was the sum total of my message.

Yet when I entered the office the atmosphere was utterly different. The office girls that normally said, 'Hi, hi,' and hurried off to make me a coffee didn't look up from their typewriters. The secretary herself, normally so warm and friendly, had a brittle grin etched across her normally sunny features. She parked me in a chair in the corner where I sat for several minutes in frigid silence.

At length, the agent himself reeled in from the Garrick, but instead of offering his hand, he merely beckoned me in without a word. The moment the door was shut behind me I immediately burst into tears and blubbed like a baby while he fumbled around in embarrassment for his handkerchief.

He was, in truth, grace and courtesy personified – of course he was, he was a member of the Garrick – and even offered me a fortifying brandy and a promise that 'if it doesn't work out you can always come back.'

Of course, that was three decades ago, before mobiles and the internet. Times have changed and there are so many ways to wield the bloody dagger. So what's the best method? Should you still go in and see them? Send a letter? Or just ping a weasly email and take refuge behind the sofa?

My departure from my next agent, two decades on, had me trying version two: the letter. Having successfully wooed a replacement, I ended up driving to my soon-to-be old one's private house on a Sunday afternoon and pushing a note through their letterbox, before scurrying back to my car like the sewer rat I was.

It was an unedifying spectacle, and I wasn't in the least surprised when their call next morning to acknowledge receipt came with hefty dose of sheet ice to it. However, time has lent a softer hue to my course of action. Going in to see your agent to tell them you're leaving is a fruitless pursuit. You go in, you cry, you weep, you embarrass yourself and possibly them, everyone ends up spouting vapid platitudes and you've rendered the whole office so jangled and unnerved that they're unfit for purpose for several more hours (and in one case I heard of, the agent was so upset they threw the fax machine at the departing client).

'Oh for God's sake, tell your readers to stay away,' one agent said to me wearily when he knew I was writing this book. 'Tell them to send an email and have done with it.' When I asked why she advocated this particular method, she replied with a stiff smile, 'Because we'll already know.'

Dog eat dog

The most graphic example of just how cut-throat the relationship between actors and their representatives on earth remains, is one related to me a few years ago by one agent.

One client of his in particular had managed to transcend the usual dance-macabre that forms the basis of all actor/agent friendships. The two of them would regularly meet for coffee and laugh together about the venal personality of most thesps, and how actors will sell their own grandmother the moment they get a sniff of the big time. Their friendship genuinely seemed to have become something richer, more nourishing and thoroughly dependable.

Then two things occurred. The actress in question suddenly got a major lead in a very tasty comedy series. And the agent's mother had a bowel cancer scare. Both things happened simultaneously and without warning and, during the next few weeks of preliminary tests, the agent was a tiny bit preoccupied with dealing with his mother's plight, while his client was equally preoccupied with her filming.

Thankfully, the agent's mum soon got the all-clear, yet he'd hardly got his feet back under his desk when his client suddenly started to prove difficult to track down. Whenever he rang, there was always a reason why she couldn't linger on the phone – she was shopping, or in make-up, or just boarding a train.

Inevitably the dread email arrived, announcing she was trading him in for a bigger and more powerful model. All the usual weasel words of course – 'Thank you for all your help over the years', 'Hope we can still remain friends', 'If I don't take this chance I may never get another.' It was only months later that the agent heard via a third party of the real reason being pedalled by the actress in question. Her justification for putting the boot in, she averred, was that her agent's mother had had a health scare and she'd been forced to go in case he 'lost focus'.

With friends like that, who needs enemas?

ACCOUNTANTS

It was George Best who said, 'I spent a lot of money on booze, birds and fast cars. The rest I just squandered.'

If you want to do the same (and who doesn't?) you need to have a good accountant. By 'good', I don't mean someone in a camel-haired coat with links to untraceable bank accounts in Lagos, but merely one who understands actors and how our tax affairs work: someone with a solid reputation who won't allow you to sail too close to the wind.

Despite the government's best attempts to alter it, the system by which actors pay tax remains a complex, not to say byzantine process. After three decades I still don't fully understand how it works (which is why I employ a good accountant) but broadly speaking, actors don't pay our tax at source but up to two years after we've earned it.

The good news is that during those 24 months between acquiring the money and handing it over, we've got ample opportunities to think of ways of correllating 'legitimate professional expenses' (as defined by H.M. Revenue & Customs) to offset the sum owed.

The bad news is that, being actors, we're feckless, easily persuaded and virtually innumerate. So we forget we haven't yet paid the tax, think the amount sweating away in our bank account is all ours, and blow it all on booze, birds and cars. Thus we can't pay the lump sum when it becomes due. Which can be damaging to our reputation.

A good accountant will see to this. They'll regularly ring to remind you that a proportion of the sum gently fermenting in your account isn't yours but the Chancellor's, and that you'd better have a care before booking that fortnight in Antigua. They may even insist on your handing over a proportion of your earnings to a special fund held in trust by them, so there's sufficient money when the time comes to cover your liability (a useful precaution, unless your accountant is himself a crook, in which case it'll be him having the luxury holiday in Antigua rather than you).

The most important investment you can make, however, will undoubtedly be the purchase of a supermarket carrier bag in which to stuff the thousands of dog-eared receipts that are now going to be part of your daily ritual.

RECEIPTS

The reason most actors have bulging wallets is not to stash their stupendous wages, but merely to keep the thousands of bits of scruffy paper they carry around with them. Bus receipts, cinema tickets, chits for virtually everything from a new shirt to hair gel. Almost anything you pay for in the course of a day's work may be useful to your overall cause at the hands of a skilful accountant.

For example: you'll need a car in which to travel to work and interviews – and somewhere to park it. Plus petrol and oil; not to mention an MOT certificate and Roadside Relay. And what about one of those dashboard air fresheners? Then there's rail and tube fares of course, taxi rides, plus books, make-up, meals out, meals in, meals out, even newspapers and periodicals.

What else? Clothes for interviews, moisturiser, hair gel, dental floss, shoe polish, new laces, a smart belt, dry cleaning, plus ink cartridges for your printer, stationery, stamps, a laptop, flowers for the first nights, a regular tip for the stage doorkeeper, another for your dresser: and then there's your phone line, and up to 80% of your mobile usage. The list, if not endless, is certainly capacious: more than enough for a good accountant to get stuck into.

Where the skilled practitioner is worth their weight in gold is in knowing where to draw the line: because the temptation is always to push your luck, and unless there's a steadying hand on your shoulder, before you know it you'll not only be including DVDs and greetings cards but also items like patio chairs, water filter cartridges and tickets to Arsenal versus West Brom at the Emirates.

After all, surely H.M. Revenue & Customs are far too busy trying to corral rapacious hedge fund managers in the city to query why you've included roast lunch for two at your local gastropub in your own piffling accounts. You're just small fry. Bung it in. They'll never know.

And inexorably the inventory will widen, each inconsequential purchase chipping away at the amount you have to pay the taxman. Marvellous! If you go on like this they'll soon be paying you! The knock on the door will never come.

Except it will. Take it from me, those official adverts with the sound of footsteps advancing down a dark alleyway, and the dark intoning of the phrase 'We're coming for you' are true. It may take some time, but it'll happen. And however good your accountant, when the knock does come, you're on your own. So his job is to make sure you don't get too greedy.

Because, in the world of tax investigations, no one can hear you scream.

In my case, it occurred back in the 1990s (and before I had a decent accountant), when I was subject of a random inspection from a very nice man who arrived in shirt-sleeves with a row of different coloured biros in his breast pockets and carrying a smart briefcase. His name, as I recall, was Gerald.

It all began so promisingly. As he was unpacking his briefcase he spotted the signed poster of Ian Botham on the wall (my tastes in home furnishings were rather less sophisticated back then), and informed me breezily that cricket was one of his abiding passions (he even had tickets to the first three days of the forthcoming Lords' Test).

Before long we were soon chit-chatting like old friends about cricket in general – whether reverse swing was aerodynamically possible or just a rumour, and the chances of our boys defeating Pakistan in the forthcoming series – while I plied him with chocolate shortbread and fresh coffee.

And then suddenly, about fifteen minutes in, it all stopped. 'Now about your accounts,' he said, opening the latches on his briefcase with an ominous snap; in an instant his face clamped shut. No more smiles. No more jovial banter. The next two hours was the verbal equivalent of waterboarding.

As we sifted through bags of yellowing chits, I was forced to account for each and every one. Fish and chip suppers in Crouch End; bus journeys to far flung corners of the capital; receipts for aftershave and stay-fresh socks, many of which I could barely recall. Yet nothing escaped Gerald's basilisk eye.

'Now, I see here you bought some olive chinos at Next on Ongar High Street in August 1996,' he said, referring to one particular docket laying between us on the table top. 'Can you explain why you needed this particular item for your work?'

I recalled the garment only too well. It'd been a ghastly mistake, one I was still trying to live down amongst my friends. Of course I hadn't bought them for work at all, merely for a forthcoming holiday with my girlfriend in Greece. But it was too late now. I spent the next ten minutes trying to explain why a pair of olive chinos might be essential to my professional advancement, but he was having none of it.

'I think we'll strike them from your accounts don't you?' he said mildly, 'describing them as "essential" rather stretches the dictionary definition of the word, don't you agree?'

But this was only the beginning. He wanted to know why I'd claimed on a cinema ticket to see the latest Pokémon movie at my local multiplex. I blathered something about needing to keep up with the cultural zeitgeist, but the fact was I'd merely taken my mate's seven-year-old while she attended to a leak in her radiator. Another item similarly troubled him. 'I see you have specified one particular meal as being "lunch with agent", yet the accompanying receipts suggest it consisted of a couple of pork pies and a Diet Coke in the buffet on Cleethorpes station. Can you explain why you chose such a curious venue?' Another flick of Gerald's biro, and another tenner down the Swannee.

During the next two hours we wrangled over literally hundreds of items, from swims at my local leisure centre to athlete's foot powder from Sainsbury's. By the time we'd got to a pair of gardening gloves I'd purchased at a garden centre in Maida Vale, I was barely offering a defence.

At length he turned his attentions to some items of women's underwear that had been troubling him. I already knew that claiming for three pairs of women's pants I'd bought my mum as a Mother's Day gift had been a mistake, but it had all seemed so easy back then. Now I shifted uneasily in my seat. 'Is there something you'd like to tell me?' he asked quietly.

Perhaps if I'd confessed to a little light transvestism I may have gained his sympathy. But I couldn't bring myself to do it, and my halting defence about the possibility of going up for the dame in panto was left hanging in the air.

Finally we came to the column marked 'Dental Work.'

'I see here you've claimed nearly £600 on some root canal treatment, two crowns and a polish and clean. Can you explain this please?'

The issue here, he assured me, was 'duality of purpose'; for whatever the cosmetic advantage, the majority of their daily usage was to masticate food, which is a necessity whether you're working at the RSC or Matalan. All but a fraction of their cost was to be struck from my accounts.

At the end he did a quick tally-up. The sum clawed back by his visit was very nearly a third. But even then he wasn't finished. 'I notice an unusually high quantity of the receipts seem to have muddy boot prints on them. You haven't, by any chance, gotten into the habit of picking up stray examples from the pavement and claiming them as your own have you?'

Our eyes locked. Perhaps it was the sight of Ian Botham flaying a lofted drive over extra cover, but Gerald softened slightly. 'Never mind,' he said, closing his briefcase. 'Let's assume it's merely due to your eagerness to put them safely in your wallet after purchase. Just as well the England slip cordon doesn't suffer from similar butterfingers, or we'd struggle to take ten wickets in an innings.'

And just as I thought I was safe from further punishment, he turned in the doorway.

'One more thing. Please don't make these mistakes again, or else we may be forced to take a less charitable view next time round. Good-day.'

You need a good accountant.

EQUITY

Put any two actors in a bar together, buy them a couple of drinks, and before half an hour has elapsed you can be certain they'll be having a stand-up row about Equity.

Equity is, of course, the actor's trade union. It is, according to your point of view, a vital legislative safeguard, fighting to ensure thesps everywhere are provided with a living wage and decent working conditions, and offering support and assistance in times of crisis and exploitation: or a toothless and thoroughly clapped-out talking-shop for actors who are only serving on the committee because they can't get sufficient work in the first place.

These days, when anyone can legitimately call themselves an actor merely by announcing the fact on Twitter, it must seem bewildering to learn that until relatively recently you weren't even able to work in the industry without being a member of the union. The absurdity of this situation was something of a black joke in the profession – the fact you couldn't work without being awarded an Equity card, and you couldn't get an Equity Card without first being offered work.

Although these prized cards were supposed to be scattered liberally and equally throughout the industry, some organis-ations were awash with them while others didn't seem to have any. For instance, there never seemed any shortage of them amongst strip clubs and cruise ship companies, whereas the recognised theatre enterprises only had two a year to divvy up between the countless drama school graduates clamouring for preferment. The more you were prepared to flash your tits or organise a wet T-shirt competition in the middle of the Med, the greater your chances of getting a toehold in the business.

I was perfectly happy to show my tits or wear a wet T-shirt whenever asked. Trouble was, there were no takers.

Then we hit the 1980s, and along with invading the Falklands, privatising British Gas and dismantling the mining industry, Mrs Thatcher also found time to break up the actors' closed shop. Suddenly you no longer needed an Equity card to work, and it was a free for all. Worse still for our solidarity, newcomers saw little point in signing away a percentage of the earnings to a union they no longer needed for advancement, and yet were happy to piggy-back on all the hard-won terms and conditions gained by Equity over a century of hard legal slog, without feeling the slightest necessity of supporting the organisation that put them in place.

Thirty years on, membership of our union is now voluntary, and like all voluntary organisations, its power is greatly weakened. This enfeeblement means more and more actors rightly complain it's useless and refuse to stump up their annual subscription because they can't see the point. The vicious circle spirals ever downwards, and hence we eventually arrive at the two actors now throttling each other in the lounge bar which I referred to at the start of this brisk polemic.

The most poignant aspect is that it's often the most success- ful actors who've let their membership lapse. Of course they have.

After all, they've got agents, personal managers and publicists fighting their corner, each one taking their own slice of the action.

The shortsightedness of those who want to pull up the drawbridge was graphically demonstrated to me some years ago by a conversation I had with one of our leading beefcakes, then playing one half of a successful cop show. Having made a number of series and now sporting both a large Porsche and an even larger paunch, the actor in question launched into this very line of attack with me one night in the bar of the hotel in which we were both staying.

'Equity… Don't get me started…' he spat the words out with as much distaste as he could muster as he clawed at his umpteenth glass of wine. 'Fuckin' hopeless. As much use as rabies in a dog's home.' When I pointed out the obvious collective benefits of having an umbrella union forestalling the excesses of rapacious managements, he roared back, 'That's what I pay my agent for', before launching into a tirade, loosely based on the Monty Python 'What have the Romans ever done for us' sketch. 'I can fight my own battles, thanks', he finished, slumping heavily against the bar.

At this point, thank God, he passed out. But if he hadn't have done so, I would have calmly pointed out the fundamental error in his logic. We don't pay our subs for ourselves – we pay them so that our union is able to afford to help out the poor chorus girl being chased round the desk by some cigar-chomping sleazebag, shouting, 'You want to work don't you, you little fool?' while slave-driving her for 14 shows a week at some end-of-pier show, all for £180 a week and no overtime.

So if you're going to be a proper actor, join Equity. And pay your subs. And if you're asked to volunteer to become Equity

Deputy in the company in which you're residing, put up your hand. And count your blessings that when finally you do break your leg in the darkness of the wings by tripping over a badly placed electrical cable, or get shafted by some venal low-life producer who never intended paying you in the first place – there'll be an organisation to turn to for help.

And now, with a final rousing chorus of 'L'Internationale' and with the two actors glassing each other out in the street, I take my leave.

Sorry? What happened to the star playing the police cop? Truth to tell, I haven't seen him on our screens for over a decade. I sort of hope he's doing summer season on the Isle of Man.

10 X 8s

Finally, you'll also need some decent photos.

Your 10" by 8" mugshot is your principal calling card, particularly when you're first setting out in the profession and nobody knows who you are; and in addition to sending copies of it to anyone and everyone who might be able to help, you'll also need to insert it in the actors' directory published by *Spotlight,* a publication regularly trawled by casting directors, and inclusion in which is considered *de rigeur* (please see section headings for some of my own examples over the years).

Getting a decent photo can be a time-consuming and expensive business, but it's well worth it. Don't be tempted to entrust your hopes to your dad's old mate Frank who's a professional wedding photographer and who will do it for thirty quid cash in hand. Such ruses rarely result in anything worth even this piffling investment. Presenting you in the best possible light (quite literally) is a job for the experts only.

There are hundreds of professional photographers specialising in the field, and a quick trawl through the internet or the journal *Contacts* will soon flush one out. Normally a photo session will cost you between £100 and £300 (including a selection of prints), and take a couple of hours to complete. For the actual shoot you'll be asked to turn up either at the photographer's preferred location (my current one is very fond of taking me into the woods near Alexandra Palace), or alternatively at their house if they prefer a more climate-controlled environment.

You'll need to wash your hair, get a good night's sleep, lay off the booze, and bring along several contrasting outfits. Sort out your wardrobe well in time before setting off, as frayed collars and straining buttons will soon mark you out as a bit of a loser (an entire batch I had taken some years ago was ruined by a gob of dried egg down the lapel of my jacket). It's not the photographer's job to resolve your sartorial issues, and in any case, they'll have a gig scheduled in another part of the forest as soon as they've completed yours.

Think carefully about the image you wish to present. A sharp suit says crisp professional; hoodies suggest athlete or thug; and jazzy patterns, wacky ties or crimson polka dots will date horribly. And there's no point glaring moodily back at the lens from a black leather jacket if your natural métier is that of an amiable bungler. Most actors go for something all-purpose, a neutral look, with an enigmatic smile peeking through a fierce intellect, blended with understated deter-mination. If you can manage that lot you'll be considered a suitable candidate for anything from librarians through to psychopaths.

And don't try anything too fancy, as I did on the occasion I had my eyelashes dyed at a nearby beauty salon in an effort to give myself a slightly smokier appearance. I ended up looking less like Daniel Craig and more like Danny La Rue. And don't be afraid to smile, even if it risks displaying a set of teeth like yellowing tombstones. After all, you never know when Mike Leigh might be on the lookout to cast his next film.

Once it's over the photographer will ping the best thirty or so samples over to you by email for your consideration. This is the best bit of the entire process, as it requires you to spend several hours poring over endless images of yourself, trying to pick the magic shot that will access all areas. Beware of Photoshopping the finished images too much: it may make you look a million dollars on the page, but you run the risk of the director screaming in horror when you walk in for real.

GOOD TO GO

So you're finally tooled up. You've got yourself a nice agent, an accountant ready to get to work just as soon as you provide him with the raw materials, a decent mugshot, and you've notified Equity of your presence on this earth.

So what now?

Let's take a close look at the various options for getting work, some of which may not have previously occurred to you…

RESTING

Why don't actors look out of the window in the morning?
Because they want something to do in the afternoons.

Resting. The word that bedevils actors whenever and wherever they go. You'll be at some family wedding, or at a dinner party, or even sitting quietly in the pub, and sooner or later someone will nudge your arm, offer a knowing smirk, and utter the dread words, 'So you're an ack-*torr* are you? Resting at the moment?'

If they do, try to smile. Cut them some slack. Don't smash your pint glass on the tabletop and brandish it in their face. It won't help.

Having said that, don't encourage them, not unless you want more of the same. Once emboldened, it'll only be a matter of time before they'll be asking, how do you learn your lines and have they seen you in anything on the telly? The following conversation will then proceed thus…

'So… have I seen you in anything on the telly?'

'Well I was in *Foyle's War* a few years back.'

'No, don't watch that. What else?'

'I did *Dr Who* last Christmas.'

'I hate sci-fi. Can't see the point. Anything else?'

'Did you see the last series of *Above Suspicion*?'

'Never heard of it. What else?'

'I was in *EastEnders* last April.'

'To tell you the truth, I never watch the telly. So what do you do for your day job?'

It may seem brutal to start a chapter about the various forms of employment available to actors with a section on unemployment: but for many, resting is as good as it gets. 92% of the acting profession are out of work at any one time, so rather than pretend it isn't going to happen, the trick is to acknowledge it, embrace it, and make it work for you.

If nothing else, resting provides a unique opportunity to get out of the exotic hothouse of actors and acting and sample the real world. There are some great characters waiting to be discovered out there, but you won't even encounter them if you spend all your free time meeting other actors for coffee. Half of being an actor is emulating, so picking up lessons from everyday life can be a valuable professional tool.

Your biggest enemy, as if you need telling, is indolence. Anything you can do to generate sufficient energy and income to continue pursuing your dream is priceless. So if you can find a job that's payable, flexible and bearable, take it. You've nothing to lose except a morning slumped in front of Jeremy Kyle.

If you already have a second skill – supply teaching, driving HGVs or speaking French – you're laughing. But even if you can't do much more than write your name, there are ways of getting by, if only you're prepared to swallow your pride and get stuck in; waiting tables, pulling pints or even selling interval ice-creams at your local playhouse.

Most actors worth their salt have their own 'worst job while resting' experience. One friend surmounted her first spell out of work by demonstrating organic yogurt mixing machines in the foyer of the Harlequin Centre in Watford, a gig that paid decent money, taught her microphone technique (she had a little electronic one draped round her neck for live demos) and gave her practice in holding an audience spellbound with sparse material. (It also helped clear up a stubborn case of aural thrush she'd had trouble shifting.)

The actress Annette McLaughlin was handing out samples of Gouda cheese slices at her local Tesco's dressed as a Dutch maid complete with clogs when she heard she'd got the lead in the West End production of the musical *Chicago*. Another friend staved off financial oblivion by spending an entire summer scraping the gloop off the insides of the Spangle-making machine at Mars confectionary in Slough, while yet another dressed as an energy-efficient house while handing out free light bulbs at a home improvement exhibition at Earls Court.

The actor Stuart Grogan still dines out on how he combined a spell as Santa Claus at Stansted airport by day with working as a security guard for a clinic specialising in providing abortions for Catholic foreigners by night. My favourite has to be that offered by suave heart-throb Tristran Gemmill, who staved off the bailiffs by carrying the official flag at the opening parade of the Massey Ferguson tractor convention in Australia.

Jobs I've taken when things have been tight include working a crate smasher at Nissan UK and selling Dorling Kindersley children's dictionaries to primary schools in Tottenham. My most lucrative, however, at least in terms of remuneration for effort, has to be the day I was hired by bookmakers Paddy Power to conduct incognito surveys at their various outlets in London. My brief (for which I was paid £50 a pop) was to visit four separate branches in the Willesden area, and in the course of placing a £5 bet, make a note of the décor, the friendliness of the staff, and whether the public areas were clean and tidy, the results of which I then fashioned into a brief report for head office.

As it turned out, three of the four premises I was sent to investigate were already boarded up. Not only did I earn a couple of hundred quid for about thirty minutes work, I also made an extra £50 when my sole bet came in at 11/1.

Whatever you do, ensure the job allows flexibility. There's no point taking a job as a glamorous PA if you need to give a fortnight's notice in triplicate every time you want to scuttle off for an audition.

PRESERVING YOUR SANITY

Remember the last time someone phoned you from a call centre? Just when you were serving up the evening meal, or settling down in front of a roaring spouse? Do you remember how you shouted at them when you realised who they were? Recollect the language you used?

Cold-calling innocent civilians to persuade them to change their electricity supplier or taking up accidental death insurance may seem a chance of easy money, but the tales related by survivors of this niche industry are horrific. Hours slogging away repeating the same brainless dialogue to disinterested punters, abuse and vitriol your only reward (apart from about £60 a day before tax), and in many such environments you even have to put your hand up to be allowed to go to the toilet (you'll also pick up repeated ear infections from sharing headsets).

'A small part of your soul is lost each time you pick up the phone,' was how one veteran put it to me, who then recalled rocking back and forth in despair on the floor of the ladies' during her rest breaks. There's simply no point taking a gig that destroys what little self-esteem you're already trying to protect. You'll only carry your failure with you into the audition room.

The important thing is to keep busy. Go for a jog, join a gym, or even go for a swim at your local baths, or refresher classes at the Actors Centre off Cambridge Circus. If nothing else, keep away from the remote control. Never mind drinks, tobacco and drugs – these three axes of evil will undoubtedly reduce you to an empty husk if you imbibe too freely, but they're nothing to the corrosive effect of watching re-runs of *Cash In The Attic*.

SIGNING ON

Jobseekers' allowance was simply not designed for actors. It was designed for normal people.

Normal people work on building sites, sell insurance, or work behind the counter at their local branch of Gregg's. They have contracts, wage slips and PAYE tax returns. Actors do not.

For actors, a nice new comedy series on Channel 4 with Stephen Merchant, or doing two nice scenes in the next series of *Whitechapel* are legitimate professional opportunities. Trouble is, you don't get much call for that sort of thing in your local jobcentre. So instead you'll be offered shift work at your local warehouse, and when you refuse on the grounds that you'd rather not because you're up for a new musical about the life of Doris Day at Malvern… Well, the person in charge of finding you suitable employment may not understand the finely-nuanced difference between the two.

And when it comes to filling out another crucial box, the one marked 'reasons for leaving your last employment', simply putting 'I ran out of dialogue' or 'I got shot in the chest half way through episode two' doesn't compute. Like Dickens' fictional Mr Gradgrind, what they want is facts. And facts are the one thing in short supply in the acting game. In any case, if you wanted to be treated as an office worker, you'd be working in an office.

In short, it's a one-way ticket to madness. They won't understand you and you won't understand them, and in addition you'll have to reveal every torturous detail of your daily life.

If you're happy to go through the ordeal just to get a few measly tenners then good luck. But take it from me, by the time it appears in your bank account you'll long since have given up the will to live; that is, if you haven't already starved to death in the process.

THE NATIONAL THEATRE

The National Theatre, on London's South Bank, is considered by most stage actors to be Nirvana – the acme of what an acting gig should be like.

Everything about the place is just about perfect – the setting, (a prime spot in central London next to the river Thames), the quality of the productions, the skill and experience of the creatives, the dizzying variety of productions and the generous funding (it's about the only place where they can still afford to make you a pair of bespoke shoes, rather than sending you off to have your feet wedged into a hired pair with Paul Scofield's athlete's foot still lurking in the inner sole). Actors want to work in it, writers want to write for it, and the public is flocking there in ever-larger numbers.

The building, designed by Sir Denys Lasdun in Soviet-chic, opened it doors in 1975 under the artistic directorship of Sir Peter Hall, who managed the task against overwhelming practical difficulties and despite sufficient setbacks to have Henry V himself phoning the Samaritans.

For decades since, the NT has vied with the RSC as the place to be: but at the time of writing, it's pulled ahead by several lengths and now occupies clear blue water. Quite simply, the place is on a roll. With three separate auditoria pumping out shows six days a week, Lasdun's austere fortress has become a cornucopia of culture.

But there's no need to take my word for it: just look at the list of critically-acclaimed smash hits that have transferred across Waterloo Bridge to the heart of the West End – *One Man, Two Guvnors, The History Boys*, and especially *Warhorse*, a show of such hare-brained audacity that you marvel anyone thought they could get away with it.

Pay is good, conditions are second to none, and employees have the added incentive of nightly performance fees, which, when added to your basic wage, can add up to a decent salary. Another boon is that the various plays are performed in repertory rather than repertoire, thus giving the actors the occasional night (or even week) off, an invaluable and priceless benefit if you've got a young family or needing to fit in other projects.

But best thing of all is the subsidised canteen.

If this seems a somewhat smartarse observation, I assure you I'm being deadly earnest. An army marches on its stomach, or so it's said, and there's nothing actors like so much as 24-hour grub. The allure of being able to have roast beef and Yorkshire pudding 52 weeks a year at competitive prices is a huge draw to itinerant actors, used as they are to making do with flaccid cheese toasties and pails of scalding coffee.

It's also a great place to socialise. When I first worked there in 1985, (one of three spells I've put in over the decades), my first ever visit to the canteen found me sharing a lunch table alongside Sir Anthony Hopkins, Sir Michael Gambon and Sir Peter Hall himself, who despite rising awkwardly at the end of his meal and upsetting both the furniture and greasy contents over the three of us in spectacular fashion, managed to escape without so much as a gravy granule landing on his own suit.

That's when I realised the man's true genius for the job.

THE ROYAL SHAKESPEARE COMPANY

I forget who said, 'I don't see what's so great about Shakespeare – it's just a load of famous quotes all strung together' – but old Bill's words are everywhere just now, not only in our daily vocabulary and the mouths of our politicians, but in our theatres, our cinema screens and even on our TV sets. Four hundred years on from his death, we've never been so passionate about the Bard.

The Royal Shakespeare Company (or RSC to give it its popular moniker), based on the banks of the river at Stratford-upon-Avon, is the pre-eminent classical theatre company in the world, employing 700 staff and turning out upwards of 20 full-scale productions each and every year. Sixty years after its inception it enjoys an international reputation second to none, and is *the* place to work if you want to immerse yourself in the classics.

And just as well, for performing Shakespeare is no matter for dilettantes. On the contrary, it requires expertise and dedication. After all, there are all those stanzas, blank verses, and iambic pentameters to worry about, as well as the soaring imagery, telling metaphor and complex similes. Such literary riches require specialist skills, especially as nobody in the audience can understand what the fuck anyone's talking about anyway due to the archaic language.

This is why the RSC is so important, for it has the most celebrated directors, vocal coaches and academic experts on tap. And when all is said and done, the Bard surely deserves our respect. You can't just busk it like one director I worked with, who was accosted during rehearsals for *Love's Labour's Lost* by the actor playing Dull.

'Excuse me, but what's the meaning of this speech I have to say in Act IV?'

'Which one do you mean?'

'"*I said the deer was not a haut credo – 'twas a pricket*"'

'No idea. Is it in the back of the book?'

'No.'

'Then just say it quickly and fuck off.'

That sort of thing may suffice in Margate and Minehead, but the cognoscenti deserves better. My own ignominious debut in RSC colours is discussed at length later in this book, so suffice it to say for now that a season at Stratford is still about as good as life gets for anyone serious about the craft of acting.

And best of all, the Dirty Duck across from the stage door does fabulous lock-ins.

REP

No simple small word separates the generations of actors with such brutal finality as the word 'rep'. To newcomers the term is a strange and bewildering one, redolent of a distant past, as quaint as the notion of smearing your face in greasepaint or sending a good luck telegram on opening night.

But just like those sticks of Leichner number 5 and number 9 (the twin-hues which, when blended together were supposed to replicate basic skin tones but which inevitably made you look as if you'd been terribly burnt) the term 'rep' still evokes a *frisson* both powerful and elegiac, of something left over from a previous era. Youngsters may mock it, but they know they can never have it for their own.

How times change. Back in the day, when nearly every provincial town had its own resident company churning out plays year upon year, rep was the be-all-and-end-all for the aspiring young actor. Anything beyond was so impossibly exotic as to be scarcely worth contemplating.

Look up the biography of any major star over 50 and you'll be astonished at how they started out. Lindsay Duncan made her debut at Crewe, Imelda Staunton's first play was at the old Swan Theatre in the middle of Worcester race course, and I myself recall seeing *Downton Abbey*'s own Hugh Bonneville as Dame

Trott at the Mercury Theatre Colchester back in 1985 ('Hello everyone, I'm Dame Trott, but you can call me anytime…')

Just how much things have altered was illustrated when I spoke to a group of students at one of the country's leading drama schools, during which I casually asked them to name any repertory theatres they knew of.

Once upon a time they could have recited the names and addresses in their sleep, if only because they'd have written so many begging letters. But now my enquiry was met with bemused silence, until some brave soul eventually put up her hand and offered a single hesitant response. 'Chesterfield?' she asked plaintively.

Chesterfield. Even by the time I was starting out back in the 1970s it was hardly functioning any longer as a rep, one of hundreds of small provincial companies who was by then awaiting the slow, inexorable approach of the Arts Council with a bloodied axe.

When I left RADA there were still 70 or 80 such regional reps you could apply to for a job: Basingstoke, Lancaster, Farnham – their names read like some theatrical version of Flanders and Swann's *The Slow Train*. Back then you were assured of at least half a dozen sequential productions if you landed the gig, with parts ranging from juvenile leads to the back end of a pantomime cow. Time to learn, to observe, to find your feet, and most crucially, to sort your emotions and your technique out before things got serious in the West End or on TV.

YORK MINISTER

My second job at the York Theatre Royal in 1979 reflected the extraordinary training ground that only repertory could provide. My 12-month contract started with a production of Pinero's classic farce, *The Magistrate*, followed by Shakespeare's *The Taming of the Shrew*, on through Alan Ayckbourn's *Bedroom Farce*, and then to Trevor Griffiths' savage indictment of culture in 1970s Britain, *Comedians*, about a group of aspiring stand-ups attending evening classes in deepest Manchester.

In the role of Eddie Waters, the club comic who is their weekly instructor, the director cast the popular local stand-up Stan Richards (later to achieve immortality as Seth Armstrong in *Emmerdale*). During rehearsals the entire cast even went over to Wibsey Working Men's Club near Bradford to see Stan perform his shtick in front of a packed Sunday night crowd ('My dog has no legs – I call it Marlboro 'cos every night I take it out for a drag'). Our evening ended with Stan taking us all for fish and chips at the original Harry Ramsden's. It was invaluable, wonderful stuff.

Next, I played a one-line reporter in Ben Travers' *Thark*, then Tony Lumpkin in *She Stoops to Conquer*, then the lead in a new play written about the newly-discovered Viking dig in the centre of the city, before high-kicking my way through Peter Nichols' musical *Privates on Parade*, about a group of soldiers touring with the Combined Services Entertainment Unit in darkest Malaya.

The season finished with pantomime; in my case, *Dick Whittington and his Cat*, starring a young Gary Oldman as Cat. During my time with the company I shared everything from digs to girlfriends with Gary, and at Christmas, unable to return home due to heavy snow, I ended up squeezing into a single bed with him at a house in Rotherham owned by the parents of the Sultan of Morocco.

Apart from appearing in the current production, we'd spend all day rehearsing the next one. Along with eating, sleeping and shagging, acting was the sum total of our lives. The company was our surrogate family, and even on our one day off we'd all go to the pub, watch a movie, or in the case of York, spend winter afternoons going with the stage door keeper, Frank, to watch his beloved York rugby league team playing teams like Barrow and Widnes.

In case you think all this sounds impossibly homespun and folksy, the standard of productions was terrific. The company was run by a curious, muscle-bound six-foot hunk called Michael Winter, who wore tight green bomber jackets and Doc Marten boots, and who drank weight-bulking drinks at the tea break. Yet despite this imposing exterior he was a man of extraordinary finesse and elegance, not to say delicacy (he spoke like John Gielgud having just inhaled on an asthma ventilator). As well as running the building he tended to handle anything with a bit of period in it – Travers, Pinero and the musicals.

His assistant, later to achieve fame and fortune as creator of *Return to the Forbidden Planet*, couldn't have been more opposite. Bob Carlton was straight from the pages of a Malcolm Bradbury novel; small, pugnacious, rabidly left-wing, with distaste of anything poncey or high-brow (for both of these read 'Tory') who was rarely seen without his trademark grubby Macintosh and a roll-up.

It was he who told me that upon returning home to see his mum after his first term at Coventry Polytechnic, was asked to explain something she'd seen many times on TV and always wondered about. She wanted to know the derivation of the opening phrase used by quizmaster Bamber Gascoigne at the start of each new round in her favourite programme, *University Challenge*, which had puzzled her for years. 'Why does he always say "Your side of the Thames?"' she asked her son, 'Is it something to do with the boat race?'

Carlton handled all the edgy stuff, the Viking play, *Comedians* and anything slightly agitprop. He and Winter were as unlikely bedfellows as you could imagine, a bit like Ray Winstone trying to work alongside Brian Sewell: yet somehow their partnership formed the perfect symbiosis.

Nonetheless, some of my casting, was, perforce, preposterous (my 60-year-old police sergeant in particular springs to mind) but the experience it offered was priceless. I learnt how to time a laugh, to hold a pause, and to know the difference between an audience of 80 at a Thursday matinee and a full house on a Saturday night. Most importantly, I experienced a crash course in nearly 400 years of British drama.

It also led to some especially piquant experiences. As well as performing *Shrew* in the main theatre, we also toured it out of the back of a van all around North Yorkshire. On one occasion we even took it to Askham Grange women's prison, where, we were assured, we'd be playing to some of the country's most notorious female prisoners, including, it was rumoured, the infamous child murderer Mary Bell.

We never met her (or if we did, remained unaware) but our production of Shakespeare's contentious play, one deliberately directed by Carlton to accentuate the misogynist tendencies of Petruchio, played to a rapt and febrile audience, many of whom knew the consequences of domination at the hands of a brutal male Svengali first-hand, and who reacted vociferously and viscerally throughout.

Afterwards we shared a few minutes with them, and despite the occasion being advertised as a Q&A, they soon made it clear they were much more interested in us all smoking fags while we talked, merely so we could pass them over surreptitiously after only a few puffs.

Having never smoked in my life, it took me several minutes to realise that you couldn't successfully light one without drawing on it at the same time. The image of me holding one queasily at arm's length while trying to persuade it to ignite from a proffered lighter got one of the biggest laughs of the evening, as well as several offers to adopt me once their period of incarceration was over.

My year at York also gave me the chance to act with, and learn from, leading actors who themselves had been schooled in this peerless tradition. What they didn't know about stage acting wasn't worth knowing. Watching these theatrical titans taught me more than a decade at drama school ever could.

REALITY CHEQUE

Nowadays the few surviving reps are lean, streamlined, and financial-savvy outfits, getting by – just – by coming up with all sorts of tricks; co-productions with nearby theatres being the preferred method of spreading expenditure. And always looming, kept only at bay with an upturned chair, is the threat of having their funding altogether withdrawn, as local councils struggle to quantify the value of a thriving local theatre against that of a swimming pool, a care home or twice-monthly recycling.

Nonetheless they're tough old buggers. You won't get a 12-month contract any longer – that's long gone. But the experience on offer is still priceless. So if you get the chance to work in rep, grab it with both hands. You'll learn far more strutting your stuff at Salisbury or even Sidmouth then you will by carrying a flaming poniard at Stratford-upon-Avon.

Like any family, life there can be full of nepotism, feuds and intrigue (my actress wife Julia recalls the director of the Palace Theatre Westcliffe-on-Sea, the inimitable Chris Dunham, screaming at her during a rehearsal of the Kit-Cat club scene in *Cabaret*, 'You're only sulking because I didn't give you Sally Bowles, now fuck off and put the kettle on...') But this sense of belonging was, and remains, its greatest asset.

Just how powerful are the memories was brought home to me a year or so ago when I participated in an 'Actors' Xmas Sale' at a community hall on Barnes Common. A wonderfully convivial affair, the event took the form of a sort of luvvie car boot fair, in which various thesps and media personalities each hired a stall and sold on some of their unwanted clobber to star-struck punters anxious to purchase Amanda Burton's cast-offs from *Silent Witness* or a desk lamp once owned by Aled Jones.

With business slackening after lunch, I left my own thread-bare stall and wandered along the aisles to see what else was on offer. Eventually I came to a stall manned by the actress Polly James, who achieved national fame back in the 1960s as one of

The Liver Birds, and who, 40 years on, was still carving out a decent career in the business. One particular item that caught my eye – in between all the costume jewellery, bric-a-brac and embroidered bedspreads – was her make-up box, the one she'd carried with her for 30 years while she was training in rep, and which she was finally dispensing with.

Polly, who was sitting quietly in a jumper decorated with Christmas puddings and with a pair of illuminated reindeer antlers on her head, was happy for me to inspect the contents. Inside, sticks of greasepaint in assorted hues lay in neat rows. Jars of cold cream jostled for space with smoothing powder, talc, and sticks of carmine and crimson, and there was even some old spirit gum used to fix wigs and sideburns, which I recalled from bitter personal experience could take the top layer of epidermis off your skin at 20 paces. The aroma was unmistakable, and so evocative that having replaced the box, I walked out onto the common and stood moist-eyed for several minutes.

I realise I may be turning into one of those rheumy-eyed old bores droning on about my halcyon days spent promenading back and forth across some tatty provincial stage but if so, I'm in elevated company. Meeting Gary Oldman unexpectedly on Hungerford Bridge a few years ago, we stopped briefly to recall our days together, nearly four decades before.

'Simmo,' he concluded, 'I do movies, I live in LA, I've had everything the business could offer me. But there are times when I'd give up all that crap, just for one week back doing *Privates on Parade* at York.'

Oldman is of course, one of our finest actors – but I'd like to think that on this occasion, he was telling the truth.

TOURING

Hermione Gingold once said, 'Laurence Olivier is a tour de force. Donald Wolfit is forced to tour.'

The poor relation of the West End it may be, but commercial touring in a show is still a great way to be in work. And in addition you'll probably be eligible for a 'touring allowance', usually round about £150 a week, intended to help you with living expenses out on the road, and which if used sensibly, can help you eke out your basic wage.

If the show is a big one you may find yourself doing several weeks in one place but usually touring means a week (at most) in each town, before lumbering bleary-eyed to another one, often at the other end of the country, ready for an opening on Monday night. I don't wish to impugn the reputations of those souls who organise such itineraries, but it's amazing how many times Aberdeen and Poole seem to occur in sequential weeks.

The legacy of life on the road, so gloriously replicated in Ronald Harwood's play *The Dresser*, encapsulates perfectly what it was once like, and to an extent, still remains. The play (and subsequent movie) draws heavily on Harwood's own experience during the 1950s when he was the personal dresser to Wolfit, the doyen of touring actor-managers and a performer who largely made his name in the provinces; and it evokes perfectly the world of itinerant actors, hurtling back and forth across the country on wheezing steam trains, their compartments piled high with wicker baskets, dogs and babies, and inevitably meeting up each Sunday morning in the waiting room at Crewe as they waited for their various connecting trains to their next destination.

It was a tough old life, one comprised of exhausting hours, withering schedules, drafty digs, unreliable transport, threadbare theatres, and in many cases, stupefying quantities of booze, if only to numb the drudgery and disjunction from home comforts.

Even though motorway service stations and Travelodges have replaced railway carriages and Mrs Goggins, Abattoir Lane, if you get a job in a touring production you'll certainly still catch more than a whiff of the life as evoked by Harwood. In fact I recommend watching a DVD of *The Dresser* before setting off.

Road trip

It took me 38 years in the business before I finally lost my touring virginity, in the form of a 15-week national tour of the stage version of *Yes, Prime Minister*, the classic 1980s political comedy, in which I was giving my Sir Humphrey Appleby. Having rehearsed and subsequently played the show at Chichester Festival Theatre in darkest January, it ended several months later in the relative warmth of mid-May, albeit in Darlington, where anything less than frostbite classifies as a heatwave.

Habitués of the touring life are always droning on about how knackering it is. I soon saw what they meant. The first weekend of the tour, in which we all had to travel from Chichester to Coventry, coincided with a ferocious blizzard, resulting in a terrifying drive up the A3 in a whiteout, my only companion the ashen-faced actor driving the car and the aroma of overheating brake pads.

For my second week in Coventry, I foolishly decided to try and save some money by putting up in a seedy motel near the theatre, advertising self-catering rooms for £18 a night. My room, which I soon dubbed the Myra Hindley suite, was dark, gloomy, and inundated with the smell of unwashed feet and stale aftershave from legions of commercial travellers who'd occupied the sheets before me: while the crockery was so sticky that you could pick up a tea cup from one of the Formica tea trays in the kitchenette without the two coming apart (I whiled away several afternoons by doing just that).

Sitting in bed in my overcoat eating chips in curry sauce out of a polystyrene tray at 2 am was, I freely admit, one of the lowest points in my adult life: though in my defence I had just consumed four pints at the local Wetherspoon's.

But that's the thing about touring. You never know what you'll encounter next. The following week the snow cleared, the sun came out and I found myself in the charming seaside town of Llandudno in North Wales. The weather was balmy, and in place of the sleazy motel, I found myself in a charming B&B with tea-making facilities and sea views. Short of rustling up my dead parents it would be difficult to imagine a more comforting environment in which to soothe away the previous week's horror.

But whatever you do and wherever you go, cancel all other arrangements. Your next few months are going to be spent travelling, performing, or mooning about in shopping arcades. Nice work if you can get it – but it's not real life.

Shitty centres

Tours are roughly codified like the various tiers of the English football league, with a Premier Division (known as 'A' tours or Number 1s, usually involving Bath, Brighton and Norwich), a slightly less glossy variant (known, somewhat unappetisingly, as Number 2s), and so on. Some venues, despite their size and importance (or perhaps because of it) can seem soulless and unfriendly, while others, hanging on by their fingertips, can make you feel a million dollars.

It's a sad fact now that many provincial theatres, far from the elegant Georgian playhouses that once graced town centres, are often sprawling leisure complexes, resembling something out of Stalin's Russia and built by civil engineers who know nothing about theatre (one that springs to mind is a building in Staffordshire which has neither wash basins nor windows in the dressing rooms).

Even if the venue is still in the town centre it'll often be part of a much bigger enterprise, aimed at everybody and catering for nobody. Here you're likely to find your best efforts being drowned out by the sound of Showaddywaddy in the adjoining concert hall, or your costume inundated by the smell of swimming pool cleaning chemicals. At one such venue on the south coast during the *YPM* tour, a trip I made out to the front of house café to request a knife with which to peel a pineapple I'd bought was refused 'in case I stabbed someone'.

And there's the nub. The nature of many town centres has also changed. Theatre goers – especially provincial ones – tend to be of a certain age and demographic, but where once the area surrounding their local playhouse was a welcoming environment, now they're often required to walk through streets knee deep in vomit and broken glass to get to it. Even if they take the car they're forced to house it in windswept and lowering multi-story car parks smelling of piss and festooned with sinister concrete pillars every few yards. It's hard to get much enthusiasm for an evening of *Uncle Vanya* or *The Railway Children* if you've got to run the gauntlet of drunken revellers and the threat of car clampers if you so much as stop to ask directions.

Bed & bored

The key to successful touring is in getting good digs. When all else fails, when the actors are no longer talking to one another and the auditorium has tumbleweed blowing through it, the place in which you've elected to stay can make the difference between survival and suicide.

The digs list is available from any decent theatre, and will normally be forwarded to you along with your contract and your measurement checklist. This spindly document, often out of date and frequently inaccurate, is your most prized possession, and like the ancient hieroglyphics which it often resembles, is worth spending some time trying to decipher.

There are many considerations in choosing where best to stay, the cost being only one. If travelling by car, does your accommodation have convenient on-street parking, or a secure garage? Is it in a nice part of town, or one in which your vehicle's likely to broken into on a twice-nightly basis? If travelling by rail, are the digs near enough to the centre? The room in some leafy Victorian suburb may seem an attractive option, but not if you've got to rely on a 30-minute bus ride out into some far flung hinterland after curtain down.

Does it accept pets? Is your partner or current amour (not necessarily the same person) welcome to stay if the need arises? As a rule, self-contained is generally always better than a room in someone's house: but if staying with a family, do they have young children who'll wake at 5.30 am and demand to be put in front of *The Tweenies* at full blast? Even if they're teenagers there are likely to be endless waits for the one available bathroom while they prick their blackheads.

If the digs in question turn out to be a stinker, either physically or metaphorically, don't hesitate to check out, even if you lose your deposit. Your own sanity is paramount. One colleague in *Yes, Prime Minister* arrived at his lodgings in Canterbury to find his so-called 'airy spacious room' to be a cavity in the eaves, which could only be accessed by climbing a ladder, squeezing through a narrow partition in the wall and stepping carefully over exposed beams interlaced with fragile plaster. The landlady coquettishly admitted that if stepped on, the plaster would have sent him plummeting into her double bed directly below.

Some actors prefer the anonymity of chainstore hotels, but they'll wipe out much of your expenses, you won't get a decent cup of tea, and contrary to the environment suggested on those adverts where popular celebrities lounge on double beds the size of Rutland, at weekends the corridors will be populated by ferocious hen parties and tribes of young men prowling around at 4 am looking to see how best to discharge the hotel fire extinguishers.

A popular scam is for cast members to club together to hire an entire house, often the best and cheapest option. But be warned. The actor who might seem your new best pal in the dizzy optimism of the rehearsal room can soon turn into a crushing bore, and the last thing you want is to be forced to spend 24/7 on the road with them.

A final thought. Don't presume that your arrival in a strange town will have the locals strewing palm leaves in your path. The uneasy relationship is best illustrated by the experience of a one friend of mine who arrived at Derby to join the cast of a touring show, then installed for a week at the local theatre.

'Can you tell me the way to Derby Playhouse?' he asked the first passer-by he met outside the station.

'Aye,' replied the man, 'Straight up the hill, left at the traffic lights, and fuck off...'

MUSICALS

'Musicals are a series of catastrophes, at the end of which everyone has a party.' I forget who said this, but his words not only describe the plot of 99% of all successful shows, but also encapsulate the experience you'll have if you ever get cast in one.

If you do nothing else as an actor, you should try above all to develop an ability to sing a song. Needn't be anything too special – we're not talking Streisand or John Barrowman – just the knack of being able to manage a tune, sustain the odd harmony when required, and perhaps make an assault on the occasional top note without sounding as if you've trapped your hand in a car door.

The reason is simple. Unless Charlie Fairhead drops dead in his hospital gown and you get chosen as his replacement on *Casualty* (a scenario I frankly find impossible to imagine) getting a berth in a successful factory musical is likely to be your only means of earning decent money over a sustained period.

And that's because there's money still sloshing around in them. Most of the top musical producers are habitually listed in the annual *Sunday Times* list of the 100 richest individuals, and they didn't get that way by producing revivals of *Zoo Story* at the Drill Hall, but by tapping into the predominant desire of all middle-aged Brits: namely to relive their youth through the music they grew up with as teenagers, before life turned nasty and they all got varicose veins.

'Gimme, Gimme, Gimme'

Musical auditions are no-nonsense affairs. No cosy chat over a cup of tea about how you see the role, followed by a sheepish suggestion as to whether 'you might like to read a scene or two'. No, think *Britain's Got Talent* organized by the Gestapo, and you're much nearer the mark. What they want to know is whether you can sell a tap routine, hold a harmony, sing in tune and grin like a bastard while doing all three.

My most memorable experience in the world of big musicals occurred in the spring of 2001 and, as with so many of my favourite jobs, came about by chance.

When I first bumped into Chris in Wardour Street, he was still laughing about it. He'd just been up for a new show which was allegedly going to attempt to string all the hit songs of the 1970s Swedish group Abba together in one improbable confection, set it on a Greek island, throw in a spurious story about a teenage girl wishing to invite all three of her potential dads to her wedding, pepper it with a load of middle-aged crones trying to rediscover their youth, and end it all with the love-struck youngsters walking off into the sunset.

Improbable? Laughable? You took the words out of my mouth. Or rather, out of Chris's mouth. Rumour had it theatrical disaster rubber-neckers were already booking their first night seats, particularly as what little street cred the whole Abba shtick may have once retained had been undermined by its subsequent association with Steve Coogan's alter ego, Alan Partridge and the show, *Knowing Me Knowing You* ('Ah-Ha!').

Yet as we parted, my actors instinct kicked in. 'Look' it said, 'It's all very well you slagging the thing off. But a job is a job.' And there was something else in my thinking too.

'Strange how potent cheap music is,' said Noël Coward, who knew a thing or two about stringing a load of syrupy old ditties together and sitting back to watch the cash registers spring into life.

In my case the whole Abba fandango was clouded by an intense emotional attachment to them and their music. I may have been too young to thrill to the wide-open plains of *Oklahoma!* or while away my youth surrounded by surfboards and the layered harmonies of the Beach Boys, but being a teenager in the seventies was most definitely all about Abba. Their melodies provided a leitmotif to all the agony and ecstasy of teenage life. The thought of being paid handsomely to relive my doomed adolescence seemed almost too piquant to contemplate. I duly rang my agent and asked her to try and get me an interview.

The reply came a few days later. I was to present myself at the Soho laundry, once an establishment responsible for providing central London with clean underwear but now a run-down warren of rooms and corridors which could be hired out for auditions. No need on this occasion to bring my own party pieces, as the audition song was, by karmic co-incidence, 'Knowing Me, Knowing You', the one ruined forever by Alan Partridge, and which had provided such an intense counterpoint to my own adolescent fumblings.

Duly armed with the dots, I turned up at the appointed time and date. Almost immediately I was ushered inside to be greeted by a line of strangers staring back at me from behind the table. One, at least I recognised – Phyllida Lloyd, the talented young theatre director deputed to spin this two and half hours of sow's ear into a silk purse. She was famously kind and approachable by disposition, and we'd already worked together some years previously.

'OK then,' she said after a brief introduction. 'Let's see what you've brought us…'

'Lay all your love on me…'

The first rule of auditioning for musicals is to make friends with your audition pianist. The young man seated glumly behind the upright piano in the corner of the room is your good samaritan: the one friend you've got. He wants you to do well, if only because it will cast reflected light back on his own efforts.

So be nice to him – spread out your pages nicely on the piano, rather than leaving him to break his nails prizing open the staples and above all make sure you inform him of the tempo you need the song played at. There are few things worse than being taken off guard and having to sing 'Younger than Springtime' to the tempo of 'The Flight of the Bumblebee'. It may get you a place on *I'm Sorry I Haven't a Clue*, but not much else.

In this case there was no need. After all, the song was ubiquitous. He struck up the famous intro, and seconds later I opened my larynx and let rip.

'*No more… carefree… laugh- terrrr…*'

Across the desk I could see Phyllida smiling encouragingly. The musical supervisor was gently rocking his foot beneath his chair. Another panellist was tapping a pencil discreetly on his notes. And then, just as I launched into the chorus, it all went wrong.

'*Knowing me knowing you, ah-ha!*'

The panel leapt from their seats as if stung by a collective cattle prod. Meanwhile the accompanist stopped dead in his tracks as if shot by a high velocity rifle.

Phyllida was the first to speak.

'Michael, there are no "ah-ha's".'

'Pardon?'

'We're not doing the "ah-ha's". They're excised from the song. Didn't you notice in the score we sent you?'

I hurried over to the piano and gazed at the dots. They weren't there. Somewhere between *I'm Alan Partridge* and the Soho Laundry, they'd been airbrushed out of existence.

'I'm sorry, I could have sworn…'

'It's ok,' said Phyllida gently. 'A common mistake. If you'd like to try again…'

I blundered through the song once more, but my fragile confidence now came apart at the seams.

A day or two on my agent called.

'How are you darling?' Downward inflection.

Never mind. A musical set on a Greek island to the tunes of Abba? It would be lucky to last five weeks.

One of us is lying

A year later, with the show now the hottest ticket in town and identical productions springing up across the planet like musical triffids, my agent called again.

'The chap playing Sam Carmichael is leaving next month. Phyllida was wondering if you'd like to come in for it. Shall I say yes?'

Look, here's a valuable truism for a jobbing actor auditioning for a musical. If you haven't kept your voice in good nick throughout the long months between auditions, by the time you get one it's already too late to get your chops up to scratch. Your vocal chords won't take kindly to being asked to suddenly sound like Bruce Springsteen or Rihanna just because your career depends on it. So be practical. Use your few days wisely. You don't need teaching. It's too late for that. You need encouragement.

I don't know who first suggested I go to Chuck Mallet, although anyone with a name such as that deserves a look-see whatever the purpose. Nevertheless, he proved just what the doctor ordered.

Nobody would claim Chuck was Andre Previn. His piano playing was bright, bold, and unashamed: but that'd not the point. This guy gave you confidence. At the end of my first rendering of the song he spun round on his piano stool, and said in voice part Bayswater, part Liberace, and wholly camp, 'Well… what can I say? That was terrific! I simply can't imagine that being improved upon. Shall we do it again?'

To listen to Chuck, you'd have thought that if only I'd stuck a blond wig on my head and dressed up in a gold spandex catsuit I could have walked off with the Eurovision Song Contest.

His optimism in my feeble powers was unequivocal, absolute and utterly fortifying.

The following day I turned up at the Prince Edward Theatre in Soho, now the established fortress home of *Mamma Mia*. This time the audition panel was camped out in the remote wastelands of the stalls. In the middle I spotted the unmistakable elfin features of Bjorn Ulvaeus himself.

Encountering such an icon in the flesh would have been enough to render me incapable of speech, let alone singing; but I was determined there'd be no mistakes. No rogue 'ah-ha's'. And each time I was tempted to look out to see if one of popular music's greatest-ever composers was hanging himself from the dress circle, Chuck's beaming face appeared in an amorphous haze over the seats like some musical Cheshire cat.

A couple of days later the phone rang with a call from my agent. I picked it up.

'How are you darling?' Upward inflection.

'I do, I do, I do, I do, I do...'

The first thing you need to know about a musical is that everything – everything – depends on your voice. From the moment you open your eyes in the morning to the time you step on stage, you'll be making vague throat-clearing noises and humming arpeggios under your breath to reassure yourself it's up for the show.

The problems of coping when your voice goes AWOL are dealt with later on, but suffice it to say here that those two tiny folds of gristle half way down your clack are now the most important thing in your life. Look after them and you'll be fine.

So, put away your passport and your driving licence. You won't be needing them. You're about to become star of your own version of *The Truman Show*, with the four walls of the building the limit of your virtual world. Soon nothing else matters – wars, famines, political upheaval – the only thing to concern you will be the minutiae of life inside your tiny toy box. Not that you'll notice, as everyone else in the building will be just as preoccupied as you.

That's the downside. The upside is you'll end up with a bit stashed in the bank, have fabulous parties, somewhere to dump your purchases while out shopping, and best of all, you'll have more fun than you can shake a copy of *The Stage* at.

'You can dance, you can jive...'

For instance, my year in *Mamma Mia* was about as much excitement as I've ever had without taking someone else's clothes off. Having never done a big musical before, I wasn't prepared for the visceral thrill of stepping out on stage for the first time to bright lights, a rock band thumping away in the pit and 1500 adoring Abba fans stretching before me in the gloom. During my year in gold spandex, I notched up nearly 400 shows, and it never disappointed.

For that's the thing about musicals – however fed up you may be, however much you've tired of the whole twice on Fridays and Saturdays treadmill, with matinees in front of a thousand bewildered German businessmen who've been given tickets as part of their corporate hospitality package and who would far rather be at the Savoy Grill or Spearmint Rhino – the music always lifts you.

I even got the chance to sing with my smouldering teenage pin-up from the original group, Anni-Frid (the brunette). We'd already been tipped off that she was paying a visit – her first – to the show, and she sent word during the interval that she was enjoying it so much she'd like to join the company for the reprise of 'Dancing Queen' at the curtain call. As senior cast member I was coveted for my opinion.

Having had a quick peek through the front cloth, my advice was unequivocal. Thirty years on from her auburn-haired triumphs, she now looked less like the burnished siren of my teenage fantasies than an elderly, if elegant, member of the Swedish royal family. If she came onstage unannounced (I argued) nobody would know who she was. In fact they'd probably assume she was the Duchess of Kent and launch into a chorus of 'God Save the Queen'.

Thank God nobody listened to me. She'd barely put a finely manicured big toe on from the wings when the audience rose as one and gave her an ovation that could have been heard in Stockholm. I lost count of the number of curtain calls we took that night.

If you'd told me back in 1972 in the depths of my post-pubescent despair that one day I'd be sharing a stage and singing 'Dancing Queen' with my Abba fantasy while wearing sequined spandex, I'd have accused you of making too free with the Watney's Party Four. But that's what musicals do – they razzle-dazzle, whether you're in the audience or up onstage.

Inevitably my sojourn in the show led to further oppor-tunities and further excursions, including five separate stints as Billy Flynn in the West End production of Kander and Ebb's musical *Chicago*, a gig that required me to sit centre stage in a tuxedo, lit by a battery of spotlights, surrounded by dancing girls, and with Leigh Zimmerman and Denise Van Outen perched on my knees. It was a filthy job; but somebody had to do it.

Musicals are glorious technicolor experiences, at the end of which, naturally, everyone has a party. What's more, you may, as I did, even get to walk about the stage each night wearing platform boots and a gold lamé codpiece.

You don't get that sort of opportunity at the Royal Court…

FRINGE

The term 'fringe' was first coined in 1948, when a leading theatre critic observing the burgeoning international arts festival at Edinburgh wrote that, 'Round the fringe of the event, there seems to be more private enterprise than before.' The term stuck, and is now used to describe virtually anything that is unpaid, experimental, or comes without the aid of a proscenium arch or a proper safety certificate. Edinburgh itself has in the meantime become the acme of the medium (at 2012's beano there were precisely 1478 new shows in addition to the official programme of events).

Typically, fringe productions are technically sparse, often on low pay or profit share, and frequently housed in venues without many creature comforts. Because of this they can offer unparalleled opportunities for actors who don't mind living on sandwiches and dreams. In fact much of the most exciting theatre currently on offer can be found tucked away in rooms above pubs and in converted railway arches.

In truth, fringe has now become so respectable an art form that the delineation between it and mainstream theatre is blurred to the point of being non-existent. Many venues are better run, better attended and offer a higher standard of work than their respectable counterparts round the corner.

The majority of the fringe projects you'll hear about will be through the theatre grapevine, or via informal approaches by friends and colleagues in the pub. They're also likely to come with the proviso 'profit share', which means that while the job itself is likely to be unpaid, in the event of the gig exceeding its outlay costs, any surplus will be dutifully divvied up among the cast.

Which brings me to the first rule of doing fringe. There's never any profit to share. So if you're seduced by the prospect of a handy cheque, forget it now.

Nonetheless, fringe provides some of the most exciting and innovative opportunities around. Because of the low overheads and informal approach, dynamic entrepreneurs can attempt projects no respectable management would dream of taking on lest it bankrupted them. It's also highly regarded. Nowadays you'll find yourself working with respected actors and directors, anxious to stretch their creative wings and who can afford the financial hit that six weeks at the Finborough Arms or the Hen & Chicken will involve.

Better still, if your show gets noticed you'll soon find the audience crammed with casting directors and agents anxious to see what the fuss is about. The leap from the Rose & Crown to The Rovers Return is far less precipitous than you might think.

The only consistent features that invariably separate fringe from mainstream are the conditions backstage. While many respectable venues are themselves hardly Claridges once you step through the pass door, you can positively stake your life on the fact that in fringe, you and the rest of the cast will be sharing an airless basement, with males and females only separated by a length of grubby curtain hung across the centre of the room.

The electrics will be a deathtrap, there'll be puddles of stagnant water in the corridor, and the wing space will be crammed with items of dilapidated furniture and even, if you're above a pub or restaurant, crates of empties or economy-sized bottles of mayonnaise.

Even if you have a window on the outside world, it'll usually give out onto a brick wall with a dead pigeon staring unblinkingly back at you from a coil of rusty barbed wire. As regards the toilet and kitchen facilities (frequently the same thing), there'll be no paper towels in the dispenser, the cold tap will have a notice stating 'not for drinking', and the one available toilet servicing both cast and crew will have a broken flush and a sign saying 'Not for Number Two's' (not that you're allowed to use it during the performance anyway as it can be heard onstage). You'll also likely to be sharing your accommodation with hot and cold running mice.

Onstage conditions are also often less than ideal, frequently requiring you to traverse fire escapes or even hurry out into the street in order to cross from one side of the stage to the other, while if you're involved in pub theatre your best efforts can be thwarted by wine bottles cascading into a recycling bin or raucous laughter from the downstairs bar.

But as Edinburgh amply testifies, that's all part of the charm. There's something terribly exciting about 'just doing the show right here' that gets the pulse racing. And an appearance in a hit can often ignite or revivify your career.

My most surreal fringe experience, and one that illustrates perfectly the sort of glorious scrape you can get into, has to be the time I accepted the offer to play the lead, for one show only, in Tim Crouch's extraordinary drama, *An Oak Tree*, at the Soho Theatre.

The plot of the play – not that I knew this when the curtain rose and I spoke my first line – was about a man whose daughter is killed in a road accident and his efforts to both deal with his grief and locate the culprit.

Crouch, as well as writing and devising the project, played all other parts. But in addition, he also fed me all my lines through a miniature earpiece a split-second before I was due to speak them: a fact also known to the audience who thus shared, albeit vicariously, my roller-coaster journey as stricken parent.

One of Crouch's intentions in devising the project was to see what would happen when different actors performed the part without recourse to choice or selection about their portrayal. Thus I was one of a long succession of guest artists for one night only, ranging from Chris Eccleston to Frances McDormand and beyond.

The various interpretations (Crouch later assured me) varied enormously according to who was appearing on a particular evening. Some proved uproariously funny, others grotesquely dark. High drama jostled with high camp. Rarely were the performances less than startling.

They say that in acting your first choices are often the best. Rehearse too long, think too much, and you can end up hemming yourself in to all sorts of unhelpful cul-de-sacs. No fear of that happening here. I barely had time to hear my next line before being required to bring it to life within the context of the scene. Panic barely does the experience justice.

So terrifying was the ordeal that I recall little other than blind fear mixed with a curious sense of liberation. When the lights went up for the curtain call, I discovered we'd been playing to a packed house of nearly 200 people, all of whom were under 25 (the only exception being veteran comedian Barry Cryer perched somewhat sheepishly in the front row).

Which brings me back to the Mecca of fringe, the Edinburgh festival and my only exposure to its extraordinary mezze of talent that comprises its many parts. Some years ago I found myself in the city on the first Saturday of the shindig, and decided on the spur of the moment to see as many shows as I could in a single day, selecting each one only with the aid of a pin stuck randomly into the listings.

Thus at 8 am I found myself watching a muscular young performer offering a dance-based interpretation of Mozart's twelve variations on 'Twinkle Twinkle Little Star' (K 265), which pumped out from a CD machine on the floor in front of him. It may have been J.B. Morton who so brutally classified ballet as 'acrobatics set to pretentious music', but this guy really was something. In fact his physical artistry was so outstanding he even received a standing ovation at the end of the gig: although that wasn't difficult as I was the only person who'd turned up to see him.

By noon I was on the other side of the city, watching another show which consisted of a man roller-skating back and forth across the stage with a live Labrador strapped to his back while reading Shakespeare sonnets (the man, that is, not the dog).

Having grabbed a double espresso, by 4 pm, I was hurtling along the main drag towards the Gilded Balloon, Edinburgh's most celebrated fringe venue, where I caught a highly-rated item called *Gone with Noakes*, in which, with the help of home-made video footage shot on location, the protagonist described his attempt to locate a much-loved but now reclusive children's TV presenter living in semi-retirement on one of the Balearic islands. At 6 pm, I was installed in a church hall watching a group of sixth form drama students from Redcar performing Gorky's classic play, a production that gave fresh resonance to the title *The Lower Depths*.

My final event was a late-night performance entitled *An Evening with Mother Teresa*. The hour-long show (was it really only an hour?) consisted of a young fresh-faced Irish comedian with a tea towel wrapped round his head doing live stand-up on assorted religious topics.

Alas, this final event really did seem to display fringe theatre at its most notorious and inept. Maybe I was missing something, but it struck me as unfunny, crass and self-indulgent. I would have left the show long before the end had my departure not necessitated my having to walk across the stage in front of him to reach the exit. Afterwards I cursed him for his lack of self-awareness. Now here really was a guy who needed to go back to his day job.

Thirty years on I came across the various programmes and leaflets pertaining to my days out, now moldering away in a box in the attic. The dancer, now in his late-forties, had presumably given up active ballet and is probably running a dance school somewhere. The Labrador too must be long gone (unless his owner had had him stuffed), and although John Noakes has continued to remain largely hidden from the public gaze, the young Cambridge undergraduate who wrote and starred in the show about him turned out to be Ben Miller. As regards the students from Redcar, I hope they've fulfilled their dreams, just so long as it isn't a career on the stage.

Which leaves only the guy playing Mother Teresa. My programme informs me his name was Graham Norton.

Any ideas…?

OPEN-AIR FESTIVALS

Open-air theatre during the summer is an increasing part of British culture. For the jobbing actor it can provide a useful source of employment and a chance to do some classical acting. No matter that the show being staged is nearly always *A Midsummer Night's Dream*. Work is work.

There are hundreds of open-air productions up and down the country during the summer months, ranging from festivals at magnificent castles right down to homespun events in your local municipal park; these are often swollen by amateurs and semi-pros, some with stupendous budgets, right down to others where the only back up is a couple of rugs and a torch.

The drawback to this sort of thing is that you can often feel as if you've wandered into a sort of dramatic offshoot of Classic FM: live theatre, but only the mellow bits, designed to soothe away the strains of the day. Alan Titchmarsh as Bottom, you feel, would be their dream casting.

You can't blame the producers – after all, if you're going to stage a play in the open air under the stars, you're hardly likely to attract maximum revenue stream if you put on *The Romans in Britain* with its scenes of male sodomy. No, you want Romeo glimpsed in tights through some distant casement, or Sir Toby Belch tottering on across the drawbridge.

And after all, it's the middle classes who tend to favour both Classic FM and open-air theatre, because they're the only ones who can afford the petrol, picnic, and admission price. The drama itself, however worthy, will essentially be an addendum to the main point of the exercise, which is to cram much fine food and wine down their necks in the space of three hours. If they can justify that extra slice of Melton Mowbray with a few sonnets or a snatch of blank verse, so much the better.

But of course, I'm talking about the UK. Life isn't quite as simple as that.

It was the great Michael Green, Big Daddy of all things thespian, and author of the incomparable *The Art of Coarse Acting*, who defined the first rule of open air festivals thus: as soon as you open your mouth to speak, 'storm and tempest will immediately descend and an enormous flock of screeching birds with loose bowels will fly to and fro over the stage area'.

His maxim sums up the problem of open-air theatre perfectly. It's a sad fact about al fresco performing in Britain that it's in the hands of forces beyond your control. Yet with the sort of insane and touching optimism that's essential for anyone looking to flourish in showbiz, the organisers always think that the gods will shine on their efforts.

'We should be fine,' they say each and every year, 'After all, we're on during the last two weeks in June.' Well I may be no Michael Fish, but I seem to remember that the last two weeks in June are normally a precursor to storms, burst drains, sandbags, firemen patrolling high streets in rubber dinghies and Huw Edwards flying over vast swathes of flooded countryside in a BBC helicopter.

Actors, too, inevitably assume a best-case scenario. Three weeks playing the Bard at a medival castle to rows of contented theatergoers? What could be nicer? And now, as the play reaches its climax, and the only sounds are of a gentle zephyr rustling the canopy of trees and the popping of another bottle of prosecco, Puck throws his girdle round the earth, while all round him on stage the lights are picking out the canopy of surrounding trees in myriad shades of green and emerald. It's a beautiful, ethereal image, that of Britain at its most magical. A midsummer night's dream in fact.

Sadly, a dream is too often all it is. The scenario is more likely to consist of an audience huddled in pac-a-macs, strafed by horizontal rain, picnic chairs already sinking in the mud, and with two members of the cast sitting in the local A&E after slipping on the stage during the prologue.

Because of their temporary nature, open-air productions can also be a health and safety inspector's nightmare. I know of two acting acquaintances who've been electrocuted by standing in puddles while resting their elbows on hastily built lighting gantries; while at one production in a 14th century castle near the Cotswolds, the entire court of Elsinore was pitchforked onto the stage from a scaffolding tower when it gave way under their collective weight.

Because of this, the three most essential qualities are the constitution of a brick shithouse, a voice like a foghorn, and the ability to display emotions such as joy, anger and despair at a distance of 1200 yards. Or Brian Blessed, to give him his proper name.

And in truth, the blessed Brian is the ultimate prototype open-air actor: hearty, implacable to cold, and able to be heard in the next county without a radio mike. The nature of acting in the open air sometimes encourages the actors not so much to flirt with the audience as to go down on them. But if the setting and the weather are kind, there's really nothing better.

By way of testimony, some years ago I played Petruchio in a production of *The Taming Of the Shrew* at Ludlow Castle. It was June, Shropshire was in full A.E. Housman splendour, and the run coincided with an unexpected heatwave. I spent the days cycling or playing tennis, and the evenings playing one of Shakespeare's most dazzling roles to 2000 rapt (as opposed to wrapped) spectators, under a blue moon so big and close you felt you could pull a piece off and eat it.

Backstage an army of volunteer helpers kept up a running buffet of soup and homemade sausage rolls. After curtain down, the cast would amble over to the Blue Boar, a 15th-century tavern on the high street, where the landlord arranged a nightly lock-in: which was just as well as there were usually up to ten different real ales to sample. Most nights I'd stagger home still in my shorts and T-shirt at 4 am through empty medieval streets, my guts full of Coalport Dodger Mild and ham sandwiches, and fall into a delicious sleep. I even tapped off with one of the actresses in the cast.

Life really doesn't get much better than that.

PANTOMIME

It's nice to be around actors at Christmas time. Look at us and you'll see our eyes fill with wonder, our cheeks flush with anticipation, and our mouths gaping with disbelief.

That's because Christmas means panto, and for most actors, it's the one time when we can be guaranteed paid employment. There are hundreds of productions round the country every year, ranging from lavish multi-million pound events with film and TV celebrities, right down to small-scale civic affairs in the local leisure centre with a mere handful of pros supported by troupes of gangly adolescents from the nearby stage school.

Such is the importance of panto to many regional venues that many rely on these few precious weeks of full houses and ringing cash tills to sustain them through the rest of the year. And its place in our national affections ensures that families who wouldn't normally be seen dead in a theatre for the other eleven months can usually be persuaded to partake of this bizarre ritual.

And a bizarre ritual it certainly is. Men dressed as women, women dressed as men, dwarves, queens, princes and genies, and with the whole glittering confection topped off with enough high heels and improbable costumes to satisfy Lady Gaga herself.

But for any actor who hasn't actually spent time as the back half of Daisy the cow or tried to persuade 500 sugar-crazed children to join in the community song sheet, a word of warning. It may seem a safe, even joyous haven from the slog of unemployment, but once you've sampled it, you'll soon change your view. Money for old rope it isn't.

Despite its apparent *joie de vivre*, panto is in fact stupend-ously hard work. For a start, cash-strapped managements will squeeze as many performances out of you as they can; wading through 80 consecutive *Aladdin and his Wonderful Lamps* with nothing more for support than a float mike and a Kit-Kat at the interval can come as a shock to the system.

Not only will you be performing twice a day, six days a week, but if the management is particularly rapacious you'll be exposed to the most exquisite form of torture ever devised for a hung-over actor: the notorious 10 am 'shoppers' matinee', when frazzled parents leave their little darlings in your tender care while they hurry off to get a last few presents.

Actors are rarely at the best in the mornings, particularly if they've been partying the night before, and standing on a drafty stage at such an ungodly hour dressed as a bellhop with a theatre full of children screaming, 'He's behind you', at decibel levels Noddy Holder himself would covet, is not for the faint-hearted.

Despite productions being cast back in September, many small-scale productions are thrown on in extreme haste, often in unsuitable venues and without much regard for the comfort of either cast or audience. I witnessed a near catastrophe many years ago in a regional production of *Cinderella* when one of the two ponies pulling the heroine's silver coach onto the stage slipped on a pile of newly-expressed manure from its colleague–in-harness and nearly dragged the entire procession into the orchestra pit. The sight of the musical director trying to conduct with one hand while holding up the splayed palm of his other to protect himself from the imminent descent of half a hundredweight of horseflesh and balsa wood will live with me forever.

At another, the fairy godmother was pole-axed when an entire section of the set fell on her while she was intoning her magic spell. 'Never mind me, dear,' she said to Cinders as she laid buried in the debris, 'You shall go to the ball...'

All in all, pantos are stressful affairs for all involved. Indeed, such was the strain of doing up to 12 shows a week that one elderly actor playing the dame in a provincial theatre some years ago expired during the interval of the final performance. Anxious to complete the show, the cast sent on Idle Jack to explain away his mother's absence in Act Two.

'You'll have to be very good children,' he announced glumly, 'Because something very sad has happened. My mum's died...'

'Oh no she hasn't!!' chorused back 500 gleeful voices.

On top of all this, there's the lack of home comforts. Striding from your stretch limo into the Groucho Club is one thing – trying to get something to eat in the Arndale Centre Doncaster when you've only got 25 minutes between the matinee and evening performance is quite another.

If I speak with feeling, it's from bitter experience. I've done several productions in my time, and even played the eponymous hero in *Hans Andersen* at Harrogate. This particular production was at an insuperable disadvantage from the start, as it's not even officially a panto at all, but a lyrical (and at times lachrymose) musical adapted from the Danny Kaye movie of the same name. And the straight-talking residents of North Yorkshire took a dim view of their traditional festive entertainment being mucked about in such a fashion.

Worse still, my costume for Hans – brown corduroy jerkin, white frilly shirt and elasticated winklepickers – made me look like the last person on earth you'd want your little ones hanging about with. In fact you'd want him electronically tagged. The sight of me with six-year-old children on my knee while crooning about an inchworm made for queasy entertainment.

But perhaps the biggest problem is simply the length of the contract. Pantomime, like the holiday season itself, tends to overstay its welcome, and by February, when many productions are still wringing the last few coppers out of their local community, the audience are no longer interested whether Dick Whittington is going to end up Lord Mayor of London, all they want to know is whether they'll have enough in their current account to cover the month's mortgage payments.

Hopefully this will be one problem you don't have to face. After several weeks of hefty overtime, your bank account should be suitably replenished. If you're frugal enough in your habits you should be able to hang on for several months, or at least until the next offer of work rolls in.

Like another panto, for instance.

UNDERSTUDYING

So you've been out of drama school for a while. You've managed a few tasty interviews, but so far nothing has come of them. You're just beginning to have the first vague stirrings of anxiety. Then your agent rings and says you've been offered understudy for six months.

The job of understudying – that of covering a role (or several) in case the incumbent is indisposed – is, one of the oddest jobs in the profession. Ninety-nine shows out of a 100 you have nothing to do except sit in your dressing room playing Angry

Birds on your iPad and keep a weather ear open for the show relay system. And once the character you're understudying has made his final entrance of the evening, theatrical custom even dictates you can pack your bags and leave for home.

It sounds a doddle. Just think, sitting about all evening for a nice, if modest, cheque at the end of it. And even if the actor you're covering has had his leg accidentally cut off while walking through a local sawmill, chances are they'll still insist on going on, if only because they're terrified lest your performance proves more assured than theirs. No actor likes to be dispensable.

But just when your guard is down, something will happen which will shove you into the spotlight – either the actor you're covering will have got stuck in a traffic jam, turned his ankle over while emerging from the tube, or, as happened to a mate of mine a few months ago, been suddenly struck down after eating a dodgy prawn sandwich at lunchtime.

At best, you'll get several hours' warning of your imminent appearance. More often than not it'll be an hour or less, just enough time to be overcome with nerves without being able to dissipate them by going through the scenes.

As if this Russian roulette existence isn't stressful enough, you'll then have to endure the audience. The theatre managers will try to break it gently, but there's simply no way to dress up bad news. 'Ladies and gentlemen, owing to the indisposition of the major star you've paid nearly 60 quid a pop to see, in addition to the cost of getting here, the meal at Garfunkel's and the overpriced interval drinks, his part tonight will be played by an actor you've never heard of and who is currently caking himself in the wings because he's not sure he's up to it.' The groan of dismay and subsequent *froideur* when you eventually enter isn't the best start to what's already a perilous evening.

But while Broadway musicals continue to pedal the image of editions of *Variety* spinning towards the camera lens with the headline, 'A Star Is Born', the reality is different. Far more frequent are incidents such as the alarming tale attributed to the bluff and baleful Lilian Baylis, doyen of the Old Vic, who, having watched an understudy go on for a major role at short notice in one of her productions, said to the actress afterwards, 'Well, dear, you had your big chance – and you muffed it.'

Of course, it may be different. You may wow them. And to be fair, there are stories – though far fewer than you might think – of the understudy entrancing the audience and transforming themselves into a major star overnight.

But going on at short notice and often with little rehearsal isn't for the faint-hearted. One understudy I saw in a West End show was so nervous onstage that while lighting a large Havana cigar as part of the action, his hand shook so much that he dropped the lit match down the front of his shirt, setting alight his chest hair.

The good news is that understudies are fighting back. No longer content to be stuffed away in the attic like dusty luggage, many nowadays organise matinée 'understudy showcase' performances of the plays in which they're involved. This prospect of a tangible performance can often be the difference between sanity and madness during the long months of inactivity.

Away from the spotlight, many understudies forestall any potential creative atrophy by writing their own screenplay or learning computer skills. One perennial West End understudy has spent his last 15 years understudying also learning an assortment of foreign languages to a high conversational standard, including Spanish and Mandarin. Only problem is, he can't get to practise any in situ – he's too busy understudying.

The other issue is that understudies are not paid to interpret the role but merely to provide a precise facsimile of the absent performer. Any derivation from the prescribed moves or inflections will quickly have the other regular actors grumbling about their own performance being thrown. And as a mere understudy, it's a brave one who has the courage to tell them to get over themselves. After all, your job is to listen to their stories, not start telling ones of your own.

Which brings me to perhaps the most difficult facet of the job. Understudies assure me the worst part is not actually going on, but when the principal actor returns. One moment you're at top table, toe to toe with the other leads, swapping bon mots in the wings, celebrating the triumphs, discussing the woes, and with your own views listened to and your personal stories celebrated – and then suddenly you're back in your dressing room up on the fifth floor, listening to Everton v Wolves on Radio 5 Live and eking out the long hours with yet another cup of tea. As one of Michael Frayn's characters famously says: 'I can take the despair. It's the hope I can't stand.'

A final thought about understudying. It's a fact all too rarely mentioned, but the more able they prove to be, the more they're ultimately signing their own death warrant. There are thousands of decent actors around, but good understudies are hard to find. It's in the producers' interest to try and keep you where you are, drip-fed on a vague diet of half-promises and airy encouragement. So don't fall for it. If the part isn't offered to you on a plate when it becomes free, don't let them string you along. Leave the gig, even if it's only to understudy somewhere else.

My favourite story concerning the life of an understudy might be too good to be true, but since when did that stop me? Urban legend has it that one young individual was covering one of the great Shakespearean roles at the RSC some years back. A few nights into the run the call duly came: the star in question had been involved in a minor car shunt on the M40 and wasn't now expected to be released from A&E, where he was being checked for whiplash. The understudy would have to go on.

Trouble was, it was early on in the run, rehearsals had been scant, and the understudy hadn't bothered to get the part under his belt. Nonetheless, there was nothing for it: he had to play the role, at least, if he wasn't to be sacked.

Yet such was his erupting terror while waiting for curtain up in the wings that he reflexively defecated into his tights. Before he could even warn the stage manager of this fresh calamity the door burst open and the star actor barrelled in, with a bandage round his head.

'Get out of my costume,' roared the actor, 'I'm going on...'

RADIO

The observation that radio drama is better than TV 'because the pictures are better' may be true or not: but foreigners marvel at the mere fact that there's any drama on the radio at all, let alone that the BBC have their own team of actors to service it.

Over in America, once the Mecca of the medium (if you don't believe me, just watch Woody Allen's elegiac movie *Radio Days*) the moment the cathode ray came around, radio drama disappeared almost overnight. But in that quaint, old-fashioned way that made this nation great, we've clasped the concept to our bosom and held it close. When Associated-Rediffusion, the predecessor of the modern ITV, was launched in September 1955, Auntie Beeb threw its most lethal weapon at the garish upstart Granada in order to spike its guns: namely, Grace Archer being burned in a fire in Ambridge. Over 20 million tuned in, and ITV only just made it through.

For jobbing actors, getting work in radio drama means either a stint with the BBC Radio Rep Company or a spell in *The Archers*.

The Archers

'Don't worry Lizzie: I've been clambering about on rooftops since I was a child.'

When Nigel Pargetter, one of the show's most endearing and best-loved characters, was savagely culled at the end of 2010 by having him slip from the roof of Lower Loxley Hall while putting up the Christmas decs, it not only created a tsunami of national outrage far greater than that at Tony Blair's decision to invade of Iraq or David Cameron's pledge to hold a referendum on membership of the EU. Even more remarkably, his long, lingering scream ended up being one of the most popular downloaded ringtones on mobile phones.

No matter that his death yell lasted a full five seconds, requiring him to have leapt from a passing jumbo jet in order to complete it before hitting the ground: Nigel was Nigel, and, like so much about life in Borsetshire, was considered semi-sacred.

Go ahead and invade Afghanistan if you will, but leave Lynda Snell's panto well alone or you'll face civil unrest in the Home Counties.

With weekly audiences still nudging over five million, gaining a berth as a regular in *The Archers* is a wonderful gig for the jobbing actor, but it can come with strings attached. Episodes are recorded six days a month in Birmingham, so if you're planning on working elsewhere on the stage or TV, you'll need to give them plenty of warning so they can fit your slots into their evermore complex recording schedules.

And while the basic fee is around £350 per episode, the average number of episodes for which you'll be required will be no more than three or four a month (you're not paid a retainer). If your character spawns a love child, loses his leg in a harvesting accident or is made captain of the Ambridge cricket team you'll get plenty of airtime and decent money; but if your only contribution is an occasional speech in the Cat & Fiddle about government silage quotas you can find yourself tied up for long periods without much to show for it.

There is, however, one great advantage about life after *The Archers* that no other soap opera can boast; for however long you stay, you won't end up leaving the series to find yourself typecast. And that's because nobody out there knows what you look like.

Wonderful if you've just fallen off a roof of course, but cold comfort for the rest of us left to deal with our grief.

Radio Rep
The Radio Rep is the colloquial term used to describe the BBC Radio Drama Company, a group of some 12 to 20 actors of

different ages and sexes, who are hired for several months at a time and whose job is to service the substantial drama output the BBC churns out on its various frequencies (apart from *The Archers*, which is entirely separate). In addition to the afternoon play, serialisations of famous books and various bits and pieces, protagonists will also be invited to fill in at *Book At Bedtime*, *Something Understood* and *Poetry Please*.

The Rep was formed in 1940, partly in response to the increasing demand for radio drama, and partly as a means to disseminate official information and raise morale amongst the civilian population during the war. Many of the early broadcasts were transmitted live, which often led to unexpected complications on the frequent occasions in which they over-ran – a famous example being the stentorian tones of a BBC continuity announcer cutting into the final duel between Hamlet and Laertes to announce, 'And there we must leave Elsinore for the evening news…'

Even now, some 70 years on, the BBC furnishes between 180-200 afternoon plays annually, plus special one-offs at the weekends, ranging from Euripides to newly-discovered talents, many of whom will use the experience of writing for radio to hone their skills on their way to fame and fortune at the Baftas. Listening figures for afternoon plays still range between 800,000 and a million, a figure that would put many popular TV drama series to shame.

Habitués assure me life within the Rep is civilised, convivial, and best of all, salaried. And with each project lasting only a few days at best, there's little opportunity for raging egotism to break out. 'Like a well-mannered party where you bump into old friends and leave before you start to get boring,' was how one veteran put it to me. The main skills you'll need in order to qualify will be an engaging voice, an ability to sight-read and a facility for dialects.

Upon arriving for your first day of work, you'll be handed a ceremonial BBC diary that will soon be groaning under the weight of assorted gigs and recording dates. And you'll find yourself working with some of the best in the business (one mate of mine who joined the company many years ago worked with Dirk Bogarde, Rod Steiger, Harold Pinter and Joan Littlewood in his first six months).

Most days start promptly at 10 am with a read-through of the proposed play. This is often followed by a brief but piquant interlude, usually referred to as *Omnes*, which is where you all stand about and gabble assorted rhubarb in the style of said project to be used later as background chatter. As well as being a great ice-breaker, custom dictates the protagonists try to slip words like iPad, Kindle and Filet o' Fish into the background action, which can be especial fun if you're recording a Restoration comedy. You then get down to the serious business of recording the play, a process that will take between a couple of days and several weeks.

But perhaps the best thing about the Radio Rep is that you don't have to worry about remembering the lines, or even moving your arms and legs. There's a special technician on hand to create all the necessary sound effects, thereby leaving you to concentrate solely on the acting. If you're dining at an Egyptian banquet in 200 BC there'll be somebody to cut up your grapes, flay your concubines and fan your brow with an ostrich feather. If you're invading France with the Third Reich, by contrast, said assistant will crunch bubble wrap to provide the hoards of storm troopers following in your wake, while the simple act of shuffling round on the studio floor on piles of old recording tape will perfectly capture Sherlock Holmes strolling through autumn leaves in pursuit of Moriarty.

There's also ample time for retakes: which is just as well, for as in all the best drama, there are frequent mishaps. One friend was cast in a play about the pioneering South African heart surgeon Christiaan Barnard, and thus found himself performing a virtual transplant scene with several other respected thesps, each clad in hospital gowns and with masks over their faces to suggest the ambience of an operating theatre. Beneath them on the floor, meanwhile, the special effects operator knelt hunched over a bowl of water with a scalpel and a cabbage, ready to replicate the sound of the requisite incisions.

'Do you think we can pull off this procedure?' ran my friend's opening dialogue.

'We have to,' replied his compatriot. 'If we don't, he'll be a vegetable for the rest of his life.'

Needless to say they had to break early for lunch.

ADS

Some weeks ago I bumped into a friend in the street, and by way of conversation asked her what she was up to. Her answer could only have come from someone in the acting profession. She'd spent the day sitting on the floor with sausage meat stuffed in both ears.

More specifically, she'd been filming an advert for Pedigree Chum; the crucial money shot, the one in which her pet dog affectionately licks her face, was only obtained when she agreed to stick some pork mincemeat in her lug holes.

It may not have been the lifestyle she'd envisaged when she'd applied for drama school a decade before, but having successfully survived it, she was now on her way to purchase some cotton buds and a new outfit from Nicole Farhi.

Her experience encapsulates the agony and the ecstasy of doing adverts. Short of being paid ten grand to be an escort for a night of passion with John McCririck, it's hard to imagine any activity where you get so much for so little, and yet suffer so much emotional damage as a result.

Despised by many in the business, loved by some, ads can make you rich and destroy your soul. They can take you to New Guinea or New Malden. They can also result in the odd phenomenon of making you very famous without anyone knowing who the hell you are (for more details please see appendix 21: *Go Compare*).

Whether or not you even go up for them in the first place will depend on whether your agent specialises in such things. Some consider ads to be a major part of their revenue stream; others wouldn't be seen dead representing a client list associated in the public eye with tampons or flatulence remedies.

By way of example, in my first decade I didn't go up for a single one. Yet the moment I changed to an agent who specialised in such projects, flatulence remedies became my daily *raison d'être*; a skill for which my long-suffering wife will confirm I was already over-qualified.

Of the thousand or so products for which I auditioned over the next few years, I was successful in about eight: a hit rate of about 1 in every 120. I also had fleeting European fame with an advert for a soap bar popular in Germany, of which more in a minute.

Early on, I noticed the same few rivals often collared the available ads. For a while I would rejoice in seeing them at each new tilt – surely the manufacturers wouldn't pick them again, especially as their faces were already on our screens day and night, often appearing in commercials for competing products? Surely it would be my turn?

But on the contrary, their success bred an easy confidence that meant they'd inevitably hoover up one after another. Take that actor in those lager ads a year or two back, the one who used to kneel on all fours to lick the toilet bowl clean while his missus stood temptingly with a can of booze just beyond reach. Until that ad I'd never seen or heard of him, yet once he'd successfully licked the rim, so to speak, he suddenly seemed to be everywhere.

And that's because getting ads is a knack. Once you've got one, the pheromones of success rub off on you: your shoulders drop, your smile is more relaxed, your hand clasp more confident – in other words, you have the sweet smell of success, and the management executives staring at you in the interview can smell a winner at a hundred paces. That's their job.

The other curious aspect about my infrequent triumphs was that they weren't evenly spread. Nearly all the pencils turned to ink in a golden period of about 18 months when it seemed I'd unwittingly cracked the code – yet my touch deserted me almost as speedily as it arrived, leaving me scratching my head as to what had gone wrong. With hindsight the difference was almost certainly that of my ageing. A few more wrinkles, a slight yellowing of the front incisors, a nose hair too many or a bag under the eye, and suddenly I didn't fit the advertising demographic. I no longer looked like the ideal consumer.

The good news about ads is that you only need to secure four or five gigs a year to make all the heartbreak, despair, embarrassment, shame and degradation worthwhile. For that's what you'll suffer. Make no mistake – any savings you accrue will be heavily eaten into by the cost of psychotherapy bills. And that's because auditioning for ads is the single most humiliating, degrading activity known to man.

Here's what you can expect. You turn up to find the waiting area crowded with numerous other actors, all looking like you, and none of whom you've heard of. When it's your turn you're shown into an interview room, where the casting director will tell you what they want you to simulate.

'So you're hacking your way through the jungle when suddenly you take a bite from your new Sprinkles chocolate bar, whereupon thousands of tiny cocoa shapes erupt from all sides and begin whirring around your head. One lands on your shoulder and turns into a lovely little elfin creature who kisses you on the ear, causing you to laugh uncontrollably. Then you float upwards into the tree tops, whirling round and round, and high-fiving your little elfin chum as you do so... before waking up to find you're still in your office at work being gazed with pitying horror by your workmates. And – ACTION!'

There's little you can do to stave off the degradation. Auditions invariably involve improvisation. I've had to endure some horrendous ordeals, including one for a brand of haem-orrhoid cream in which I had to mime going over Niagara

Falls in a barrel while suffering from acute piles. Nothing in my seven terms at RADA was of the slightest help. Contemplating the repeat fees, however, proved immensely fortifying.

On another occasion, I turned up to find that the screen test involved planting a long lingering kiss full on the lips of an actress paired up with me beforehand. But in my ignorance of the job spec, I'd previously wolfed down a liver sausage sandwich with mustard in the café opposite the premises. The sensation of kissing a beautiful woman and knowing she was trying not to breathe or gag during our embrace revived painful memories of adolescence I'd been trying to subdue for many years.

All actors have their own stories of the agony and ecstasy of doing ads, so I'll limit myself to my own, which, if nothing else, illustrates the sort of scrape you can get yourself into.

By chance it was my first ever success, a German soap bar called *Irischer Frühling,* (Irish Springtime) that smelt strongly of industrial lemons and which, I was assured, was big in mainland Europe, for whom the ad campaign was intended.

God knows what the director thought he was doing casting me in the role of a wholesome Irish larrikin, though at the time I was still in my mid-twenties, with a mop of sandy hair and a plethora of freckles, all of which presumably made me ideal for the popular notion of what a young Irishman might look like – at least if you're German.

The audition was typical of the humiliation I've described – in this case having to mime for a group of strangers what it might be like to gambol through a grassy meadow with my betrothed, laughing and joking, and smelling the sweet fresh Irish air, before stepping barefoot into an ice-cold stream, and finally setting an imaginary paper boat down an imaginary stream, and smiling gaily as it bobbed downstream to where my true love was waiting to receive it.

As commercials go, the terms and conditions seemed entirely benign, not to say inviting – a one-day shoot in southern Ireland, plus a day's travel each side, all of which came to several thousand smackers for a little under three days' work.

On the day of departure, I was picked up by a sleek Mercedes, the only other passenger being a stupendously beautiful model called Vanessa who was playing Colleen to my larrikin. We were both flown first class to Cork, transported to a grand country hotel in the countryside, and told to order whatever we liked from the à la carte menu in the restaurant.

Having unpacked, I spent an hour relaxing in the heated indoor swimming pool before joining Vanessa for a candlelit dinner, finishing off proceedings with an Irish coffee of lethal potency. Nonetheless by 10 pm I was back in my room and preparing for bed. Just as I was brushing my teeth I heard the familiar rustle of a script being pushed under the door of my room and hurried across to open the envelope. It was then that I received my first shock. I had dialogue. And it was in German.

'Irisher Frühling – so kuehl und klar mit ein Bergsee, und auch ganz sanft auf Ihren Haenden!'

I settled down to try and learn the words, but it proved impossible. My knowledge of German was confined to the war comics I'd read as a child, and thus anything more sophisticated than 'Hande hoch', 'Donner und Blitzen' and 'Aaiiiieeeeeeee' was beyond my powers. Whatever I tried – mnemonics, word association, parroting the phrases endlessly in my bathroom mirror – it was hopeless. The jumble of syllables and consonants simply refused to coalesce in my head.

After an anxious night during which the dread phrase careered round in my subconscious without ever quite landing, I was woken at 5 am, and kitted out in an outfit best described as Gilbert O'Sullivan chic – cloth cap, moleskin breeches and flannel shirt.

As we travelled by car out to the location, the director, who rejoiced in the name of Erasmus, explained the storyboard in halting English. As with the improv, I was to run barefoot down a grassy meadow festooned with wild flowers, hand in hand with Vanessa, looking happy and carefree; a progression he'd capture on a master shot from an adjoining hillside.

Then we'd cut to a medium and two shot of Vanessa and I arriving at a pearling stream, into which I would set a tiny paper boat. As it bobbled down the various currents and eddies, I was to jump from boulder to boulder until I, too, reached the far end. Finally I'd take Vanessa's hands in mine, lift them to my lips and utter the deathless phrase…

'Irischer Frühling – und kuehl und klar mit … ein… um …'

Whatever.

The first problem was the location. The field in which we were filming had been rented out from a local farmer, who'd only that morning vacated his herd of cows; animals which evidently were suffering digestive problems. Our route down the hillside was festooned with enormous puddles of foul-smelling excrement, which, if touched, discharged clouds of plump bluebottles into the air. Worse still was the gradient, which would have had Evel Knievel himself reaching for the smelling salts.

Yet every time Vanessa and I so much as glanced down to make sure we didn't sprain our ankles or step barefoot into pools of newly expressed slurry, we got furious instructions from Erasmus on the opposite hillside to keep our heads up and smile.

Somehow we got through it without breaking our necks. The next sequence merely required me to squat in the stream and set the paper boat in motion. Compared with what we'd endured it should have been a doddle; but the temperature of the water was such that within seconds of setting foot in it I'd lost all feeling in my toes. Whenever I was required to stand up and skip daintily to the next boulder I found myself moving with all the dexterity of Douglas Bader.

At length we got to the close-up: and my line of dialogue.

'Irisher Frühling – so kuehl und klar mit ein Bergsee, und… um… *something about ganz saft….*'

The shooting of this one line of dialogue remains the single most embarrassing interlude of my professional life. I must have had 30 takes at it, yet on each successive attempt I always managed to dry on a different syllable. With the light fast fading and Erasmus threatening to unleash the Luftwaffe if I didn't get my line in the can, I was forced to endure the ultimate ignominy for any actor, reading my words phonetically from a set of giant idiot boards placed behind the camera.

I wasn't the least surprised to hear from a friend living in Hamburg that my voice was subsequently dubbed by an authentic German speaker.

With luck you may successfully get many tens of ads in your career without ever having to endure any of the horror of my two days in the Ring of Kerry. But be warned – your experience may be even worse than the one I've described.

Finally, you'll recall I mentioned the unseen emotional cost. Nearly two decades on from my dalliance with *Irischer Frühling,* usually when I'm stressed or overtired, I still occasionally find myself being shaken into life in the middle of the night by Julia. My pajamas are soaked in sweat and my mouth tastes like I've just swallowed a newly expressed cowpat.

'For Christ's sake,' she usually mutters on such occasions, 'You're bellowing that line about that bloody German soap again.'

Never mind. A few more goes and I reckon I'll have cracked it.

AUDIOBOOKS

If, like me, you can't imagine ever becoming sick of the sound of your own voice, I have a simple remedy. Try recording an audiobook. It'll cure you forever.

There are now upwards of 60,000 titles available on Amazon, with hundreds more coming on stream every month. With the explosion in the use of Kindles and e-Readers, they're a massively lucrative market, and if you can gain a reputation for being able to deliver 250 pages of crisp, finely-turned words of aural prose in something under three days a pop, without deviation, hesitation or belching midway through the paragraph, you can soon make a name for yourself.

Normally you'll be expected to record a book in three to four days; more if you're recording *War and Peace*, less if it's a simple child's story. Leading specialists can record up to 30 separate volumes a year. But a word of warning. Audiobooks are not for the ill-prepared.

Each book represents a verbal Everest, with each paragraph a tiny handhold in the rock face. Every para has to be negotiated, secured and tied off before you can even think of moving on to the next. At the end of each brain-numbing and tonsil-crunching day you take off your headphones, try and nurse your ears back into life, and bivouac for the night, hoping that the next day you can urge yourself back to continue the unremitting climb.

I only discovered for myself quite how difficult they were when I recorded my first, a novel about a young teenager living in the fictional northern town of Blackport, who, by dint of a freak accident that affects his right foot, becomes the most lethal footballing centre forward of his generation.

That, at least, was the story as described to me by the producer in our initial correspondence. Once we'd agreed terms, the producer sent me a hard copy of the book on A4 paper for me to familiarise myself with before the recording. And honestly, I really did intend to read it thoroughly. It's just that there were so many other things to prioritise – my tax returns, a couple of interviews, and the unexpected descent of some relatives. In the end I skip-read the first two-thirds and promised myself I'd cover the rest once I was on the case. In other words, I thought I could busk it.

Lack of preparation and hubris; the twin nemeses of the mountaineer and jobbing actor.

Just before 9.30 am on the Monday morning, I was positioned in a tiny studio off Marylebone, with my ears braising nicely under a pair of headphones. In front of me, suspended from the ceiling and lit by a single unblinking desk lamp, was a microphone: and on the green baize table beneath, the book, each pristine leaf with its staples removed for silent turning. On the other side of the glass were my producer, Alan, and an engineer called Terry.

It's probably worth recounting the first couple of minutes in full:

'OK Mike, when you're ready...'

'Chapter One. Jimmy Young had fallen off his bicycle. Yet he could hardly recall how it had happened...'

'Sorry Mike, it's young Jimmy.'

'Pardon?'

'It's "Young Jimmy."'

'What did I say?'

'Jimmy Young. You made it into his surname. It sounded as if we were talking about an octogenarian ex-radio presenter.'

'Sorry, I hadn't noticed.'

'No probs. Let's go again...'

I took a swig from my plastic bottle and cleared my throat.

'Young Jimmy had fallen off his bicycle. Yet he could hardly recall how it had happened.'

'Mike again. Sorry, you said "how it had 'appened."'

'Pardon?'

'You said, "How it had 'appened". You elided the last two words. We lost the final H. It came across a bit like Jimmy Savile. And we don't want that do we?'

By 10.30 am, we'd barely crawled to the end of page one. Far from keeping the read fresh, my lack of preparation was now coming back to plague me. Quite apart from the innumerable fluffs, elisions and pops that now bedevilled every phrase, my attempts to bring the novel to life were further thwarted by the rush of different characters which inundated the narrative, each requiring a new voice, a fresh cadence and a specific timbre, none of which I'd prepared.

Indeed, from being the bucolic idyll it had seemed on my initial read, Jimmy's home town of Blackport now seemed a grossly overcrowded conurbation, with a huge and socially unsustainable demographic of immigrants muscling in from all parts of the civilised world. Urban unrest could be the only possible outcome.

Long before my hero had scored his first hat-trick, I'd already exhausted my shallow pool of popular celebrities I could impersonate in order to differentiate the burgeoning cast list. The games master I'd already allocated to Max Bygraves, the headmaster to Michael Caine, the first team coach to Blakey in *On the Buses*, and Jimmy's mum and dad to politician Anne Widdecombe and game show host Dale Winton. Rather than a thrilling children's adventure story, the book was beginning to sound like a nightmare version of *Dead Ringers*.

Yet even when I did get it right, the narrative kept coming back and biting me on the bum. After one passage, in which young Jimmy's games master runs out of petrol while taking him to a trial for first division side Newtown Wanderers, he finishes by saying, '*Never mind lad. I always carry a spare can of petrol in the boot. Where I come from in North Wales this sort of thing happens all the time.*' The whole section had to be re-recorded, with me now dragooning a highly iffy Windsor Davies into the unfolding drama.

The day ended with me running full tilt into Winston Cummings, a Jamaican International and star player for Newtown, who takes young Jimmy under his wing. Along with Geordie and Glaswegian, a Jamaican accent is well known in the biz as being one of the hardest to replicate, and my Winston was soon careering over much of central Europe and the Urals, with momentary touch downs in India and Mexico, until he finally crash landed somewhere around Paris.

'No, ze thing ees where I come from in Kingston...' I heard myself saying. *Ze thing ees*? I looked through the glass to find the technician stuffing a hankie in his mouth and the producer shaking his head sadly.

You'll be pleased to hear that after this chastening first day, things began to improve, though only by re-reading the subsequent pages long into the night, highlighting the various characters in fluorescent markers, and by throwing myself on the mercy of my wife. Julia's always been a dab hand at accents, and in return for a promise of a candlelit supper at the local restaurant she offered to take me phonetically through an authentic Caribbean patois. Slowly, and with immense care, I started to acquire the knack. But it cost me nearly 40 quid plus drinks and a cab home.

In conclusion, should you ever get asked to do one, learn from the unpleasantness in Blackport and follow these few simple rules. Mark up the characters, allocate your voices, and never accept a project that features characters from the Caribbean.

Unless, of course, you're from the Caribbean.

And a final tip.

Read the book.

But there's no need to take my word for it. If you go to YouTube and type in 'Judy Geeson Audiobook', you'll have a grandstand seat for an example of just how bad it can get when you don't do your homework.

In truth I don't think Miss Geeson's decision to bring her asthmatic pet dog Tara into the recording booth helps her cause – but even without this added distraction her effort is a perfect example of what can happen when you have a bad day in the recording booth.

VOICE-OVERS

Whether it's the voice of Lloyds TSB, or just a few brief phrases announcing a sofa sale at your local department store, laying down voice-overs for adverts is a good way to make a lot of money.

I'm not talking here about providing commentaries for documentaries, which is another field entirely, and a highly select one. Adding the vocal narrative for a five-part series about prohibition or the life cycle of the emperor penguin is a specific niche market, one in which the protagonists are usually already well-known, with a distinctive vocal tone to match. I'm talking now about radio ads, TV promos and brief, 30-second jingles; a separate skill, but nonetheless a lucrative one.

Nowadays you don't even have to go into a city centre studio to lay down the track, for with an ISDN phone line (Integrated Services Digital Network), a compliant partner and a soundproofed coat cupboard, you can transform your home into a one-man recording studio. As a result you can become a millionaire without having to get out of your pyjamas.

My mate Patsy is one such example. She's cornered the market in friendly mums – warm, silky, a hint of a giggle, nice and gentle, nothing to be afraid of. Consequently she's cornered the market in Mothercare, Pampers, Weight Watchers and Toys R Us. She consequently has a second home in the Dordogne and goes on three luxury cruises a year. All the rough stuff – car auctions, carpet warehouses and building supplies – she leaves to those with estuary vowels and a vocal quality suggestive of imminent violence.

Proper studios, however, are rarely booked for more than an hour a pop, so you've got to nail it. Not much time for niceties either – 'Do it again, but better', 'Less bloody acting', 'Stop sounding like *Listen with Mother*'; or Patsy's personal favourite, 'We need it more lazy and languorous, but faster.'

In order to get started you'll probably have to put down a demo for one of the leading voice-over agencies, after which, if successful, you'll be pencilled in for a few tentative offers. Once you've got a foot in the door things can quickly escalate until you're racking up several gigs a week.

There is, however, one supreme drawback. With modern technology allowing everything to be arranged at the last minute, your mobile phone can rapidly become your jailer.

I used to meet one of the most successful voice-over practitioners during the summer months at Lords, where he'd customarily while away the summer hours in between prospective bookings. Despite sporting the latest summer suit and a stupefying range of credit cards, he always looked as if he hadn't seen the light of day for several months; which he hadn't – he'd spent all his time under the stairs.

Despite his obvious trappings of wealth, there was always a distracted air about him. At the slightest sound of a ringtone, even if it wasn't his, he'd be scrabbling for his iPhone, checking it constantly between deliveries to see it was still working or whether he'd inadvertently switched it to mute.

More than this, he'd be pathologically obsessed with talking about what was going on in the rest of the business: auditions, castings, new dramas and West End plays – all the stuff he could no longer contemplate going up for in case he missed being the next voice of British Airways or Coca Cola.

And of course, the call would come – just as he was tucking into some fruit cake, or thinking of wandering across to the Tavern stand for a pint – can you be ready in 20 minutes to do a voiceover for Müller Rice or Homebase? However much he tried to relax and enjoy his wealth, his time was never fully his own.

And after the request came, he'd be off, always with profuse apologies and assurances he'd be back in time for the final 20 overs. But he never was. Because even as he'd be scurrying in through his front door, Tetley Teabags would want him for a booking at 4.30 pm, after which he'd have to there again at 6 pm to do another for John Lewis or Nescafé.

If the idea of becoming very rich in such a manner appeals, I can thoroughly recommend it. But let me add a word of warning. However successful you become, and however many gigs you notch up, never suggest irony, either on mike or off. One well-known actor who regularly features on a dizzying range of household brands once told me how he lost a lucrative contract for a leading brand of dog food after he momentarily forgot this golden rule.

He'd fronted the firm's campaign for several years and was laying down yet another voiceover for its latest commercial ('prime chunks of tender chicken, juicy kidney, all in a rich, rich sauce') over footage of golden retrievers wolfing down great mouthfuls of slimy meat from a metal bowl. As usual he nailed it on his second take – sport-on timing, silky authority, and all utterly persuasive.

As he took off his headphones the company executives applauded warmly from behind the glass. 'Thanks, guys,' he said. 'Much more of that and I'd have to throw up.' He knew instantly his mistake. Their faces collectively froze. He never heard from them again.

Doing voiceovers is nice work if you can get it. But never forget who's paying your mortgage.

Namely, the Man from Del Monte…

PRESENTATION COACHING

Do you remember that conference speech Iain Duncan Smith made back at the Conservative party conference in 2003? With the Tories trailing in the polls and rumours abounding that his halting, stiff-limbed public persona was in danger of wrecking the party's chances at the forthcoming general election, IDS's entire political future was utterly riding on his performance on the podium during the next 50 minutes.

You may not recall the speech itself, except for perhaps one moment; the instant he screwed his eyes up with the look of a middle-aged man trying to climax against insuperable odds, fixed his gaze on the middle distance as if awaiting the arrival of Winston Churchill on a golden chariot, and declared, 'The quiet man is here to stay, and he is turning up the VOLUME!'

He was removed from office within the month.

That's what presentation coaches do. Make sure people like him don't give speeches like that.

If there's one thing actors know about, it's how to deliver a speech, persuade people to listen, and ensure that what you're saying lands with clarity, integrity and clout. Until the late 1980s, the interface between theatre and big business was virtually non-existent. And then, about a decade ago, industry cottoned on to the fact that it could learn a thing or two from Equity. Now there's big money to be made for actors willing to help maximise a corporate message.

In actuality, helping businessmen to hone their presentation skills is not strictly a branch of showbiz at all, but a highly specialised field. Thus it's not essentially something you can dick in and out of, because if you're any good at it, word will soon get round, and before you know it you'll find it's become your full time career.

For many actors it's an agreeable way of earning a living; certainly better than sitting in an unheated bedsit with no carpets reading the back pages of *The Stage*. Before you know it you'll be spending more time in the arrivals hall at Schiphol Airport than your own sitting room. Your days will be spent coaching some of the most important people in the FTSE Top 100, and your nights in bleak Novotels wondering whether to fork out for the hotel porn channel or break open the minibar.

One seasoned professional told me that such is the testosterone-fuelled culture of big business that the only way to persuade its protagonists to take you seriously is to chronicle how many famous actresses you've snogged. This, after all, is language they understand. Thankfully my mate had once screen-tested for a Johnny Depp movie and got through

Catherine Zeta-Jones, Samantha Janus and Emily Mortimer in a single two-hour session ('that normally shuts them up,' he assured me).

In fairness, it's usually middle management who is most resistant (senior bosses have already twigged that you can make a difference, which is why they're bosses and not surly apparatchiks).

Yet the problem stubbornly remains one of the clashing cultures. Most of your clients will only be there under sufferance, and will regard being taught by a luvvie with all the enthusiasm of Mike Tyson approaching a cake-decorating class. They'll also expect you to be able to transform them from Steven Gerrard into Barack Obama in a few short hours. Worse still, nearly all of them will have girlfriends – usually called Debbie – who want to have a go at acting. 'Who should I call?' is usually their parting shot at the end of an initial session.

The trick, I'm assured, is not to make your charges feel vulnerable and picked-on. Go in with the attitude that you're going to show them how it should be done, and you'll be branded a twat before you've opened your mouth (or they theirs). 'Softly, softly, catchy monkey' runs the old saw; by gaining their trust and working closely with them over a number of sessions, you can genuinely help to transform both their own personal presentation, and their company's profit sheet. You'll also vastly improve your own finances at a single stroke.

It was actress and self-help guru Dorothy Sarnoff who said, 'Make sure you've finished speaking before your audience has finished listening.' It's a handy quote to have around, whether you're a performer, a businessman... or Iain Duncan Smith.

ROLE-PLAYS

One of my favourite moments from British films – or from any film – is the scene in the 1954 comedy *Doctor in the House,* when Sir Lancelot Spratt (definitively played by the inimitable James Robertson Justice) is taking a group of hapless medical trainees round the wards off his hospital in order to give them some experience in diagnostics.

He holds up the hands of one stricken patient, who is suffering a severe pain in his abdomen and turning to his quailing audience of trainee GPs, decides to put them through their paces.

'What's the surgeon's worst enemy?' he barks. 'Blood of course! And the period between the initial incision and a clot forming is known as the bleeding time.'

He turns to Dirk Bogarde.

'You! What's the bleeding time?'

'About ten past ten sir,' replies Bogarde after a glimpse at his watch.

Sir Lancelot may be a figment of author Richard Gordon's delicious imagination, but medical role-plays are a ready means for actors to earn extra cash. Medical students on the cusp of completing their training and about to be released on the unsuspecting public have to be judged not only on their knowledge, but also on their ability to communicate with the paying public. Simply giving them a written examination can't assess this latter quality; so what better way to judge their inter-personal skills than with a dummy run on virtual patients?

This is where you come in.

The best news about doing medical role-play work is that

the pay is good (usually £150 a day). You'll also get a fabulous lunch (whoever it is in the BMA who's responsible for hiring actors has obviously done their homework – thesps never turn down the offer of free nosh).

The bad news is you'll have to spend considerable time becoming versed in your chosen malady so that you can stand up to scrutiny. One friend of mine has cornered the market in blackened stools, while another is considered pre-eminent in undescended testicles.

You'll also be given a thorough steer beforehand as to the type of personality you're portraying: monosyllabic, garrulous, angry, scared, or someone who's hypermanic and can't stop talking (the latter will be a doddle for most jobbing actors). You may even find yourself portraying a pain in the arse who's got a pain in the arse.

With four to five years of backbreaking academic slog resting on this brief interrogation, some students pass with flying colours, while some fold quicker than an IKEA picnic chair. Veterans of role-plays often attest that the hard bit of the job spec is not replicating the illness, but soaking up the nerves and anxiety radiating from the students.

Some will ask all the right questions, get to the point, and be off well within their allotted span with a gold star next to their case notes. Others will gulp, press the top of their biro up and down for minutes on end, and then suggest/insist/plead that the ailment you're describing is not the one you've got at all but something else entirely, one they know about.

But if you're already salivating at the prospect of getting stuck into some real old-fashioned barnstorming ham (think Frankie Howerd having been knifed by a rubber dagger in

Up Pompeii) think again. It might seem fun to be awarded epilepsy as your supposed ailment, but eight hours of mowing and gibbering in the corner of the room can soon pall. Pray you get given ingrowing toenails and you'll have a far easier time of it.

But even if you choose not to sample this curious backwater of the acting game, I can thoroughly recommend James Hogg's breezy account of James Robertson Justice, who in addition to being one of our finest character actors, spoke 20 languages including Russian and Gaelic, was secretary of the British Ice Hockey Association, and briefly served as a policeman for the League of Nations. I suspect he'd also have been a dab hand at medical role-play.

The title of the book?

What's the Bleeding Time?

EXTRA WORK

Do you recall those curious glassy-eyed individuals who used to populate the reception desk of the Crossroads Motel back in its heyday?

I was a huge fan of the series when young. Yet even back then, it intrigued me why the nation's favourite motel seemed to be staffed by people with verbal diarrhea, yet catered exclusively for guests suffering from tracheotomies.

Scenes would invariably start like this:

Meg Richardson: *(handing a couple of departing guests their receipt) 'So have you enjoyed your stay here?'*

Couple at desk smile maniacally back while nodding their heads.
Meg: *'Was everything to your satisfaction?'*
Couple grin at each other like mental defectives before more
  furious nodding in the direction of their host.
Meg: *'I'm so pleased to hear it. And have a safe journey home.'*
Couple wave as if bidding farewell to a much-loved relative
  departing on an ocean liner, before exiting in complete silence.

Of course, I realise now the reason for their sinister behaviour. They weren't real people at all. They were extras.

One question I'm often asked by actors struggling to get going is, 'Should I take some work as an extra?' Though in truth, it's a term you'll rarely hear nowadays. Nowadays they're called 'Supporting Artists' or 'Background'. After all, the term extra comes with all sorts of unsavoury connotations, suggesting slabs of unfeeling humanity to be shoved about without regard for pleasantries or personal welfare. Nonetheless there's a reason Ricky Gervais called his coruscating TV satire on the profession *Extras* rather than *Supporting Artists*. For at bottom level, that's what you are.

The benefits are obvious. Once you've signed up with a reputable agency (some will demand a small upfront fee, others will merely take a slightly higher commission off your daily rate), you'll be put up for a wide selection of TV drama, ads, and feature films. As well as earning up to £80 per day, you'll mix with various high-flyers in the business (even if none of them are prepared to talk to you).

It also allows you to examine at close quarters how a film unit operates, a real boon if you're thinking of ending up behind the lens yourself one day. You'll get a magnificent lunch, and your Auntie Hilda will be thrilled when she spots you playing darts in the Queen Vic. The only thing you won't be able to do is to speak. Speaking means they have to pay you more.

The best supporting artists, those with regular background roles to fulfill, are highly skilled. Watch *Waterloo Road* or any of the big soaps nowadays and you'll see the same select few week after week; opening the main gates of the school, pulling a pint, or frying bacon in the café. These elite troops form close bonds with the regular cast members and can make a tidy annual income.

Even these, however, are not actors. You, on the other hand are. And that's the problem. I've only ever crossed the divide once, but it was sufficient to deter me from ever wanting to do so again.

It occurred when a neighbour of mine was asked if her pet dog, an asthmatic pug called Rolo, could be used as part of a TV advert for home insurance being shot in Bushy Park.

Rolo's owner wasn't free on the day of the filming, so asked me if I'd mind standing in as minder and filmic dog walker for the day. Everything in me told me not to do it. I'd witnessed the life of extras too many times, standing hunched and dispirited for hours on end in the freezing cold, stamping their feet for warmth, their only concern how much overtime they might earn and when the next meal break would relieve the mind-numbing tedium. But then I reasoned why not? Nobody would know, and it would be a chance to spend an entire day with my furry chum.

The job began with my being rung by the third assistant director the night before the shoot, telling me to be at the park gates at 6.30 the next morning so wardrobe and wigs could check me over. No parking was available, so I'd have to get there by public transport. Rolo wasn't called till 8 am, and arrived in the front passenger seat of an otherwise unoccupied people carrier.

After checks, I was ordered to wait in a catering bus with no heating with twenty or so other shivering recruits, while Rolo was personally escorted to the make-up truck for a personal grooming.

The trend continued. Rolo was allowed to go for a pee in the bushes while a runner held an umbrella over his head. I, on the other hand, had to hang on until an official break, when I'd stand in a long queue for the notorious 'honey wagon', a portable toilet servicing about 80 people which, from the aroma emanating from its depths, hadn't been emptied for some days. At lunch I had to stand in a queue, watching the principal actors and creatives pushing in and nabbing all the best grub. Rolo, needless to say, had his meal specially prepared for him in his trailer.

The filming itself was even more chastening, consisting as it did of walking back and forth along the towpath with Rolo while being occasionally screamed at by the second AD, who'd managed to learn the animal's name but not mine, preferring instead to bawl out, 'Oy, you with the dog!'

But worst of all, the elderly actress playing the principal role in the foreground of the ad was one with whom I'd previously worked as an actor. The look of pity on her features when she eventually recognised me was to haunt me for many weeks.

And this is the problem with crossing the line. Film crews won't know that you're an actor who's slumming it. They'll think it's what you do. And that can be deeply humiliating after three years' training.

Never forget. You may not be a successful one. But you're still an actor.

IT'S AN OFFER

Alan Bennett, in answer to a question as to whether he was gay or straight, replied that it was like asking a man who'd spent days crossing a desert 'whether he'd prefer Perrier or Evian.' For most actors, the question of whether to accept a job is a similar situation, for turning down paid work is a luxury few in the business can afford. Nevertheless, it's worth having some sort of methodology to help to determine if you should say yes or not when the call comes.

My friend Robert has a handy procedure he often employs on such occasions. He maintains there are three essential criteria to be assessed in any job offer. Is the money good? Is the part good? And is the director good? If the answer to two or more of these queries is 'yes', you should probably accept. If fewer than two, it may be better to pass.

While not foolproof, the strategy is a good rule of thumb. Money may make the world go around, yet the best professional investment you can make is to hitch your wagon to an up-and-coming director, one who'll remember you when they're eventually running the National Theatre.

But this works only if the part being offered gives you the chance to strut your stuff. Whether it's in the Cottesloe or the Crown & Anchor, it's never easy to make an impression if your only contribution is delivering a scroll of parchment in Act 1 scene IV. Money is essential of course, but if you're artistically frustrated for months on end it won't do you or your self-confidence much good, however healthy your bank balance may become as a result.

My tip – if you can afford it – is to judge each gig on the size of the part and quality of the director alone. Get these two components right, and contentment will follow. Of course, if Sam Mendes offers you a year understudying Hamlet at the Civic Theatre, Pyongyang for 2k a week, this simple maxim might not help. But, trust me, it's not going to happen.

SIGNED, SEALED, AND DELIVERED

A last word on job types. Whatever it is, and whoever it's for, never spend the money till the ink's dry on the contract.

Some years ago, during a particularly pesky spell of enforced loafing, I was called by my agent to tell me she'd got me an interview for the next morning – at the unearthly hour of 9.30 in fact, just the time when I'm normally wondering whether to have another hour in bed, or watch *Location Location Location*.

Things were bad.

'I'm assured it'll be a straight offer subject to a courtesy meeting,' she explained. 'But you're ideal for the part, the director knows of your reputation, and it's starting in less than a month. Sorry about the timing, but he's directing another play and rehearsals commence at 10 am. Good luck – though for once I don't think you'll need it.'

In all my 30 years, I'd never before heard the phrase 'offer subject to a courtesy meeting'. Maggie Smith gets roles offered subject to a courtesy meeting. Michael Gambon gets roles subject to a courtesy meeting. It all sounded too good to be true.

The next morning I found myself on a gusty North London Street vainly ringing the doorbell of a small property set back from the pavement. After several minutes the director himself arrived clutching a vat of Starbucks coffee and a set of keys. 'Come in,' he said cheerily, opening the door and beckoning me in, 'Sorry to keep you waiting.' I sat quietly on a nearby sofa while he took a swig of coffee and checked his iPhone.

'Have you had a chance to read the play?' he asked at length.

'I have.'

'So what do you think of it?' he continued.

'I think it's great.'

'Interested?'

'Extremely.'

'You think we've got a potential hit?'

And I remember thinking, 'When you say "We", do you mean "You", or "Us"?' But of course I didn't say that; it would have been presumptuous. So instead I said,

'I do.'

He leaned forward.

'You want to know who we've got as the lead?'

And I remember thinking, 'When you say "We", do you mean "You", or "Us"?' But of course it would have been impolite. And in any case it was all going so swimmingly.

He then rattled off the name of a major Hollywood star whose presence alone would guarantee full houses and a likely transfer to Broadway.

'There's something I'd like your opinion on,' he continued confidentially, 'Do you think we should have an interval, or play it straight through without a break?'

And I remember thinking, 'When you say "we"...?'

'Straight through, I suspect.'

'I agree. Anything else you think we should consider?'

And I remember thinking…

'Nothing I can think of.' I picked up a copy of the script laying on the coffee table between us. 'Would you like me to read for the part?'

'No need,' he replied, 'In any case, I've got to go – I'm due in rehearsal in 10 minutes.' He rose and showed me to the door. 'Thanks so much for coming', he said as he shook my hand, 'I think we're going to have some fun with this, don't you?'

And I remember…

It so happened I had to travel down to Maidstone in Kent to take part in an expenses-only workshop for a new musical set on the roof of the Empire State Building. When I finally called my agent at the end of the day she had no news. 'I've spoken to the office and they're out', she explained, 'but they've assured me they'll confirm first thing tomorrow.'

By chance, another competing job offer came in the following day. Thank God I was able to turn it down – I'd have kicked myself if I'd already sewn myself up.

Two and a half weeks later my agent finally got a reply, namely the news that the job had 'gone in another direction'. Apparently some leading West End actor of my age and type had unexpectedly become free; but they appreciated my time and hoped they hadn't inconvenienced me.

The moral is that we're all filling somebody else's boots. I know full well if Robert de Niro had been free for any of the myriad parts I've picked up during my four decades – Hans Anderson at Harrogate, the musical workshop set on the

Empire State building, or even working as a crate-smasher at Nissan UK – I wouldn't have got a sniff at any of them.

So before you crack open the bubbly, remember: it isn't starting till you've signed the contract. And when they ask you whether we should play it straight through or with an interval, keep your mouth shut.

Because you never know who 'we' might be.

HOW TO GET A JOB

Here we go. This is the nugget you've been waiting for. This much, at least, is easy. It's sure-fire, never fails, and is the most useful piece of information you'll find in the entire narrative. I'll stake my professional reputation on it.

Book a luxury round-the-world trip of a lifetime for you and your partner. Non-refundable and non-transferable.

I guarantee the phone will start ringing the very second you've confirmed your three-digit security number.

PART THREE

Get Me Michael Simkins!

MICHAEL SIMKINS

Scott Marshall
44 Perryn Road
London W3 7NA
0181-749 7692

Height 6 feet 1 inch   Blue Eyes

For most actors – certainly for those who grew up before the internet – success in showbusiness means the West End.

'Theatreland', that glutinous title coined by Westminster Council to encompass the area of playhouses clustered around Soho, is still what most people think of when they hear the word 'actor'. For two centuries it's been here, within this square half mile of the capital (with outposts in Victoria and now on the South Bank) that the great and good of the acting game have strutted their stuff.

My own first glimpse of this magical and highly exclusive kingdom was as a ten-year old, when my Uncle Harry and Auntie Gladys took me to see The Black & White Minstrels at the Victoria Palace. And while the entertainment on offer was hardly representative, the glamour of both the occasion and the environment made a deep impression. This is where I wanted to be; my name picked out in coloured light bulbs, jostling for attention with Big Ben, taxicabs, Routemaster Buses and Angus Steak Houses.

My notion of the place as some sort of acting Shangri-La was further buttressed throughout my time at RADA. As drama students, we frequently got offered cheapies and freebies to a dizzying assortment of London shows, from *A Chorus Line* and *Privates on Parade*, to *Macbeth* and *Once a Catholic*. I saw tens of productions during my three years' training, and everything about them screamed, 'Get Me Michael Simkins'. Dream time.

For a while it looked as if it would remain that way. For though I'd been carving out a decent if unspectacular career in the provinces (and racking up nearly 50 separate productions in the process) the West End still seemed a distant, impenetrable fortress.

Then in the spring of 1985, having already seen me inflict untold commercial damage on Harrogate Theatre with my portrayal of Hans Andersen, the artistic director of the company (whom I can only assume was intent on bankrupting the place), invited me back to play Frank-N-Furter in *The Rocky Horror Show*, a part that would have required me to cross-dress for the first time in my adult life. I was on the verge of saying yes when salvation (both for me and Harrogate) came in the unlikely shape of John Gale, artistic director of Chichester Festival Theatre.

Gale had already built a healthy reputation (and an even healthier bank balance) with West End hits such as *No Sex Please, We're British*, and his tenure at Chichester was equally populist. His offer to me was to 'play as cast' in a season of plays throughout the summer, starting with Noël Coward's bloated, tub-thumping junket *Cavalcade*, continuing with *Anthony & Cleopatra* (starring Denis Quilley and Diana Rigg) and ending with an opulent new adaptation of *The Scarlet Pimpernel*.

The idea of dropping back to the dread ranks of 'play as cast' (a job spec I hadn't countenanced in over five years) wasn't something I relished, but Gale assured me I'd be one of a number of similar unknowns taking a punt in the company – among them a young hopeful called Alex Jennings and another called Michael Grandage. The director of the Pimpernel gig would similarly be some aspiring individual I'd never come across called Nicholas Hytner. I decided to take a chance.

It was obvious from the start that projects at Chichester were on a far grander scale than anything I'd previously experienced. Coward's lumbering musical pageant (a blend of *Upstairs, Downstairs* and the Edinburgh Tattoo) required the services of two dozen professionals, 150 local amateurs and even the Bosham Town band. Indeed, the whole quivering concoction coalesced each evening for a final eardrum-bursting chorus of Parry's *Jerusalem* at the curtain call (if you're wondering how it went down, remember, it was Chichester).

Luck was with me from the off. I got a couple of nice scenes in the Coward, an amalgam of several small roles in the Shakespeare that collectively amounted to a half-decent role, and for Hytner's dazzling production of *Pimpernel,* starring the legendary Donald Sinden (an actor who I regarded with something approaching awe, if only because he'd featured in the, 'What's the bleeding time' sequence in *Doctor in the House*) I was given the part of the juvenile lead.

The show proved such a hit that it transferred to the West End, where it enjoyed a solid run at Her Majesty's Theatre in Haymarket. The show might be running still, were it not for US President Ronald Regan's decision to bomb Libya, an act that sent most metropolitan theatregoers scurrying for their basements and which scuppered half the West End productions at a stroke.

But I'd got a toehold. A lengthy stint at the National Theatre followed, which led to another transfer, and over the next 20 years I was to appear in three major musicals and 12 separate plays in town, and work in the process with Stephen Sondheim,

Tim Rice and Andrew Lloyd Webber, Arthur Miller, Michael Frayn, Harold Pinter and (several times) Alan Ayckbourn.

Lest this seem like hubris, let me also point out that in between times I also did roleplay workshops for Severn Trent Water Sewage East Division, compered trade shows for Vauxhall Cars at the Camelot Theme Park, Chorley, and even returned for a brief stint as a crate-smasher at Nissan UK. But beyond doubt, I was now where I'd always wanted to be.

This section deals with theatre and the whole West End shebang: the people you're going to be working with (and for), the rehearsal process (from read-through to getting your notice), the lifestyle, the rewards, and the perils and pitfalls – plus a few practical tips for good measure. It's also applicable if you find yourself on the equally hallowed turf of the NT or the RSC.

But while most of my stories are taken from my time as a 'West End Wendy', they're just as appropriate whether you're appearing at Drury Lane or the Druid's Head. At least I hope so.

In the event of another airborne attack on Libya they probably won't prevent you from getting your notice: but in most other circumstances, they'll make you virtually bombproof.

Let's start by examining the dos and don'ts of audition protocol, and whom you'll be working with.

AUDITION PROTOCOL

It was Gore Vidal who said, 'It is not enough to succeed. Others must fail.'

Interviews are tough. Your future hangs on them. But there are some simple do's and don'ts of auditioning, things you can do to improve your own chances and make the whole experience marginally less horrendous, both for you and your adversaries: and it's best you learn them in these paragraphs rather than via a right hook.

Timing your entrance

It may seem counter-intuitive, given my old-fashioned, Alan Sugaresque insistence on punctuality, discipline and self-reliance: but the very worst thing you can do is to arrive for your audition before your allotted time. If you do, you'll see the competition – and that's the kiss of death.

I have a small group actors who are always up for the same parts as me – my 'nemeses squad' I like to call them – some of whom I rate, others I don't, and this same small group of individuals has dogged my every audition since virtually the day I left RADA.

It's almost as if they know the innermost secrets of my private diary. Wherever I go they're waiting for me, like theatrical stalkers. A fair few of them are good friends, while others I can take or leave, but the mere sight of their names alongside mine on the audition list is enough to make me want to throw myself under the nearest train.

No doubt you'll have your own nemeses, even if you don't know them yet, and if you insist on turning up before your appointed time you're bound to run into them, sitting there grinning stiffly back at you in the waiting room. Once their turn comes, you'll almost certainly be able to hear snatches of their interview, and they'll always sound far better than you, combining the economy of Daniel Day Lewis, the mystique of Marlon Brando, the charm of Hugh Grant and the gravitas of Paul Scofield.

So stay away. Do your warm-up on the tube or the bus on the way in, even if it means emptying the carriage. Arrive just in time to sign in, brush your hair in the toilet and arrange your thoughts for a few minutes. Confidence is the only weapon you've got on your side – do everything to protect it.

Arrival

Of course, sometimes you can't help arriving early. The interviews may be running late, or it'll be raining so hard so you can't kill time outside on the pavement. Should you do so, show some sense. Don't blather on to the poor sap already waiting his turn, because he doesn't want to hear where you went for your holidays, or which of your mutual acquaintances are working, or what shows you've seen. He's trying to concentrate. He doesn't need to hear chapter and verse of your own footling existence.

And in any case, it'll soon be your turn to sweat, and the last thing you'll want is to fend off the same crushing bore as you are being.

Departure

The same rule about economy applies when you leave. The overwhelming feeling upon exiting from any interview (apart from an overwhelming craving for sugar) is one of gut-wrenching relief – and where better to expend all that surplus adrenalin than to dump it on the people still waiting to go in?

Don't. Don't throw your arms around them (especially if you don't know them), don't puff out your cheeks and raise your eyes to the heavens to demonstrate just how pleased you are it's over, and don't sit down and start telling them what to expect when their own turn comes. ('They're absolutely lovely, really friendly, you've nothing to worry about' etc etc.)

Most important of all, don't slap them on the knee and announce 'Well this part's got your name written on it.' Give a brief gladiatorial smile as you pass by, just sufficient to recognise your mutual suffering, and leave without further ado.

There'll be time enough to compare notes properly when you run into them in a few minutes' time in Dunkin' Donuts.

DIRECTORS

Directors are many things – according to Billy Wilder, a policeman, a psychoanalyst, a sycophant, and a bastard. In my experience they're frequently all four at once.

And no wonder. They have the hopes of producers, audience and cast resting on their shoulders. Everyone is looking for a sprinkling of fairy dust with which to transform their own trundling efforts from the journeyman to the sublime. And that's before they've even started directing the actors.

The director's initial task is to give a physical framework to a play – 'blocking the moves' as it's referred to in the biz, after which the process becomes more intangible, in which they join with the actors to transform this two-dimensional scaffolding into a three-dimensional entity.

And here's the first snag. Some actors respond to the smack of firm government, others want to be loved, while some just want you to piss off and leave them alone. The director's job is to meld all these disparate parts into one seamless and memorable whole.

In a previous book I described the two different types of director (three if you include a largely defunct sub-division, known as 'bastards.'). The main two are either 'Blockers' or 'Wankers' – the latter a term first coined not by me, but by the then-director of the renowned Abbey Theatre Dublin, Patrick Mason, with whom I worked at Bristol in the early 1980s. In fact the best ones are both blockers and wankers; individuals who can both help you time a laugh and elucidate the socio-historical context of the play. They're a rare breed.

Blockers

Blockers will turn up on the first day with the framework of the play already formulated. They've been pushing tiny cubes of different-coloured wood round in their brain (or on a plan of the set) and will have it all mapped out. Thus they will treat you largely like automata, telling you where to stand, what to think, and how to say the lines, which leaves them just enough time in which to annexe the Sudetenland.

Once they've stood it up, the good Blockers will then allow you to deconstruct their masterplan, until, like a fine pair of shoes, the role will feel entirely yours. Michael Winner famously defined a team effort as being, 'A lot of people doing what I say', and indeed, it's often said the best directors are the ones who get you to do their bidding whilst making you think it was your idea in the first place.

The bad blockers, by contrast, don't have the slightest idea what else to do once they've got you standing in the right place.

Having arranged the moves, they'll then insist on endless runs of the play on the spurious pretext of 'allowing things to bed in', but in fact because they don't know how else to fill up the time. At the end of each run, they'll give you notes such as, 'I wonder whether you might take off your wedding ring. It's catching the light.'

In one play in which I was involved with a few years back, the director in question actually pulled out his book of moves for a previous production he'd done 40 years before and blew the dust off it. Another stopped me 30 seconds into my first attempt to get my part on its feet to ask if I would like some 'suggestions for appropriate hand gestures now, or in a few days' time when I felt more familiar with the role.'

I pointed out that if he was going to start offering hand gestures, I had a couple of choice examples I could think of in return. He backed off, cut me some slack, and we ended up the best of friends.

Wankers

Wankers, on the other hand, will sit round for days discussing the script, getting the various cast members to read one another's parts, allocating animal types to the various characters, and playing trust games such as asking you to fall backwards off a table for the rest of the cast to catch you. (I wouldn't trust most actors of my acquaintance to catch a cold, far less protect my cranium.)

The story of Michael Bryant at the NT may be apocryphal but even if it's not true, it should be. Legend has it he was given several days off rehearsals for the role of Badger in *The Wind in the Willows* to go and study the behavioural traits of his chosen animal. At the end of the enforced hiatus he returned and was asked by the resident choreographer what he'd learnt during his studies. 'It's odd,' he's reported to have said, 'But I discovered they move exactly like Michael Bryant.' He wasn't bothered again and needless to say, turned in a sublime performance.

The Bastards

This largely forgotten sub-genre of the directing profession used to proliferate in British theatre and contained some pretty fearsome specimens: John Dexter, William Gaskill, and Peter Wood to name but three, each combining fierce intelligence and directorial genius with a savage wit and an intolerance of perceived shortcomings.

One knight of the realm who cut his teeth working with Dexter as a young rookie, related to me of the time during rehearsals at the Old Vic when he woke one morning to discover he'd overslept. Upon arriving hot and dishevelled (and nearly an hour late), he was duly given the anticipated verbal flailing by his employer in front of the rest of the cast, along with the warning that if he ever transgressed again he'd be sacked on the spot.

The following morning his alarm clock let him down again and thus his only recourse upon blundering into the rehearsal room was to blurt out the only excuse he could think of which might forestall instant dismissal – namely, that his mother had died.

Dexter stopped the rehearsal, took the actor aside, expressed his profound sympathy, and insisted he went home and on no account return until the funeral was over and he felt strong enough to continue. My friend spent the next ten days lying in bed at home watching TV.

Sadly this breed of martinets that once bestrode British theatre is now extremely rare. Their replacements are tractable, conciliatory, and above all, encouraging: the single most important quality in any director.

REMEMBER ME

One of the most common laments amongst actors is that powerful and influential directors whom they've known since infancy never seem to employ them professionally. 'I can't understand it,' they wail, 'I'm godfather to his two kids and we shared a room together for three years at college, but he won't see me for his new play.'

To which, I reply, 'Would you?'

The point they're forgetting – which all actors forget in the red mist that descends when the call doesn't come – is that directors don't want people around who know where the bodies are buried. And if you've known them since you were both 17 and anxious, you're a ticking time bomb. You know who they've had, their bathroom habits, their grubby peccadilloes.

Directors need to be able to create an air of mystique in the rehearsal room. They don't want their carefully honed image undermined by you telling anecdotes over the tea urn about how they used to be called 'skid marks' or how they were once expelled from school for shafting the principal's wife in the bike shed.

So, spare a thought for directors. Unlike actors, they're essentially solitary animals, moving quietly in the shadows from job to job, rarely meeting others of their species, and in most instances, reluctant to comment on a rival's work, particularly if it's been a hit. They daren't come to the pub with you as they know that's when you need to let off steam by slagging them off, and once they attain any status, the mere approach of an actor towards them in the street is a blaring klaxon that they're about to be hit on for a job.

In any case, they don't always need much time in which to work their magic. The very best ones will often unlock an entire part for you with a simple word or two. It may be at the read-through, or in the gents, or even walking back to the tube at the end of rehearsal. So whatever you do, keep an ear open for what their pearl of wisdom is. Or shut the fuck up, as it's sometimes known.

Alan Ayckbourn and Harold Pinter, two of the most brilliant and deft directors I've ever come across, often used to employ this method of directing by casual anecdote to brilliant effect; but if you're spending all your time trying to think of an even funnier bon mot to respond with, you won't be listening, and your chance to gather gold dust will vanish along with it.

Of course, the vital phrase that suddenly unlocks the part for you may never come. A friend of mine was playing the title role of *Richard II* some years ago in a production that was as ill-conceived as it was under-prepared. In fact, they'd barely got halfway through their only available dress rehearsal before they had to break off to allow in the first night audience.

My friend recalls sitting in the backstage green room, still in his crown and cloak, forcing down a sandwich and trying to subdue a rapidly ascending sense of panic. He was about to face one of the most chaotic and catastrophic evenings of his professional career. Then he spotted the director approaching him between the tables with a cup of tea.

'I want a word with you,' said the director.

'At last,' thought my friend. 'Thank God. This is the moment when he gives me the note that will unlock the part for me, and give me the confidence and understanding to go on.'

The director sat down next to him, put his head in his hands, and said, 'What the fuck are we going to do?'

But my favourite story about the genius of directors was actually told to me by Alan Ayckbourn. Many years ago when still an actor, he found himself playing Stanley in a production of Pinter's *The Birthday Party* at Scarborough, directed by the author himself – only the second ever production of the play following its disastrous initial run at The Lyric, Hammersmith.

Ayckbourn, along with the rest of the bemused cast, was mystified by the provenance of these strange characters in the drama. One day he plucked up the courage to ask Pinter where this sad, failed concert pianist came from and then afterwards, when Goldberg and McCann had carted him away in a van, where on earth Stanley went to?

After a lengthy pause, Pinter replied, 'Mind your own fucking business.'

An invaluable lesson in both acting, and directorship.

PRODUCERS

It was the American impresario, Max Gordon, who, having suffered yet another disastrous flop on Broadway, this time with a play about Napoleon, said in despair, 'Never, never again will I do another play where a guy writes with a feather…'

Producers are the Isambard Kingdom Brunels of show-business. Whether they're mounting a multi-million-pound production at Drury Lane, or merely raising a couple of grand for a performance under the arches at Waterloo station, their driving ambition is to put on shows and make sufficient money from them to fund even more shows. Their job spec ranges from finding the script and hiring the director, to booking the theatre, co-ordinating publicity and seat prices, right through to securing sufficient investment to nurse the show through till word of mouth or critical acclaim gives it the impetus to fend for itself. They are important people.

Some producers are larger than life (David Land, one of the most powerful and flamboyant producers, always averred that one of his ambitions was to call his production company 'Hope and Glory' so he could answer his phone by saying 'Land of Hope and Glory'); while others will seem as anonymous as your local building society manager.

The first time you're likely to see them is at the initial read-through, when they'll turn up to welcome everyone on board and say how thrilled they are to be working with such an incredibly talented bunch. Then, sometime around 10.30 am, they'll check their Blackberries, ease themselves gently out of the room and escape into a waiting limo to be whisked away to some other crucial rendezvous.

The next time you'll see them is on opening night, when they'll knock on your dressing room door at the half, with a bottle of champagne or bouquet of flowers. Three hours later you'll see them again at the first night party, when their previous smile of encouragement will have been replaced by a look of malevolent greed (it's a hit) or a glassy stare (flop).

Should they turn up in the interim to watch a run in the rehearsal room, or even a dress, it's usually a sign of trouble.

Someone has tipped them off that there are problems, and despite the blithe assurances and boxes of designer muffins that will accompany their arrival, there'll be an element of fire-fighting to their attendance. Producers don't have time to waste.

One friend who directed a new and ludicrously ambitious production in London several years ago, recalls sitting in the stalls during the technical rehearsal (one that had already lasted three days and still not made it to the first interval), only to discover the producer sitting next to him in the adjoining seat. No words were spoken for several minutes, until at last, the action onstage ground to another juddering halt while yet another unforeseen problem was addressed.

Eventually the producer leaned across, and without taking his eyes off the stage, muttered quietly. 'You do know how much this is costing us, don't you? It is going to work, isn't it?'

'Of course,' replied my friend mildly.

Months later, when the show had become a huge hit and something of a global phenomenon, I asked him whether he'd been as certain of success as he'd previously claimed.

'Of course not,' he assured me, 'I was cacking myself.'

DESIGNERS/COSTUME DESIGNERS

A few years ago I attended a public masterclass given by the great American character actor William H. Macey, star of *Fargo*, *Boogie Nights* and countless other major movies. A leading light of the celebrated Atlantic Theatre Company of Chicago, during his 90-minute talk he provided a detailed and fascinating insight into creating a character and building a role from the bottom up, according to the celebrated Steppenwolf style; one which involves the exchange of impulses, a generous cohabitation of the physical and psychic space, and a dynamic and visceral method of listening.

Afterwards there was an opportunity for questions from the floor.

'What if,' I asked him, 'You've spent four weeks discovering your psychic space, exchanging your impulses and listening with as much dynamism as you can muster, and having decided the part you're playing is a traditional alpha male with issues of abandonment, an ungovernable temper and a deep psychological need to be top dog in any given situation, you then find you've been given a costume to wear consisting of flared jeans, a cheesecloth shirt with mother of pearl fastenings, and a wig that makes you look like Donald Trump?'

I wasn't being a smart-arse: my question was based on an actual occurrence. The fact is, nowadays many of an actor's choices have already been decided for them before they've so much as signed the contract. Once upon a time, designers were basically there to provide the actors with a serviceable set and an appropriate costume. If the play was set in 1930s' Mayfair you could expect an elegant flat and a suit; if based in ancient Rome, a toga and some Doric columns could generally be relied upon to make an appearance, while anything mid-Victorian would almost inevitably involve a foggy street and a stovepipe hat.

No more – nowadays you're just as likely to be wearing a toga in Victorian London, a Savile Row suit in the coliseum and a stovepipe hat in the lounge bar of the Dorchester. Designers have mapped it all out long before you've put in your pennyworth.

And frankly they're getting a bit full of themselves.

'I've set this production of Emlyn Williams' *The Corn Is Green* inside a rat cage in a vivisection laboratory, to accentuate the stifling effect of poverty in the small Welsh coal mining village and the impossibility of the protagonists ever being able to escape from the cultural iron hoops that hold them trapped inside their epistemological tribal norms,' they announce on the opening day. And one by one actors are invited to stare glumly at the illustrations, while being given a monologue on how the designer envisages it. 'Yes, this is your costume. Like all the others it's a boiler suit, and as with all the others you'll be carrying a ball and chain round with you to denote the slow pace of life in rural Wales and the impossibility of accessing cultural change.'

Any misgivings or suggestions are met with a tight-lipped stare. Discussion is rarely invited.

Lest I'm beginning to sound an old fart, let me state that good designers can be the making of a play, realising it afresh for both cast and audience, scrubbing away the collected varnish of stale tradition and bringing it up as fresh as paint. Many of the best ones I've worked with – Mark Thompson, Christopher Oram and Anthony Ward to name but three – have conceptual abilities far beyond that of mere mortals.

But you'd better hope the designer does know what they're doing, for unless you're above the billing there'll be precious little opportunity to influence matters. And there's no point turning to the director for help. They're in on it.

The overall concept was signed and sealed between them many months before you were hauled on board: and if the director is minded to set his production of *Cat on a Hot Tin*

Roof on a corrugated iron sheet surrounded by scaffolding poles, you can be sure he'll already have sanctioned the designer's decision to put your Maggie the Cat in dungarees and a pair of Caterpillar boots. By the time you come across their fiendish plans, they're already onto the next project.

And in case you're wondering what Macey's reaction was when I finished describing the costume I'd been saddled with, he smiled back sadly and said, 'You've worked with that designer as well, have you?'

ANGELS

What's the best way to become a millionaire?
Start as a billionaire and invest in theatrical productions.

Theatre backers, or 'angels' as they're commonly known, are rarely seen or heard. To common mortals like you and me, and much like their celestial doppelgängers, it's perfectly possible to go through life without ever catching sight of one.

These venture capitalists of showbiz can range from multinational conglomerates who have an eye to fasten their funds to some fashionable theatrical event (thus Goodyear's rumoured sponsorship of the RSC's forthcoming production of *Pericles, Prince Of Tyre*), to star-struck individuals still living at home with their collection of Richard Clayderman LPs, who've inherited a few grand and want to experience the roar of the greasepaint, the smell of the crowd.

Most angels have a tendency to only stake sums they're happily prepared to lose. Normally the minimum sum required to become a backer is £2500 for a straight play and £10,000 for a musical. If the show turns out to be *Les Miserables* they can expect to spend the rest of their lives lighting cigars with fivers. If however, it turns out to be *Bernadette, Moby Dick* or *Metropolis*, they'll lose the lot. It's a bit like playing roulette but with more turns.

Such people are invaluable to the lifeblood of the business, so if you ever find yourself being accosted at a first night party by someone who tells you his profession is in making ducts for ventilation units, please treat them with courtesy rather than scanning the horizon for the nearest exit.

It may be his vol-au-vents you're scoffing.

STAGE MANAGEMENT

'How many actors does it take to change a light bulb?'
'None – stage management can do it darling…'

Although I've left them till last, stage managers (you can also include stage crew in this amalgam) are the most important of the lot. The theatrical equivalent of the poor bloody infantry, they work colossal hours, often for meagre pay, hold everything together, are the nub of everyone's temper when things go wrong, and then have to sit in the pub while you hold court and call them darling, when a few short hours ago you were calling them cunt.

Worst of all, they usually get left off the guest list for the celebratory nosh at The Ivy, and then have to endure all the actors droning on about what a wonderful time they had the following day.

Despite this, the vast majority of stage managers are salt of the earth types who love theatre and theatricals, and who will bear stupefying amounts of bad behaviour with grace and fortitude simply in order to ensure everything runs smoothly. Most of them, I suspect, would make wonderful social workers if ever they gave up showbiz.

Officially, stage management's duties are to run rehearsals, organise the get-in of the set to the theatre, and run and maintain the smooth running of the production. This entails checking the set, checking the props, checking the sound, checking the lights, sweeping the stage, dealing with unexpected emergencies such as fire alarms going off and actors going AWOL and, most crucially, 'calling the show' (the name given to the task of co-ordinating appropriate cues for lighting, sound, and scene changes). They'll be in the theatre long before you've arrived, and will still be tidying up long after you've ordered your second pint.

They are, in short, saints.

And like saints, they can enhance your time on this earth. If they like you, they'll go the extra mile to make sure you're happy and content, including making tea, providing a shoulder to cry on when your agent/marriage/affair goes belly up, and even nipping out to the shops for some paracetamol if you've got a headache.

They are not, however, your skivvies.

I've asked around various stage management acquaintances to canvass what most endears them to actors and, more importantly, what makes them want to burn down the Garrick Club. Their responses were bracingly consistent with what I suspected.

Items included in their love list include:

1. Making them an occasional cup of tea instead of expecting them to make it for you all the time.
2. Asking them how their weekend went, instead of forgetting they didn't have one as they had to take down the entire set on Saturday night, transport it from Bath to Wolverhampton through a blizzard and then erect it again in time for a Monday evening show.
3. Learning their actual names instead of referring to them as 'darling', 'crew' and in the case of one notorious actor, (who I think might secretly be a member of UKIP) 'That stage manager girl', every time you want something done.

Not so difficult, is it?

The list of hates is, predictably, rather longer.

One acquaintance waxed long and lyrically to me about the subject of actors and props. She was continually gobsmacked by how many performers turn from normal human beings into complete cretins the moment they're handed a stage prop.

Instead of applying our feeble brain power to work out how to turn a handle/uncork a decanter/pull a trigger, we stand like big girls' blouses in the middle of the stage yelling 'Stage Management!!!' in a querulous tone and then complaining we had no warning of the task to be accomplished.

A neat variant on this theme is the predilection for many thesps to spend 20 minutes searching out stage management to tell them there's no milk for their coffee in the green room fridge, instead of taking the three minutes it would have required to nip next door to the convenience store to purchase some. By far the most common complaint however (and one I've been rightly taken to task for myself) is leaving our mug unwashed at the end of a break, only to complain there are no clean ones when it comes to the next interval.

But perhaps the hardest part of the stage manager's job, and the one that leads to most friction between them and us, is in the delicate art of offering prompts.

It's customary for actors to require occasional assistance in recalling their lines when running a scene in the rehearsal room, particularly when we're first attempting to perform it without the script. Prompting is an intangible art form, and the successful protagonist is something akin to a clairvoyant. Knowing when an actor is struggling for a word and when they're merely filling the moment with a dramatic pause is a fine divide; and they're not mind-readers.

Actors are wont to plump out our portrayal with meaningful looks once we've got on top of things, but to the poor beleaguered deputy stage manager following the text in the prompt copy, there's often precious little difference between a profound silence and a stonking dry; and they won't take kindly to you screaming back, 'I'm fucking acting,' when they offer up a line in good faith.

Best policy is to agree to the rules beforehand. If you do need a prompt, always indicate your predicament clearly by uttering, 'Line?' Clicking your fingers in their direction is the quickest way to have them dispensing the arsenic pills at the tea break – that is, of course, if they can find a clean mug in which to put them.

Be warned. If you do take advantage of their good nature, they can really piss you off, quite literally in some cases.

The story of the backstage staff at the London Palladium ceremonially urinating into the overhead water tank providing the raw material for the signature number in *Singin' in the Rain* may or may not be apocryphal: but there are other, less overt ways for stage management to remind you of common manners.

One actor who'd pushed his luck (and their forbearance) too far once found himself requiring a prompt mid-performance. After two hissed enquiries for a line had been met with stony silence, he screamed, 'Can I have a bloody prompt please?' into the wings.

'Hang on,' came the reply, 'I'm doing something...'

THE JOB

Airline flight crash investigators attest that the most dangerous part of any flight is the take-off. Catastrophe is most likely to occur while attempting to get the whole unwieldy structure airborne.

Similarly, the first hours of rehearsal of a new job are likely to be the most anxious interlude of the entire contract. The success of both the project and your personal happiness will be defined by the assortment of oddballs and eccentrics you're about to encounter, many of whom will become your close friends, sworn enemies or passionate lovers (and sometimes all three) during the coming weeks.

Because of this you'll have slept badly, woken up at some ungodly hour and already consumed sufficient coffee to keep a small South American nation solvent for several months.

You'll also be stalked by the possibility, however remote, that your casting in the role has been a ghastly mistake. The scenario is only too easy to envisage at 4 am, when you're staring out into the darkness from beneath your duvet. You enter the rehearsal room to discover a sea of horrified faces, waxy smiles and impromptu huddles in the far corner, followed by the director walking stiffly across. There's been a mistake. They didn't mean you at all.

You think it unlikely? One actress acquaintance turned up to begin filming a series for Yorkshire TV, only be told by a quavering producer that there'd been a terrible howler in the admin department and that they'd meant to book another, even more famous actress for the role, one who shared the same Christian name. She was paid off for the contract but nevertheless found herself back on the 12.30 train to King's Cross, and was walking her dog in Richmond Park by 4 pm.

Hopefully you'll be woken by the alarm clock just as you're climbing on board. But nonetheless, these first few minutes of a new job are an anxious period. Luckily there are a number of steps you can take to make the whole experience slightly less painful.

Meet 'n' greet

If the meet and greet is at 10 am, make sure you don't turn up any earlier, so you're not the first person to arrive and are thus forced to swap desultory chit-chat with the producers, many of whom won't have the first idea who you are.

Take comfort from the fact that everyone else standing around with inane grins pasted onto their features, gorging on biscuits and laughing hysterically at anything and everything, will be feeling every bit as vulnerable as you. So there's no need to grasp at it, or to behave like what a friend of mine described with admirably Chaucerian phraseology as 'Coco the cunt'. Dump your bags, find a friendly face to shelter alongside, and wait for the bigwigs to come to you. If nobody does so, you can always make yourself look in demand by pretending to check your messages.

Remember, it's a marathon, not a sprint, so pace yourself. Don't be too keen to identify the friendliest face in the room (your selection is bound to prove faulty under such straightened circumstances). Similarly, don't make a beeline for the star turn and gush on about how working with them is the pinnacle of your acting career – that can come later, when you may well no longer feel that way in any case.

And whatever you do, make sure you avoid the individual who turns up in a bright pink fluffy sweater with a tray of cakes specially baked for the occasion in their Aga the night before (unless of course you're working with Jane Asher, in which case tuck in).

The design

We've already covered designers and their mores. Suffice to say that at some point on the first morning you'll be invited to inspect the model for the set. This will be a small cardboard facsimile, perfectly created in miniature and with lots of dinky little scale furnishings and props that wouldn't look out of place in a doll's house – chairs, settees, doorways and tables – all of which will immediately fall over if anyone so much as breathes on them.

Your job is to stand around as part of a large enthusiastic semicircle and coo with enthusiasm. The irony is that the people who really need to see the design, namely the stage management team, will either be forced to stand at the back staring at a load of dirty necks, or be pushed off to the kitchens to wash up everyone's dirty coffee cups and thus miss the demonstration entirely.

The read-through

The next stage is the read-through, when the cast gathers round a table to read the play out loud for the first time.

The question here is one of judgment. Do you deliver your role with all the enthusiasm of Christopher Biggins, or bury your head in your chest and attempt to look mysterious? Some actors dive straight in, giving pretty much a facsimile of opening night. Others sit in a distant corner mumbling their lines as if having recently been the victim of some complex lobotomy: accenting nothing, and intoning each phrase in a dull whisper which will leave you craning forward in an effort to try and work out when it's your turn to speak.

Don't be fooled – art has nothing to do with this – it's almost certainly an attempt to make themselves seem dark and mercurial, while simultaneously forcing you to look like a deaf twat. If not, why is it that they inevitably position themselves at the furthest end of the table?

If you do find yourself being cast as their unwitting stooge, just look blank, keep schtum when it's your turn to speak, and when everybody turns to look, calmly announce that you thought we'd stopped for coffee. Once the smooth reading of the script is abruptly stalled a few times the director will soon step in and suggest everyone gives it a bit more wellie. A bit like standing up to the school bully, you'll immediately be marked down as someone not to be trifled with.

Suits you sir

At some point on the first morning someone with a tape measure strung across the shoulders will approach you.

This is, according to the scale of the project, either the designer/costume designer/head of wardrobe/director's current squeeze named Debbie who's offered to help out. They've come to secure your measurements so they can start preparing the costumes.

If, like me – like most men – you kid yourself you're still the same weight you were 20 years ago, and that the suit you bought at Next last month is only too tight because you didn't follow the washing instructions, the temptation during this brief ceremony is always to lie.

Don't. When the tape measure is held around your waistline, it's vital you don't hold yourself in. All that'll happen is that you'll be given a costume that you can only struggle into with the help of an orthopedic corset or a block and tackle. Apart from the fact you won't be able to breathe, you've always got the even greater danger of buttons exploding onstage and putting somebody's eye out. Good if you're in a farce but not otherwise.

Please also remember it's theatrical protocol for you to hold the top end of the measuring tape yourself when your inside leg is being assessed: especially, but not exclusively, if the designer is not of the same sex.

That's lunch folks!

Sometime around 1 pm the director will declare it is lunchtime.

If the gig is a swanky one, there's a good chance the management will provide either a specially-imported buffet or a meal at a local restaurant. If it's the restaurant combo, stay on your guard. The heady brew of nerves, adrenaline and the fact you're not paying for it, can make you lose your sense of judgment.

Don't do what I did when taken out by leading West End producer Michael Codron and drink so much alcohol that you are unfit for purpose in the afternoon: and however great the temptation, don't take foolish risks by selecting something unfamiliar on the menu that you wouldn't normally dream of ordering.

In an effort to look sophisticated I once ordered something called *steak tartare* at such a shindig. It wasn't until it arrived that I realised I'd ordered raw mince with a freshly cracked egg on top. Of course having ordered the bloody thing and with the director sitting directly opposite me I had no alternative but to eat it, condemning me to a worm's eye view of the toilet bowl throughout the afternoon.

The most likely scenario is that you'll all be sent away while the creative team remains in the room for a production meeting. Their privacy is crucial, so make yourself scarce. Don't hang around on the perimeter of the room eating your meat paste sandwiches: you'll only likely force them into speaking in urgent whispers, as well as filling the rehearsal space with noxious fumes.

Most of the cast will repair to the local boozer for a burger and coke and a little early bonding. Whoever arrives at the bar first will be expected to purchase a round, and with 15 thirsty actors piling in after you, your generous gesture could wipe out most of your first week's pay. So hang back – you can stand your turn later on in the week when it's all a bit less frenetic.

The afternoon

So. You've survived take-off. Now's the time to unfasten your seatbelts and check out the in-flight entertainment.

If your director is a Blocker you'll need a set of sharpened pencils and some highlighters for the afternoon session. For Wankers, several cases of Red Bull are indispensible. Bring both just in case. And try not to drop off.

With luck the rehearsal will end sometime around 4.30 pm. Now comes the final dilemma of this torturous first day – do you siphon off back to the pub with your new friends or slope off home? If you go for the pub option, a word of warning. In the post-coital glow of having survived unscathed, the temptation will be to spend all evening there, tanking up on white wine and getting through several hundredweight of Cheesy Wotsits in the process. It'll be fun, no doubt – anecdotes of past gigs will be trotted out, mutual acquaintances discussed, and you'll end up knowing much more about your new friends than you did when you entered the premises at opening time.

But be warned, your partner back at home won't take kindly to you rolling in at 11 pm with the aroma of various brands of cheap aftershave or Twiglet breath clinging to your shirt on your first day. The last thing you want to do is to suggest trouble further down the line. So have a couple, but make sure you're back in plenty of time for *Emmerdale*.

And sleep well. You've a long road ahead.

REHEARSALS

It was the great Sir Tyrone Guthrie who once defined the art of theatre directing as, 'Filling everyone with a yearning to get back at 10 the next morning'. It's as good a definition as I've come across.

In Andy Nyman's pithy and illuminating handbook, *The Golden Rules of Acting*, he describes perfectly the attitude actors should acquire during the rehearsal period, which is to give everything a go and don't worry about making a prat of yourself. A good maxim for life too, come to think of it.

'When a director asks you to try something new,' he argues, 'Always try it at least three times. The first time will feel terrible, the second less terrible, and the third time will allow you to judge it properly.'

He's right. Some of the most surprising work I've ever produced (and you can take that adjective how you will) has been through trying something that made me cringe first time round.

A legendary and much-loved tutor at RADA called Ben Benison used to run a two-hour workshop on Friday mornings called 'Action', but which was universally referred to by its more popular moniker; 'Just Say Yes'. Ben's genius was in getting actors to live dangerously, to accept rather than deny, to run with the ball rather than hold it close. Actors by nature cling to old familiar habits when they feel vulnerable, yet as a rule, once you've committed to a director's suggestion, you'll soon know whether it's a winner or a shocker. So stop slagging them off and give it a go.

Then you can slag them off.

In any case, directors are often trying to nudge you towards something only they can see. One celebrated artistic director of my acquaintance, currently bestriding both the West End and Broadway, told me he knew his young trainee assistant was going to be one of the best in the business when he dropped into rehearsals of a play his protégé was directing, to overhear him telling the leading actor, 'We've seen you do this performance hundreds of times. Get out of your comfort zone and show us something new.' The young assistant is indeed himself now one of Britain's tastiest talents.

Rehearsing a play is a bit like trying to organise the caucus race in *Alice in Wonderland*. Actors will zoom off in all sorts of different directions, at different speeds and with different destinations in mind. Some will be off the book by the end of week one, while others will still be mumbling into their script at the end of week three. For the director, the process is akin to herding kittens.

My overriding practical tip is to get off the book as quickly as you can. Learn the lines. You can't start to throw the part about until you can speak them with speed, flexibility and myriad changes of tone – just as would do in real life in fact.

I realise many thesps will throw their hands up in horror at this suggestion. 'Oh no,' they cry, 'If you learn them too quickly they become set like concrete before you've mined their meaning.' Maybe, but in my experience the ones who are still clutching the script in week three are the ones who'll have made the least interesting journey.

Not that they'll realise this themselves of course – they'll kid themselves that an increasing fluency through simple repetition is evidence of a deepening understanding of the inner workings of the role. It's not – it's speaking the lines quicker, which, if they'd pulled their finger out they could have managed by day ten and enjoyed a further fortnight in which to have fun and explore.

The most extraordinary illustration I ever witnessed of the power of being fluent was during an early rehearsal room run-through of a play called *Burn This*. I'd been a late addition to the four-man cast, and thus was still feeling my way with the part when we did our first stagger-through.

The lead actor John Malkovich, by contrast, had already played his role hundreds of times on Broadway before coming here for the London version, so by contrast with my fumbling efforts, had his role already assimilated into his bloodstream.

At one point during our initial run-through he ambled over, mid-speech, to the table at the side of the room, where the stage manager, a girl called Gillian, was sitting surrounded by stopwatches, ring binders and (naturally) pencils. Malkovich then removed a tea pot which was perched on the table top, before carrying it back in to the acting area and popping a tea bag into it.

His acting – and the speech he was intoning at the time – was so seamless throughout this manoeuvre, that the table, the girl, and even the detritus surrounding her momentarily became part of the play. The reason for his brief diversion soon became apparent – he needed the teapot in the scene, and she'd forgotten to set it in its correct place before the run commenced.

Perhaps you needed to be there. But if any performer could convince me, despite my knowledge of the play, that a teenager from Sevenoaks in paint-splattered dungarees might just be perched in the corner of a fashionable Manhattan apartment at 2 am in the morning, Malkovich was that man.

That's not to suggest the third-week mumbler should be discounted as a waste of space. On the contrary, I've lost count of the number of individuals I've worked with who can hardly string a sentence together in rehearsals, and then just when you're tearing your hair out and thinking of making an anonymous call to Age Concern, they stomp on at press night, drill the part to within an inch of its life, steal all the reviews, and leave you for dead.

THE TECHIE RUN

This is not be confused with the 'tech', a different event altogether and one that occurs slightly later in the process. The techie run is the occasion, usually a week or two before opening night, when the various heads of department and backstage support team are allowed in to see a run of the play.

Up till now the rehearsal room will have been your own private cocoon, a play box where you and your pals can muck about, experiment, dry, waste time, drink tea, tell improbable stories and totter uncertainly in the direction of finding a performance you can charge money for. But now, at the techie run, your Wendy house is about to be invaded.

You might think that having an audience, however impromptu, would be a tremendous fillip for the cast, akin to a glass of water to a thirsty traveller. After all, you've been pegging away at the play for some weeks with only the increasingly wearied director for company. The thing you need most now is feedback from actual human beings – be it a laugh, a gasp, even a shocked silence. Anything to help you decide what you've got and where to go next.

So who better than an audience in miniature on which to try out your new creation – especially one whose own future is wrapped up in your own endeavours? Let them in, for God's sake!

Yet, ironically, you're about to face the worst house you'll ever play to. Because the one thing this lot won't be doing is watching the play. Or at least, watching it with the uncomplicated, disinterested eye of the punter. They're not here to enjoy themselves; on the contrary, their interest is entirely forensic.

The production manager needs to see when and where pieces of scenery will have be to shunted about so he can decide how many staff he'll need to accomplish the process. Wardrobe and wigs will be looking to see how their outfits and hairpieces are going to stand up to the action (for instance when the heroine gets pulled by her hair across the floor), the lighting designer will be looking to see where you're positioned at certain integral moments of the action so he can plan the positioning of his lighting grid, while the head of sound needs to know where best to place the miniature loudspeaker to provide the sound of the ringing telephone or the noise of distant thunder. Even the box office staff needs to scrutinise the product to see if it contains nudity, violence, swearing or explosions.

Thus techie runs are almost inevitably monumental disappointments. Uproarious comedies will be played out to barely a titter; taut thrillers will receive an absent-minded waggling of a pencil stump in the ear; heart-wrenching tragedies will be played to nothing more sonorous than stifled yawns or the scratch of a biro on a jotter.

It doesn't mean you've failed, or you've ended up with a dud. They've come to cover their arses, not yours. In the unlikely event that you do garner a reaction, you can rest assured you've struck theatrical gold. I've only ever known the occasion to happen once, and I won't forget it.

The occasion was during rehearsals of Arthur Miller's drama, *A View from the Bridge* at the NT. The play is one of his finest, if weightiest pieces, a modern spin on a Greek tragedy set among the factories and dockyards of the New Jersey shoreline.

In 1986, I was playing Marco in a production in the Cottesloe, directed by Ayckbourn and, with the exception of the great Gambon in the role of Eddie Carbone, a largely unknown cast. Miller is always an exciting, if portentous dramatist. Heavy on symbolism and clanging metaphors, his plays can still exert a powerful and cathartic effect on audiences. However, they're not to be trifled with – written nearly 60 years ago, his powerful blend of symbolic drama overlaid with direct-to-audience soliloquies must be handled with skill if they're not to seem preachy. With so much horsepower under the bonnet, a light touch on the pedal is desirable. Less is more, in other words.

Luckily in Ayckbourn and Gambon we had the perfect combo. Gambon, a famously anarchic and gifted comic actor, had the role of his career in Eddie, the tragic longshoreman who loses his only daughter to an immigrant teenager over from Italy to start a new life in America. At the age of 46, he was in prime form for the role.

As rehearsals progressed and Gambon started inching his way into the part, we all felt we might just be onto something special: but it was impossible to know. Then came the techie run. A week or so before our first preview, a procession of weary heads of departments plodded sheepishly into the room, some clutching folders, others dressed in overalls, and none of them meeting our gaze. They took up positions on a row of chairs arranged along one wall and sat waiting glumly for something to happen.

The final moment of the drama sees Eddie, who has surreptitiously shopped the young immigrant Rudolpho to the authorities rather than endure the romance between him and his daughter, is prowling the street. But Rudolpho's elder brother (me) has realised the identity of the informer and seeks Eddie out. A fight ensues, at the end of which Eddie is fatally stabbed. He lies bleeding to death, his head cradled in the arms of his distraught wife, while his daughter Beatrice stands looking on with a mixture of horror, hatred and disbelief.

The techie run ended. After a brief moment, Gambon got up off the floor and dusted himself down, while the rest of the cast broke out of their characters and made their way sheepishly towards the tea urn. Normally at such gatherings there are a few embarrassed coughs, a smattering of desultory applause, after which the various heads of departments troop out in utter silence.

But on this occasion nobody moved. Instead, they sat rooted to the spot like a row of window dummies. And there were sounds unfamiliar at such occasions. Instead of the scraping of chairs, the snapping of ring binders and the unfastening of zips on handbags, there were snuffles and the blowing of noses; and was it my imagination, or was that the sound of a woman crying?

So it was. The watching group sat red-eyed and silent. One or two caught the eyes of the actors and nodded in mute approbation. Meanwhile at the far end of the line, a female front of house administrator wept into her handkerchief.

The drama had somehow overwhelmed their professional concerns and utterly gripped them. That's when we knew we were onto something.

And so it proved. The play became one of the greatest successes in the history of the NT, playing to stupendous critical acclaim and enjoying a sell-out run in the Cottesloe followed by a transfer to the Aldwych Theatre. On the first preview, such was the ovation at the end that we were back in our dressing rooms and removing our costumes before we realised the sound of static crackling over the tannoy was in fact the audience still applauding.

Dressing hurriedly, we blundered back on for yet another call. Olivier nominations flowed over the show like confetti. When Miller himself came to see a performance a week or two into the run he described it afterwards as the finest version he'd ever witnessed. If I say that the cast took all this in their stride I'm not being arrogant. It's just we already knew. We'd moved them at the tecchie run.

If you can get the head of the stage crew to crack his face, you know you've got something special.

TECH & DRESS

The 'tech' is the bridgehead, sandwiched between the end of your time in the rehearsal room and the first dress rehearsal, when the play you've been working on moves into the auditorium, to be adorned with costumes, lights, props and scenery, ready for the paying public.

The first rule of techs is that they're inevitably a shambles. If they're not, something's very wrong.

Like most actors I've enjoyed some techs and endured many more, from affairs lasting barely more than a couple of hours, to monsters which have lasted three, four, or in the case of a production of *How To Succeed in Business Without Really Trying*, five days. At first they're new and exciting occasions, not to say a bit of a larf.

After all, you've got your costume, you're exploring your new world like an excited puppy, and because techs proceed at a funeral pace due to the myriad problem-solving to be done, there's plenty of time for standing about and gassing with your fellow actors.

But be warned, like the fairground ride that loses its charm because the bloke in charge has wandered off for a fag and left you on it for too long, techs soon pall. You've just got your performance together, and now suddenly doors won't open, props won't work, lighting cues will be in the wrong place, the phone will stop ringing when you're still three feet away from picking up the receiver, and your own portrayal will be played not to a respectful silence, but to a cacophony of noise from the stalls, as the various HoDs wrangle over whose problem it is that the whole thing's such a technical crock of shite.

Keep your cool. It's going to get better. The part you've lost in all this mechanical mayhem will slowly re-emerge back during the subsequent dress rehearsals. And meanwhile the hinges will be oiled, the carpet will be fixed, the door handle will be screwed in properly so it doesn't come off in your hand, your shirt cuffs will be lengthened, the flaming torches in the upstage arch won't fizzle out with that terrible farting noise halfway through the scene, and the bloke up the ladder fiddling with those electrical cables just where you're supposed to do your downstage soliloquy will disappear. Trust me. It's going to get better.

Whatever you do, don't succumb to the desire to stand in the middle of the floor, shouting, 'STAGE MANAGEMENT??'

FIRST NIGHTS

Dame Judi Dench's recollection perfectly sums up the tribalism and partisanship that are the hallmarks of these tortured events. Apparently her first line upon stepping onstage was, 'Where are you, Mummy and Daddy?' On the first night in question, her mum shouted back from the audience, 'Here we are darling, H 24 and 25!'

According to scientists, the amount of stress endured by the average actor on an opening night is roughly equivalent to that experienced in a minor car crash. Thus it remains the bitterest of ironies that the performance by which you'll be forever judged will be the least typical. On the contrary, the whole gruesome conceit conspires to make the experience a grotesque parody.

And that's because first night audiences are like no other. On every other night, people turn up, pay their money, watch the play, hope they enjoy it, and if they don't, will have forgotten about their disappointment long before they step back in through their front door.

On first nights, however, the world is utterly reversed. There are no disinterested punters at all – instead, the house is filled by two warring camps, 'them' and 'us': people who are either desperate for you to fail, or whose own prospects utterly depend on your succeeding.

The response is consequently a nightmare blend of people reacting over-vociferously in the hope of convincing those around them, surrounded by others who wouldn't be impressed even if you'd offered them Glenn Miller and Lord Lucan in drag singing 'Sisters'.

In the 'us' camp will be producers, spouses, agents, friends, relations and publicists, plus all the support and ancillary staff whose own future hinges on the evening being a 'hit'.

In the 'them' camp are rival producers, actors who didn't get the gig (or worse, turned it down) plus assorted hangers-on, rubber-neckers and liggers, many of whom are only there in the first place because it's a freebie and there's a party afterwards. In other words, hardly anyone will have paid for their ticket: which, as any actor knows, is always a recipe for disaster. And that's even before you get to the critics.

For the poor actor it's sometimes difficult to know whom the occasion is designed to serve. Although the designated start time is invariably 7 pm (to allow the critics to file their reviews in time for tomorrow's first editions), such events rarely commence till 7.15. First you have to persuade the audience to dump their coats, finish their conversations, stop air-kissing every damn fool within a ten-foot radius, and take their seats.

Once the curtain goes up the feeblest *bon mot* will be met by gales of artificial laughter by the 'us' camp, while the 'them' camp will watch your best endeavours with a look of weary condescension. After a first half of inexplicable silence, punctuated by occasional crazed guffaws, you'll finally arrive at the interval.

While you sit in the dressing room wondering whether the nail file in your make-up box is sufficiently sharp to slash your wrist with, the human caravanserai has moved back into the bar. Cue more air-kissing, more rubbernecking, and an interval of nearly 30 minutes while the beleaguered ushers try to prize the wine glasses from the audience's grip and persuade them to regain their seats. If the second half is a tad less frenetic, it's only because the audience's preconceptions have been loosened by a couple of glasses of wine.

At the curtain call, the 'us' crowd will be on their feet, cheering, clapping, and turning ostentatiously to nod vigorously to each other in the style favoured by audiences in countless MGM musicals. The 'thems' will meanwhile be applauding with all the enthusiasm of a commuter complimenting a Romanian busker who's invaded their Underground carriage with an accordion.

But even then your ordeal isn't over. Now you've got the first night party to contend with.

Your friends of course will, quite rightly, make a fuss of you. Your enemies, meanwhile, will offer stiff congratulations, while making it perfectly plain by their body language that they thought the whole thing was something they'd inadvertently stepped in.

But worse than having to pick your way between the gushers and the gainsayers is having to deal with the hangers-on. For these are the ones for whom the party is really for. This is their reward for having endured the play. So don't think the first night party is for you. By the time you've showered, put on a decent jacket, zhuzhed your hair, and hurried over to the venue, the party will be in full swing and you'll be lucky if there's so much as a Wasabi peanut left.

I recall one first night in town – for *Burn This* in fact – in which it took me a full 20 minutes to shoulder my way to the bar and another 15 to get served, and where my only glancing encounter with the advertised 'finger-food buffet' was a desperate claw at a passing crabstick from the one remaining tray as it swept by me, only to see it disappear into the maw of the deputy editor of *Tatler*.

If I sound a tad curmudgeonly, I apologise. First nights are exciting, wonderful things, and of course, if you're in a huge hit, none of the above will matter, as these tribal factions will coalesce into one, adoring whole. But best prepare yourself. First nights are grand occasions, but they're not for you.

A final, comforting thought. However bad your experience, it will be unlikely to match that of a friend of mine, who finished his own first night of a West End play and was getting ready for the party back in his dressing room, only to find himself overhearing via the tannoy the various comments of unsuspecting punters as they filed out of the auditorium.

'Well', he heard one woman say to her husband, 'After that performance, all we need now is for the dog to have been sick in the car...'

REVIEWS

Some years ago I received a phone call from the editor of a leading national newspaper. He was calling to inform me that their much respected theatre critic was retiring at the end of the year, and would I like the gig?

The juxtaposition of the offer and my personal circumstances were especially piquant, as I was badly out of work at the time. Yet, in the way the business so often works, I'd suddenly been offered a unique, unlooked-for and utterly life-changing offer out of the blue.

The post, he assured me, was a permanent one. It would require me to visit and review up to four theatrical opening nights every week and chisel out 500 finely-turned words of criticism by midnight in time for tomorrow's copy. There'd also be a fortnight at the Edinburgh festival, plus two guaranteed trips each year to Broadway. In addition to my salary there'd be a healthy expense account and enrolment into the company pension plan so I'd get a small stipend when I finally hung up my fountain pen.

'Anything else I need to consider?'

'Only two further stipulations,' he assured me, 'Both of which are non-negotiable. You have to give up acting. And you must tell the truth...'

Twelve little words; but a veritable Encyclopedia Britannica of implications. Actors are by disposition not good at either giving up acting or telling the truth, and I felt like one of the perspiring entrepreneurs on *Dragon's Den* who's been offered half a million pounds by Theo Paphities, only to be informed he wanted 50% of the company. I think I even asked if I could I have a moment to consider?

'Of course,' said my contact. 'I can give you 24 hours. Give me a call tomorrow, and if the answer is yes, I'll put the process in train.'

I put the phone down and relayed the news to Julia. Her reaction was to go to bed with some headache pills. She assured me that having wasted her best years hanging around with self-employed, self-absorbed, largely impecunious actors, the idea of having a partner with a regular salary, a pension plan and two guaranteed trips to New York per year was more than she could bear to hope for. She told me to wake her once I'd made my decision, as long as it was yes.

I decided to phone a friend or two. Once I'd canvassed their views, I'd make my decision. I picked up the receiver, and began dialling.

SLING & ARROWS

Critics are a necessary evil of showbiz. Catch their collective eye, allow them to build up a head of steam on your behalf during each subsequent outing, let them feel as if they are your sole champion, and you're half-way to becoming a star.

What I'm trying to say is, critics matter.

And because of this, they are also kind, tender, unbiased, fiercely intelligent, hard working, tolerant and perspicuous individuals whose brilliant and eclectic knowledge of actors and acting is a true gift. They're also kind to animals and happy to stop to help elderly ladies cross the road.

The oddest thing is that crits and critics are entirely a phenomenon of live theatre. You'd think that television or film reviewing would matter nearly as much, if not more so, but TV criticism, although a finely tuned art form, doesn't have the same clout. You simply can't imagine the cast of *Game of Thrones* or *Dr Who* quaking in their boots lest they get strafed in the *Observer* or *TV Quick*. Yet in live theatre, crits still wield real influence. Love them or loathe them, they can't be ignored.

HOLD THY PIECE

It was P.G. Wodehouse who said, 'Has anybody ever seen a critic during the daytime? Of course not. They come out at night, up to no good,' and indeed, theirs is a funny old world. As the rest of humanity is trailing back from work on the 17.23 to Penge, they are strapping on their coats, filling their pockets with biros and their favourite moleskin notebook, and setting off in the opposite direction to commence their deadly work.

In some ways, being paid to see live theatre is a bit like eating cherry liqueurs – wonderful when it's a bit of a treat, but not so nice once you're strapped into a chair and forced to continually gag the stuff down, whether you want it or not. After all, what could be nicer than going to see a stirring production of *Romeo and Juliet* or *Hedda Gabler*, especially if you're given the best seat, a drink before the show and another during the interval? Sounds heavenly, doesn't it?

But what if you had to watch *Romeo and Juliet* every other month or so, year after year, on into eternity. Or *Hedda Gabler*? Or, God forbid, *Twelfth Night*? That terrible knowledge when you took your seat that you were going to have to watch three hours' worth of the same thing you'd seen only a few weeks before; the same drunk scene, the same shemozzle with the letter in the garden, and then that deathless Sir Topaz shtick.

And finally the discovery of those dreaded words: *Approximate running time: three and three-quarter hours.*

In the old days, when critics had to bellow their review down a public telephone to a copywriter, the possibilities for misunderstanding were legion, as exemplified by one review in the *Guardian* for the opera *Boris Godunov* which was published next day as being for '*Doris Godunov*'. Or another occasion when the principal character in *The Merchant of Venice* was consistently referred to in the finished newspaper as 'Skylark the Jew'.

But even now, filing reviews can be a bloody business. Even if the show commences promptly at 7 pm (and it won't), that leaves them barely an hour and half to get out of the building, find some Wi-Fi, bang out the words and send in their finished piece before the proposed deadline for next day's edition. That is, if their vehicle hasn't been broken into or towed way, as happened to one leading critic of my acquaintance.

Benedict Nightingale, until recently the theatre critic of *The Times*, began to seriously doubt his calling when he found himself sitting in his car at around 11.20 pm pounding out a review for Pamela Anderson in panto at Wimbledon, only to realise he had an £80 parking fine slapped on his windscreen.

And even if you find something fresh to say about this particular *Twelfth Night*, there's another production to see a week next Monday at the Young Vic. Then the RSC have their own version planned for their autumn season, and rumour has it Liz Hurley might be having a bash at Viola in the New Year. There they are, like planes stacking up over Heathrow, a never-ending conveyor belt of yellow stockings and cross-garters circling above you into eternity.

In my experience, there are only two sorts of actors – those who read their reviews, and those who do but pretend they don't. I know of one leading man who eschews the temptation to read a single word of his notices until curtain down on the last night, when he goes through them all meticulously over a glass of brandy before setting fire to them one by one. But he's an exception, and in any case you may be contravening fire and safety regulations if you attempt such a stunt yourself.

For actors, reviews are like pornography. You don't want to look at them, you feel abased and grubby by doing so, but you can't help yourself. What's more, if they're favourable, you can find yourself becoming strangely aroused. One leading American actor, seen a great deal in London's theatreland in recent years always claims he never reads crits, but a friend of mine assures me he saw him in a café in Muswell Hill, shrouded in dark glasses and with a baseball cap pulled low over his forehead, trawling through an entire stack of them the day after an opening night at the Old Vic.

So how best to deal with them?

Forgive me if I start to sound like Rudyard Kipling here, but my advice really is to treat the twin imposters just the same. Any half-decent actor already knows whether they are good or not in a particular part, and receiving the approbation or ridicule of a few select strangers shouldn't make any difference. I've had some raves simply because the critics in question hadn't happened to have seen my particular box of tired old tricks before; while by contrast, some of the most daring stuff I've attempted has been misunderstood or let down by influences or individuals beyond my control.

I used to get particularly good notices from the late lamented critic of the *Daily Mail*, Jack Tinker, although what the general public didn't know was that I lived upstairs from his mother in Brighton and often used to pop down to help her on the numerous occasions when she locked herself out of her flat, or when the flush on her toilet cistern stopped working. Tinker never forgot his friends.

But perhaps the healthiest attitude to reviews is that of a mate of mine who lives in Finchley. Meal times in his house are always hugely enhanced by a poster displayed on his kitchen wall for a West End production he once witnessed, and whose attendant reviews he subsequently printed out and added to the poster before framing. A small selection of the dozen or so is worth repeating.

'The worst play I have ever seen...' (Daily Express)

'As joke after joke sinks to its knees, you wonder if anything will ever seem funny again' (Sunday Telegraph)

'A turgid draining evening' (What's On)

'A pathetic squib' (Observer)

'My astonishment that it had not closed by Thursday is exceeded only by my incredulity that it actually opened on Wednesday' (Mail on Sunday)

And my favourite:

'There's no start to the fun!' (Independent)

As you may have guessed, my mate had played the lead in the show. The strategic placing of the poster over the dining table reminds him each morning that today's stinker is not only tomorrow's fish and chip paper, but quite possibly tomorrow's wall decoration.

FIT FLOPS

And what of me?

As it turned out my friends' advice was sufficient in itself to dissuade me from taking up the offer. 'It'll warp you,' said one,

'You'll end up in Joe Allen's, sitting by yourself, eating the best food and drinking the best wine, and staring across at tablefuls of your old mates. We'll be sure to say hello, but don't expect us to ask you to join us at our table.'

That did it. I wasn't sitting by myself at Joe Allen's for any amount. I rang the editor, told him my decision, had a Scotch, and went in to wake Julia with the news. Though in truth, having announced it, it took me a further while to explain my reasoning.

Not that we weren't speaking – it's just that I wasn't quick enough to interrupt…

LONG RUNS

So. The critics have pronounced the show a palpable hit. What now?

Now you have to perform it again. And again. And again.

Albert Einstein once defined insanity as being the act of, 'Repeatedly doing the same thing over and over again and expecting a different result.'

Anybody who's endured performing a long run of a play will know what he's talking about.

And you don't have to take out a lifetime subscription to *The Mousetrap* to experience it for yourself. Commit to any production for six months or more, and unless you read on, you too will one day be found in a foetal position in the dressing room sucking your thumb and babbling that the butler did it.

By 'long run', I'm referring here to anything numbering over 100 shows. I can claim to be something of an expert in this department, as, at the time of writing, I've enjoyed runs numbering 812 shows (two separate stints in *Mamma Mia*), 374 (*Yes, Prime Minister*), 278 (*Donkey's Years)* and 198 (*Democracy*), plus several other extended stints each nudging three figures.

Most young actors nowadays look upon anything longer than a few weeks as akin to theatrical incarceration, but they can thank their lucky stars they weren't born a generation ago. Until the mid-1960s, the clause in most standard acting contracts specifying 'run of play', meant just that – for as long as the play lasted. So if you were unlucky enough to take a small part in some terrible old tram smash intended to tide you over Christmas, that then became an unexpected hit, you were stuffed, often for several years.

Even now, in this so-called enlightened age, I sense managements would simply love to nail you down for the duration if they could arrange matters. Just think – no pesky re-rehearsals, programme reprints or costly new advertising hoardings: just wind you up and let you go, while they swivel round and round in their office chairs and shouting, 'Yee-Hah!!'

Happily, producers can no longer persuade star-turns, on whose shoulders their commercial hopes rest to agree to go on for more than a few months; and in any case, the penny has dropped that compelling actors to go on for years on end against their will may not be good for the show.

Such existential concerns will seem no more than a distant dream to you when you sign the contract. There are so many things conspiring against a play's longevity that the possibility of endless repetition won't cross your mind. You'll be too busy trying to get the bugger on. But once it's a smasheroo, your perspective steadily, if imperceptibly, alters. And 200 shows can suddenly seem a long way off if your only role in the play is to come on as the taxi driver in act two and say, 'Thank'ee guvnor.'

Stage one

The good news about stage one is that you won't know you're in it. The play you've committed to till this time next year may well not make it to the end of the week, so why worry? Let fate take care of itself. And if the show proves a roaring success? Well, there are worse prospects...

Stage two

This is the best of times. You've done six to eight weeks, the show is a smash, the tills are ringing, queues for returns are snaking round the wall of the building from 4 pm each afternoon, and your future is assured. You've chummed up, you've money in your pocket, and you've hit upon a handy routine (pub Monday, Wednesday and Thursday, meet up with a friend Tuesday, back home for Wossy on Friday and perhaps a club or a take-away with the missus on Saturday).

Best of all, the part, which once felt so alien and uncomfortable in the rehearsal room, is now beginning to feel like a tailored suit – smart, bespoke, and now without any chafing in unwelcome places. The critics have given both you and the product their benediction, and while you're still visited by a frisson of nervous anticipation at beginners, it's no longer anything more than a pleasurable anticipation.

And it's about to get a whole lot better. By performance number 60 you'll be able to walk onstage as easily as flicking a switch. No need to prepare. It'll be available for you, whenever and wherever you need it, instantly. Effortless, secure, yet newly-minted each night.

People visiting me in shows often ask how actors do it: how are we able to manage to perform the same thing, again and again and twice on matinée days, without exhausting ourselves or getting bored? All I can find by way of response is to reply, 'It's a knack.' The performance is there, in our bloodstream, and once we're secure, we can inhabit it perfectly well without having to agonise over it beforehand.

A similar effect will also have inundated your colleagues. That scene of your first entrance, for example, when as the estate manager you're showing the first guest into the main room and explaining why he's been summoned here for an urgent family summit. That bit of business which the actor playing the guest opposite you was exploring in rehearsals, that of glancing airily round the room as he listens to your opening speech, will now be working wonderfully well, fanned by constant repetition and full houses.

And why shouldn't it get a laugh? Those chuckles when he runs his finger along the mantelpiece to inspect it for dust, or straightens the portrait on the back wall, are now gaining in strength and regularity. You have to admire him. When all is said and done, invention is what stuffs the pillowcase of the text with the goose feathers of dramatic inhabitation. It's frankly a pleasure to be on stage with him.

Enjoy the feeling. It won't last. Because within this fruits of familiarity, the seeds of your ultimate destruction are already germinating.

Stage three

Around performance 80 is when minor irritations will begin to erupt. The journey into work each night will seem more tedious, the attractions of the pub after curtain down less alluring, and while the show will almost have lost a couple of minutes' playing time, your onstage colleagues will be starting to irritate you just a tad. Eccentricities and mannerisms in other people's performances, ones that seemed so deft and enchanting a few weeks ago, will start to grate.

That business in the first scene for instance. Where once the actor playing the guest was merely adjusting the frame of the portrait and mopping his brow with his handkerchief while you spoke, now he looks like somebody from Pickfords attempting to master the intricacies of Morris dancing.

The hankie business is still very funny, of course it is, but does he really need to flourish it quite as much during your lines? Or blow his nose luxuriously at the end, thus hijacking the whole focus and turning it back on himself? Especially as the noise he's making now resembles a car horn. You're trying to expound the plot for God's sake!

Perhaps you'll have gentle word with him in the pub. Except you don't go to the pub so often as you did. Those bar room anecdotes which once seemed so funny during rehearsals are starting to reoccur with monotonous regularity, and frankly if you have to sit next to that elderly character actor again, who's always droning on about train timetables back to his home in Letchworth, you'll shoot yourself. Funny. He seemed so wonderfully courteous and old-fashioned a few weeks ago. You've only just realised he's actually a crushing bore.

Stage four

Somewhere around performance 120 is where it begins to lose its sheen. And it's also when you really begin to earn your crust as an actor. However hard you try, your concentration will no longer be quite so subservient to your will. Whenever you have nothing much to do or say for longer than 15 seconds at a pop, your mind will start wandering all over the place like some frustrated puppy spotting a rabbit in the distance.

There are other travails. That tosser you have to act with in the opening scene for example, the one playing the guest. His deft business, once so admired, has grown and grown until it resembles Freddie Starr on the Royal Variety Show. Knocking his toe on the footstool, making gurning faces at himself in the stage left mirror, and now waving that bloody handkerchief about as if trying to assist a Harrier Jump Jet to alight onto the deck of an aircraft carrier: quite apart from the fact that it's blatant upstaging, he's also adding a good half a minute to the scene. The whole play is being dumped on its arse before it's even got going.

If he doesn't stop it soon you're going to deck the fucker.

Stage five

Round about performance number 200 is when it gets nasty. Acting is now like performing on sheet ice. The slightest thing – someone coughing, the sound of a door banging or even a passing motorcycle in the street outside – will now be sufficient to upend you. Your brain, the obedient puppy of a few weeks ago, has turned into something resembling Tigger. The slightest moment of repose and it'll be haring off all over the place.

You're also now prone to paroxysms of helpless laughter at the slightest deviation from the text. Mistakes and fluffs that normally wouldn't cause so much as a raised eyebrow now send you in spasms of reflexive giggling, while more substantial howlers will have you facing upstage with your handkerchief stuffed into your mouth (for practical advice on how to deal with such an emergency, please see the end of the section: *Corpsing*).

Thankfully you no longer have to deal with that little shite in the first scene. Not that he's not still doing everything within his power to derail your performance – far from it, his acting is now about as subtle as an earthquake. It's just that you're no longer looking at him. By fixing your gaze determinedly out front and bellowing each phrase, you're just about able to hold your own, even though the gales of laughter punctuating your dialogue suggest that somewhere behind you he's turned into a one-man Cirque du Soleil. You're already spending your time on the tube home each night trying to estimate the most likely outcome were you to dare take him on in a fistfight.

You're now paddling in the shallows of stage six.

Stage six

Stage six is stage-fright. And stage-fright is no laughing matter: so much so that I've provided a separate heading for it.

Hopefully it won't get to this. By now, the end will be in sight, just a few precious weeks away. And that mere fact will be sufficient to act as a safety valve. The lines will start to return, your fury will abate to a dull ache, and the moment the curtain falls on the last night you'll all be swearing undying friendship once more, reminiscing about what fun you all had, and laughing afresh at anecdotes from the company duffer about the 22.43 via Welwyn Garden City as if he's Peter Kay performing the 'Garlic Bread' sketch.

Which brings me to my final thought. Don't, whatever you do, be fooled into staying on for yet more of the same. 'We're taking it out on tour' or, 'Have a couple of weeks off and then come back for another three months' are both scenarios likely to be suggested by the management if there's still money to be made, and you may be fooled into thinking a quick wipe down with a rolled up copy of a *Lonely Planet* guide will be all that's needed to restore your equilibrium.

Resist.

I don't know what stages seven to fourteen are, but I don't recommend them.

STAGE-FRIGHT

Stage-fright is one of those terms ('nodules' is another, 'panto with Louie Spence' a third) which you rarely hear actors discuss, even between themselves. If it's not taboo, it's perilously close. Not just because you can't earn a living any more, but also because the process by which you discover you've got stage-fright in the first place is so horribly unimaginable.

Think of it. You're on stage, and you can't recall a single word. Everyone's looking at you (including the other actors), and you haven't got a clue what you're supposed to say next. And even if you do manage to blurt out a facsimile of the printed text, the same agonising ordeal is waiting for you like a spring trap on the very next line. And the line after that. And so on and so on.

Compared with the usual nightmares suffered by those in the business (hearing your cue approaching and not knowing your way to the wings, or finding the stage has become a giant Dunlopillo mattress on which you can't keep upright), stage-fright is far worse than anything else you can imagine. And it's all too real.

There have been many celebrated instances in the past, the most famous being that suffered by the great Laurence Olivier himself. Olivier, who succumbed for nearly five years whilst at the peak of his powers, later wrote of it as being the worst crisis of his career (though in fairness, if I'd been married to Vivien Leigh I'd have felt a bit seedy myself).

Things got so bad that while playing Othello, he sometimes had to be forcibly pushed onstage by the company manager in order to commence the performance. At the height of his neurosis he even had to implore his fellow actors not to look him in the eye (though I've worked with a number of performers for whom such a regime is already second nature).

Stage-fright, sometimes known by its glossier appellation of 'performance-related anxiety', can occur at any time, and often without warning, but it'll certainly crop up if you stay too long in the same production. It also inevitably seems to strike when an actor is at the height of his fame – and no wonder, for overwork and anxiety are usually the most common trigger points.

Other side effects include a fluttering or pounding of the heart, tremor in the hands or legs, sweaty hands, facial nerve tics, dry mouth and erectile dysfunction (all of which I've suffered at various times, but not at the same time and never onstage).

So what causes it? Long runs undoubtedly, but also overwork, marital breakdown and physical illness. Sometimes a break from work is all that's needed to restore your internal machinery to full working order. The problem is, you won't know whether you've licked it until you attempt it once more.

And don't confuse this condition with a mere inability to remember lines – a separate issue entirely. One actor of my age famously suffered a collapse of seismic proportions some years ago while working at the RSC. One night he was sailing along happily, the next he couldn't put one line in front of the other. His answer was to resort to a prescription of beta-blockers, which cured the stage fright but added about 20 minutes to his performance.

Thankfully, the good news is that it can be surmounted, a fact I witnessed first-hand a few years ago. In 1990, I appeared in the National Theatre's production of Shakespeare's *King Lear*, a dramatisation stuffed with the great and good of British theatre, and starring as the eponymous King, Sir Ian Holm.

One of the brightest talents of the 1960s and '70s, Holm had enjoyed a spectacular career in all forms of the business before succumbing to stage-fright during a performance of *The Iceman Cometh*. So profound was the attack that he disappeared from live theatre for many years. 'Something just snapped,' he later recollected in an interview he gave to an American magazine. 'When the concentration goes, the mind just closes down.'

Well, Holm was back on for it, and Lear was to be his great comeback. It so happened that I was alongside him for his very first entrance on the very first public performance.

Playing Lear is regarded as the ultimate challenge for any actor, the pinnacle of their ambition. To attempt it after having suffered from a very public case of stage-fright was tantamount to trying to cure yourself of vertigo by climbing Everest. Yet Holm didn't blink at the prospect.

You will remember that the play opens with a brief duologue between Gloucester and Kent, as they discuss the likely outcome of the imminent division of the ailing king's substantial kingdom. Then the entire court files on for the actual divvy up; Lear himself, of course, his three daughters, Goneril, Regan and Cordelia, as well as various lords and attendants, including Cornwall, the part with which I was entrusted.

It so happened that I was immediately in front of Holm in the queue for the grand entrance. We stood there, in the dark on the first preview, contemplating a packed and expectant audience on the other side of the curtain, and listening as Timothy West and David Burke intoned the first brief exchange out there under the lights ('*I thought the King had more affected the Duke of Albany than Cornwall*').

Holm's recent personal history and the peak he was about to very publicly scale, had not been mentioned during rehearsals, yet there were none amongst us shivering in the wings that night, who wouldn't have entertained some private speculation about what might occur once we strode on. With the cue approaching, we gathered our robes, steadied our swords, and prepared to enter.

Just as I was about to stride on, I felt a tap on my right shoulder. I looked round. It was Holm.

'What's my first line?' he whispered, with only the faintest hint of a twinkle.

Needless to say, his performance proved a triumph, one of the great modern Lears. The production played to huge critical success both in London and abroad, and cemented his reputation as one of the great actors of the 20th century. But my abiding memory will always be of that brief moment when, faced with the ultimate ordeal, he still found time to briefly send himself up.

In my book, that's class.

LAST NIGHTS

So you've survived rehearsals, the opening night and the critics: you've bedded down, sampled the six ages of the long run, and now the day has finally arrived when it's all ending.

In acting, perhaps more than any other profession, you form rapid and intense relationships with the people with whom you work. The 'us against them' syndrome is a necessary part of getting the show on, and it's all too easy to forget in the heightened intimacy of live theatre that friendships, for the most part, will lose their raison d'être once the curtain falls.

Last nights are curious affairs. For some weeks now you've been willing the bloody thing to end, ticking off each fresh performance on a hastily scrawled chart on the dressing room wall, and approaching the theatre for the twice-weekly matinée days as if shod in diving boots.

Yet when you come to the final performance, there's always a temptation to linger, delay your departure, and stop to admire the view. After all, it's your last chance to time that laugh, to wring the last drop of pathos out of your big moment. If you're not careful you can find yourself striving too hard to achieve the perfect performance that has so far eluded you.

Don't bother. You won't manage it.

In any case last-night audiences themselves will militate against achieving cultural nirvana. The punters for this event will comprise friends and family who may well have seen the show before (possibly several times), intermingled with normal civilians who are entirely unaware of the cosmic resonance of the occasion. Thus last nights can be jumpy affairs, and entirely atypical of what you'd normally expect. Best to just let rip and take what comes.

The one exception is in the world of musicals. Here, the atmosphere in the auditorium on last nights is often super-charged, not to say overwrought, and the last rites can often seem like some semi-Masonic ritual rather than a live performance.

In 1996 I appeared in Sam Mendes' production of *Company*. Sondheim fans are by their very nature prone to coming over all peculiar at the mere mention of his name, and thus the last night audience at the Albery Theatre was comprised exclusively of hard-line fanatics who'd already seen it ten times and who in many cases knew the show better than we did.

Laughs were activated before we got to the punch-lines, applause burst out in the middle of songs without us ever knowing why – it almost seemed as if the show was out in the auditorium and that we onstage were the spectators.

The whole heady confection that evening was topped off by Adrian Lester (playing the lead role of Bobby), who marked the final beat of the final encore with an impromptu back flip of such brilliance and daring that in many countries it would have had him fast-tracked into the national gymnastics team for the Olympics. It was a stunning virtuoso gesture to round off a stunning virtuoso performance. Given the emotional demographic of the audience, I need hardly describe the reaction.

Yet even in heightened environments such as these, the moment the curtain comes down the bubble bursts. No sooner have you left the stage than a veritable posse of blokes all looking like refugees from the Hairy Bikers will attack your pasteboard world with crowbars and grappling ropes. This pillaging army only has one thing in mind – to get the set trashed and transported outside before closing time. No time for swapping anecdotes or waxing lyrical about old times. They've got a beer to catch.

I used to dread such occasions, and would try to prolong the experience by diligently taking down the names and phone numbers of everyone, from the front of house manager to the car park attendant, swearing undying love to all and sundry, and promising to meet with each and every protagonist for a coffee in a few days' time.

But meeting other actors in the cold light of day can be a sobering experience. A bit like the holiday romance, things can be much more mundane once you've swapped the luxury resort in Saint Lucia for a Thursday morning in Kentish Town. Once you've got past the, 'Wasn't it funny when…' and, 'So what are you up for?' conversation can often be distinctly sticky.

So don't bother.

Clear your dressing room before the last night, come in for the last show wearing a sharp suit or a sassy outfit, have a drink or two in the bar or at a nearby pub afterwards, organise for some sandwiches and a few bowls of those nice thick rustic chips to be provided to soak up the booze (remembering, of course, to leave some for the poor stage management in case they make it before closing time) and then, sometime about 11.30 pm, turn on your heel and leave.

Those of your number with whom you genuinely want to stay in touch will crop up again, have no fear.

And the others?

Well, I'm going to miss them terribly, of course I am.

Until the next job comes along.

ALARMS AND EXCURSIONS

I'm finishing this section with a few tips and wrinkles, designed to assist you with various emergencies that every actor will face from time to time. Hopefully you'll never experience any of them, but if so, I sincerely hope the next few pages will help.

BEING OFF

Of all the horrors the fates can drop on an unsuspecting actor, the most traumatising is being 'off' – actors' shorthand for missing your entrance.

It's the ultimate professional betrayal, condemning your onstage colleagues to stand gaping like fish, without words to speak or anybody to speak them to. When Harold Macmillan insisted, 'A week is a long time in politics' he'd obviously never been stranded alone on a stage.

Being 'off' is every actor's nightmare, involving shock, shame, guilt, and quite possibly a coronary thrombosis or broken ankle as you hurtle down to the stage in an effort to spare your workmates further embarrassment. But nearly as bad as being 'off', is being the 'offee' – the one left marooned onstage when it happens.

There you are, onstage, motoring through the dialogue as if nothing was more natural in the world, and then – there's no knock on the door.

And in an instant the world is a terrifying place. You're alone, quite alone, without a single coherent thought in your head. Suddenly, from being cock of the walk you're just a cock, your cardboard pretence crumbling like papier-mâché left out in the rain. You're just another hapless luvvie standing in a borrowed suit being stared at by 500 uncomprehending – though if that knock doesn't come soon they won't be for much longer – spectators.

Luckily such crises rarely occur, and even when they do they rarely last for more than a few seconds. Usually the miscreant has simply been yakking in the wings, and the ensuing silence is sufficient to jolt him to his senses and propel him through the door as if shot from a cannon.

As long as the audience don't realise anything's wrong there's no harm done. So the trick is to be able to stall for the few vital seconds it'll take for the offender to be located. Half a minute should amply suffice.

One actor of my acquaintance claims he was left onstage for nearly five minutes during a production of *A Murder Has Been Announced* in Bridlington, but assured me he bought precious time by announcing, 'I feel so happy I'll sing a song', before breaking into a chorus of 'Feed the Birds' from *Mary Poppins*. He even claims several audience members joined in: a preposterous claim, until you remember it was a midweek matinée at Bridlington.

But let's mark this sort of instance down as a cosmic aberration. Usually your task will be to simply buy a few precious seconds while the miscreant is found.

So how to buy those few precious seconds? Available courses of action depend on the type of play. If you're appearing in a Shakespeare, you can always eat up precious seconds by unsheathing your sword and swishing it menacingly in the air. Not only will it keep the audience rapt but it'll enable you to imagine what you're going to do to the actor who's shafted you, as soon as the performance is over.

If the culprit still hasn't appeared, the all-purpose stanza, 'See yonder Pembroke through the trampled corn,' will suffice as a suitable stop-gap to justify you marching offstage to see where he's got to (remember, there's always a character called Pembroke, and there's more often than not some trampled corn).

But what if you're not in a Shakespeare? Let's take the most likely scenario: a conventional drama. And there's no knock at the upstage door. What to do?

Shooting your cuffs can buy a second or two. Adjusting your tie, a couple more (please substitute cracking your knuckles and adjusting the toggles of your hoodie if you're appearing at the Royal Court). Still no knock. OK, look at your wristwatch. If it's a period drama, wind it. If it's a comedy you can always try putting it to your ear and then shaking it, but not if you're doing a play about enforced child circumcision in Northern Sudan.

Still no knock?

Rest assured, help is on its way. The stage management will be doing all they can. The important thing is not to panic. It's time for the Knick-Knack Alternative.

This may sound like a previously undiscovered novel by Robert Ludlum, but it'll save your arse. You walk round the set in an unhurried yet determined manner, picking up any available item of set dressing. If the play is a Coward or a

Rattigan, there'll be no shortage of items you can pick up and investigate, but even if the play is set in a rat-infested crack house in Deptford there's likely to be something to inspect, even if it's only a urine-stained mattress.

So. There's that china dog/picture of your nana/discarded heroin needle. Stroll over, pick it up, turn it over as if searching for some distinctive hallmark – and then put it back.

Still no knock? No need to worry. See that painting/print/poster over there of The Hay Wain/Che Guevara/tennis-playing cutie scratching her naked arse? Wander across and smile appreciatively. Admire the brushwork/straighten it/secure the drawing pins.

By now you should be able to hear the thundering of feet as your errant colleague hurtles down the backstage stairs, four at a time.

If they still haven't appeared, something serious has obviously occurred. They've either fallen asleep, had a stroke, or, as happened during the run of Yes, Prime Minister, have inexplicably turned off the tannoy and are oblivious to your plight.

It was during a Wednesday evening show at the Everyman Theatre, Cheltenham, when the actor playing the Kumranistan ambassador failed to appear. I was at least in one sense fortunate, as the actor playing Prime Minister Jim Hacker was also left marooned onstage along with my Sir Humphrey, allowing us to implement a rarely seen variant, the 'Double Knick Knack', whereby we both wandered around shooting our cuffs and inspecting items of set dressing. The missing actor meanwhile, was three floors up and regaling his friends in his dressing room about the correct way to grow coriander.

Eventually (as happened in this instance) there comes a moment when the audience realise something's wrong. One moment they're as good as gold, the next, you can sense anxiety spreading like a contagion through the auditorium. In the case of *YPM* we eventually had to activate the nuclear option: not in our case 'Feed the Birds' but a chorus of 'There's No Business Like Showbusiness.'

I'm pleased to report the audience twigged what the problem was and thoroughly enjoyed our impromptu chorus, so much so that when the ambassador did eventually blunder on he got the biggest round of the night.

The golden rule is not to panic, not unless you want to end up in the sort of hole I once witnessed happening to two actors during a performance of Shakespeare's *King John*. With the minutes ticking by and the monarch nowhere to be seen, despite several interludes of furious sword swishing, the younger of the two performers left onstage lost his nerve, and without warning blurted out to his senior colleague, 'Where is the King, my lord?'

After a slow burn that would have rivalled Jack Benny himself, the older actor finally unfurled a dark, sardonic smile.

'You stay here,' he said. 'I will go seek him.'

BEING ON

Almost as bad as being 'off', if much less common, is being 'on'. Namely, the act of blundering onstage before your allotted time.

The necessary conditions for this rare occurrence have the same root as its more famous sibling: that is, by losing your place in the play. Which brings me to the incident of the Royal Shakespeare Company and Rolf Harris.

The RSC and Rolf Harris are of course, both uniquely positioned at the opposite ends of the showbiz spectrum. One is a venerable old institution which has been part of the British way of life for many decades, esteemed for bringing high art to an audience in their millions.

The other is a company of actors based in Stratford-upon-Avon.

The occasion in which Rolf Harris tumbled into my life occurred during a stint with the RSC at the Savoy Theatre in London. I was appearing at the time in their celebrated production of *Richard III* (starring Robert Lindsay as the eponymous villain) in the small but showy part of Richard's brother Clarence, the bloke who's drowned in a vat of malmsey wine about ten minutes into the play.

On the night in question, we were giving a special gala performance for the great and good of subsidised theatre. All the bigwigs were present – Adrian Noble, the incumbent artistic director, plus the chairman, trustees, sponsors and assorted members of the Arts Council. Just to add further spice to the event, both my missus and my agent were in the audience: a factor not lost on me as I stood in the wings, waiting for my first brief entrance (the cue for which is, rather conveniently, Richard announcing, 'For here comes Clarence.')

It all started so well. The house lights dimmed, the stage lights came up, and a second or two later I heard Lindsay purring smoothly into action: 'Now is the winter of our discontent. Made glorious summer of this sun of York.' In a mere 32 lines I'd be walking on too, surrounded by a phalanx of guards and monks, headed by an actor with the suitably Shakespearean name of Dickon Tyrrell.

For Julia, the evening was something of a mixed blessing. Notoriously suspicious of any play in which blokes with paunches stand about in sagging chain mail waving swords and uttering phrases like, 'Hie thee hither', she views an evening in the company of the Bard as about as appetising a prospect as a visit to the clap clinic. Yet she'd been happy enough to come along tonight, not only because there was a glitzy reception at the end of the evening but also because, unusually, I was in her good books just now.

The previous day had been her birthday, and as a special treat I'd taken her to Dingwalls in Camden Town to see Rolf in concert, the details of which I now conveyed to Dickon when he asked me in a hurried whisper if I'd, 'Done anything nice over the weekend?'

As I related to Dickon, it had proved quite an experience. Supported by a peppy five-man combo, he'd started his set with his highly individual remix of 'Stairway to Heaven' and culminating in a rendering of his iconic ballad, 'Two Little Boys', the tale of two brothers, who as children play with wooden swords and a shared hobby horse in the back garden, but who soon find themselves playing their childhood games for real in the horror of No Man's Land during the Great War.

As the drum roll commenced, we'd joined in as he crooned the most famous lyric in the pantheon of easy-listening favourites...

'Do you think I would leave you dying..?'

It was just as I was describing this to Dickon that I heard an unexpected guffaw from the auditorium, followed by a round of applause. So intent had I become in conveying my previous night's excursion to Dingwalls that I'd utterly lost track of

Lindsay's opening soliloquy. Where were we? And why was everyone laughing?

There could only be one answer. I was off. Disastrously so. Upon finishing his opening speech, Lindsay had clearly turned upstage to intone, 'For here comes Clarence', and nobody had appeared. Maybe he'd repeated the line. Maybe he'd tried to ad-lib. Maybe he'd even come up with a witty aside to cover the fact his cousin had gone AWOL less than a minute into the drama. Whatever the result, the cause was all too apparent. I was off. And on a gala scale.

I hurtled on as if fired from a catapult, chains clanking, eyes rolling, and accompanied by a posse of monks and warders in various stages of dishevelment. The sight that greeted me left me in no doubt. Lindsay turned to face me with the sick, sweet smile of an actor who's been left for dead.

The next couple of minutes seemed to last a lifetime. I played the short scene with the air of a condemned man awaiting execution. Lindsay, by contrast, looked at me with the glassy stare of someone whose mind was concerned with other matters – like imminent violence for instance. I felt sick.

Afterwards I shambled off, my cheeks aflame and my head bowed. I sat down heavily in the wings and put my head in my hands.

'Well,' whispered the actor playing the Lieutenant of the Tower in a gleeful *sotto voce*, 'That was a shocker wasn't it?'

'I feel dreadful,' I answered feebly. What on earth was Bob going to say about this?

'Never mind,' said the Lieutenant, 'No harm done.'

'No harm?' I rounded savagely, 'I've ruined the whole bloody evening. It was like the Castle Players Farnham out there. How long was he waiting before I came on for fuck's sake?'

The truth, it transpired, had been vastly different from my supposition. While I'd been waxing lyrical about my weekend exploits, Lindsay had no sooner begun his opening speech, than a drunk in the front row of the stalls had staggered to his feet, turned to the rest of the auditorium and begun declaiming the lines along with him.

For the next 32 lines it was a battle between the two of them as to who could shout loudest. Eventually a couple of ushers had intervened, escorting the miscreant up the aisle and out of the crash doors, with Lindsay calling out, 'We'll let you know,' at the departing figure (thus prompting the gale of laughter and the subsequent round of applause). Whereupon he'd promptly forgotten his next line.

Just as he was about to ask for a prompt, brother Clarence had suddenly shot on, rescuing the scene and jolting the play back onto its runners.

It seemed an impossible scenario, but the Lieutenant assured me he'd witnessed the whole thing. And to prove the fact, when I approached Lindsay's dressing room at the interval he was already on his feet and preparing to embrace me in a crushing bear hug.

'Simmo,' he said, 'Thanks so much, buddy. I didn't know where the hell I was for a minute. Thank God you came on when you did. Quick thinking. I owe you one.'

I unfurled a smile of infinite indulgence.

'Do you think I would leave you drying...?' I replied.

Actually I didn't. This wasn't the time to push my luck.

LOSING YOUR VOICE

Your vocal chords are perhaps your most precious, and if you're as stiff-limbed and generally un-coordinated as I am, arguably your only asset.

A pair of identical, quivering slivers of cartilage, pale and gristly in texture and separated only by your clack, they are two lovelorn orphans whose only aim in life is to meet and embrace, and whose futile attempts to achieve congress provides the constantly fluttering curtain through which you blow the air from your diaphragm and produce the sounds which make up your mortgage payments.

They are also invaluable. So what do we do with them? We yell, scream, cough, yosk, smoke, drink wine, drown them in corrosive acid reflux due to eating too many takeaway curries, and generally live in the big city where we inhale lungfuls of exhaust-polluted, cement-filled air that goes straight down our throat and says hello.

After which we expect them to get us through back-to-back shows, Fridays and Saturdays.

At some point in your career, you're going to lose your voice. Whether it's a minor nasal irritation that just makes you sound like Ed Miliband, a husky cough, or the full-blown laryngitis that takes you out of work for weeks on end, is largely up to you. Most of the time the problem will clear up with a couple of early nights and an easing up of your bar bill. But you can be sure the problem will soon escalate if you don't take pre-emptive action when it first occurs – or put a sock in it, as it's sometimes known.

Pretention and cure

If you do lose your voice, the next few paragraphs can save you a lot of money, because basically there's nothing to be done except keep quiet and do lots of steaming. You can either do it yourself at home or pay to go and see a qualified specialist who'll give you the same advice and charge you nearly £200 for the privilege.

What you don't do is go to see your GP, or worse still, hurry off to the chemist for some throat lozenges. Doctors are kind and caring people, and are excellent at spotting everything from impetigo to hiatus hernias, but vocal experts they're not, and their diagnoses are almost certainly likely to be at best useless, or at worst, positively counter-productive.

Similarly, lozenges are to be avoided. You'll find them at the front of the counter, and they always come with comforting encomiums such as 'Doctor Foster's patent pills for the projection of the voice, as recommended for Members of Parliament, public speakers and purveyors of light operetta', and will almost certainly come with a reassuring illustration on the tin of some bloke in a top hat bellowing into a gramophone horn. But they are all basically no more than a gentle anesthetic, and while you'll experience minimal relief for the first few minutes, you'll knacker your voice completely on the mistaken principle that if it no longer hurts it must be fixed.

The one supreme advantage of seeing a specialist, however, is that you'll get ladlefuls of reassurance. And reassurance is the one thing you need, because the biggest threat to a speedy recovery is anxiety. After all, the show must go on, and for performers with laryngitis it's their only topic of conversation – or would be, if they could talk in the first place.

I first lost my voice on New Year's Day before a performance of *Mamma Mia*. With the problem persisting and me sitting at home in despair, lest the whole western economy collapse as a result of my absence, I was eventually sent to one of Britain's top vocal experts, a jolly and rotund gentleman who was an avuncular blend of Johnny Morris and the man who owns the shop visited by Mr Benn.

This is what you can expect for your 200 quid: he'll take a full description of your symptoms and then stick a cold metal tube like a large lolly stick down towards the back of your mouth, on the end of which is mounted a tiny lens that can broggle about and record a full vistavision image of your vocal chords as they try desperately to perform for the camera. He might well ask you to try and speak in falsetto, which won't be easy with him clutching the end of your tongue and a stiff cold rod half-way down your throat, but if nothing else it'll give you a more sympathetic understanding of the exigencies endured by the average porn star.

Afterwards he'll play the images back on a monitor. The chords should be pale and sharply defined. If they're red, inflamed, and have sticky mucus adhering to their edges so they can't meet cleanly in the middle, you've got an infection or have been overusing them.

Finally he'll throw in a few jokes, remind you of the wonderful opportunity you're giving your understudy, and send you home to rest. As regards treatment, he's unlikely to suggest anything more stringent than frequent steaming in a warm shower.

Yet this breezy reassurance will be enough in itself to start the healing process. After all, if he's unconcerned, then why should you be? No talking, plenty of liquids (sugary tea always seems to do the trick for me) and a slice of fresh, juicy pineapple every few hours, and your vocal chords will soon be copulating like a good 'un.

And steam, steam, steam...

Finally, if you're susceptible to such maladies, it's sometimes worth taking a look at your overall lifestyle. Some years ago, I was teaching at a drama school and happened to mention to a fit young male student during rehearsals that his voice seemed perpetually hoarse. It didn't matter what he did and how much he warmed up beforehand, the mere act of hearing him speak was enough to provoke everyone else in the room into clearing their throats and reaching for the nearest jug of water. There seemed no reason for it – he got eight hours' sleep a night, he didn't drink or smoke, and he'd never missed a class.

It was a chance conversation in the canteen about the dulcet tones of the veteran football results announcer James Alexander Gordon that unlocked the problem. The actor in question revealed that he, too, loved the sport – so much so that he played competitive football in Regent's Park every Sunday. This simple two hours' worth of frenetic fun was strafing his poor chords to buggery and rendering him utterly unfit for purpose the next week.

Having identified the culprit, I persuaded the student (albeit reluctantly) to hang up his boots and re-prioritise. His voice cleared, he graduated with flying colours, and the last I saw of him he was playing Sally Webster's love interest in *Corrie*.

CORPSING

One of the most commonly-asked questions of actors is, 'Has anything ever happened to you onstage that has made you want to laugh?'

'Corpsing' is the slang term used by performers to describe the act of giggling uncontrollably onstage when they're not supposed to. It is a terrible and wonderful thing, if only because it's impossible to resist. Think of Brian Johnston in the infamous leg-over sequence on *Test Match Special* ('Aggers, do stop it'). Of all the bodily functions that can inundate your performance – from sneezing to farting to hiccoughing – nothing is so destructive and yet so hideously exquisite.

It's also difficult to conceal from the audience. Without warning, your shoulders are lurching up and down like a bad impersonation of Edward Heath, while your voice is squeaking as though you've just sucked on a helium balloon. There's usually nothing for it but to yield to the whole delicious shame and take the consequences.

There are several ways of trying to stop yourself from corpsing and none of them work. Some actors bite their lip, while others try to imagine their entire family being wiped out in a head-on car crash. Good luck. Nothing will make the slightest difference, and such desperate measures often only make your situation even more hilarious and prolong the agony.

The only accepted method of ameliorating your plight is to take the audience with you. If you can somehow let them in on why it is that you're laughing, they'll gleefully enjoy your distress, and yet happily pick up the play where they left off once it all subsides. Audiences just love sampling a touch of *schadenfreude*.

The most memorable and illuminating example of how to turn uncontrolled corpsing to your advantage, was in a production of the hit comedy *Big Bad Mouse* I saw many years ago in the West End. The show had been running for some time when I saw it, namely by dint of its two leading actors, Eric Sykes and Jimmy Edwards. The night I attended the show coincided with one of those glorious, all-too-rare occasions in which the entire company lost the plot, never to regain it.

Not that it mattered, because what we got in its place was far better. Almost as soon as the show had got going, the actors' collective equilibrium was holed below the waterline when Sykes somehow got his tie caught in the drawer of the office desk he was sitting at. With him unable to move, his fellow cast members were soon reduced to helpless convulsions, and the situation was only remedied when a gleeful Edwards marched off into the wings and eventually returned clutching a pair of scissors.

After that, a collective hysteria seemed to sweep through both cast and audience. With the fragile conceit of the play now shattered, the corpsing fed on itself, until it reached epidemic proportions. Eventually, with the genie out of the bottle and the play last seen disappearing up Shaftesbury Avenue, the two leads simply decided to rip up the script and begin again. Edwards began insisting on an audience round each time he appeared and eventually climbed into the Royal Box, from where he kept up a running commentary on his fellow cast members gamely soldiering on a few feet below him.

They in turn were by now so helpless they could barely get their words out. It was one of the most exhilarating evenings I've ever spent in a theatre. By taking the audience with them, these two old warhorses had turned an unexpected setback into glorious triumph.

In fact, I enjoyed the show so much I decided to see it again the following year. Of course I knew it wouldn't be so funny again, but nonetheless I was still anxious to see the play as written, and to enjoy these two comedic titans at work.

Early on during my second visit, Sykes somehow managed to get his tie caught in the desk, and was only eventually released with the aid of a pair of scissors fetched from the wings. Edwards insisted on audience rounds each time he appeared, and in a final brilliant flash of inspiration climbed into the royal box. The rest of the cast was – it goes without saying – so convulsed with laughter that progress was nearly impossible. I, meanwhile, sat in silent fury. Both this and my previous trip – and presumably each and every performance in the interim – had been both a fix and a fake. I felt like asking for my money back.

But I'd actually learnt an important lesson about corpsing and showbiz. An utterly ordinary play had been transformed into something truly memorable simply by the actors managing to convince the punters they were witnessing spontaneous comic gold, when in fact it had been rehearsed to buggery.

It was George Burns who famously said, 'Acting is all about honesty. If you can fake that, you've got it made.'

YOUR NAME IN LIGHTS

The story goes of a dilapidated and impecunious actor hitching a lift from London to Birmingham by way of a canal barge that's carrying a load of animal fertiliser. At each stop on the route the lock-keeper leans out of his window and asks the bargee to confirm the nature of his cargo. 'I've got a load of shite and an actor,' he yells back.

After the fifth instance, the actor finally speaks up from the prow. 'Could I have a word about the billing?' he says.

For most actors, there are only two states when negotiating with a potential employer. Either they want you, or you want them.

If they want you, the world's your oyster. You can name your fee (within reason), specify how long you want to do the job for, and have your pick of the dressing rooms (they may even redecorate it in your preferred colour). And throughout this labyrinthine process, your thoughts on each and every facet of the project will be listened to as if you were the Dalai Lama. It's a nice feeling.

If, on the other hand, you want them, then you're stuffed. The producers can smell your need; a pungent aroma combining panic, excitement and hope. Once they realise this, your most feeble demand will be met either by a hollow laugh or a hastily contrived explanation as to why it's just not possible in the current climate. One by one your various demands will collapse like sandcastles in an incoming tide, until you eventually cave in and accede to their initial offer.

If your agent can't get the money up, there are thankfully a few other subtle ways of saving a scrap of self-respect, the main one being the question of billing. This is where your name is featured on the poster, included in adverts, and perhaps even illuminated in bulbs on the front of the building.

I've only ever seen my own name in lights once, in a play at the Aldwych Theatre in 1990, and I confess I never tired of emerging from the Underground and seeing those two precious words blinking back at me from the far end of the Strand. Not that I had much chance to – the play closed in three weeks.

Perhaps it's just as well, for electricity can be a fickle thing. I was once assured by the actor Hugh Hastings that while appearing in a play called *I Killed the Count*, he noticed that the 'O' of Count disappeared for some days after a bulb burst, thus transforming the production from a taut detective thriller set in fogbound London to a brutal slice of life on a cattle ranch in the Australian outback. No wonder Diana Fluck changed her name to Diana Dors – she'd obviously taken advice from an electrician.

When negotiating, the best place to ask to be on any poster is top left, immediately above the title (for some reason top right is genuinely considered marginally subsidiary). Bottom right and left are nearly as good, and if you can't manage these you can sometimes negotiate to have your name at the bottom framed in a special rectangle.

As in life, size matters. Stars usually manage to get their names in the same size lettering as the title of the play, with the next tier confined to 7/10ths, and so on until the makeweights at the bottom reads like the equivalent of a supermarket bar code. Sometimes, as a sop to some hot young starlet, producers will add the words 'and introducing'; but for anyone over 40 this can often lead to ridicule.

If you can't manage the billing, there are myriad other piffling considerations that can provide a fig leaf with which to cover your bruised ego. You may be able to negotiate your own dressing room, your personal shower cubicle or even a mini fridge. Such things matter when you're walled up for months on end. In the case of one elderly star with whom I worked, the deal breaker turned out to be the issue of whether she could have her pet dog in her dressing room during the performance. I'm pleased to say the management conceded, and the little chap not only proved hugely popular backstage but also helped keep the mice down.

But even if you're unsuccessful in any and all of these requests, don't let petty dissatisfactions and grudges sour what will be an otherwise unique experience. You're in the West End, where you always wanted to be, and the only reason your wishes weren't granted was because you wanted the producer more than he wanted you. What more could you have done?

Apart from, of course, killing the count.

REAL LIFE

Before we leave *Get me Michael Simkins!* forever, this may be a good time to talk about actors and real life. Or rather, actors and relationships. For while it's easy to generalise, the fact remains that going out with someone who's also in the same profession is not always ideal.

Everything about the acting game is designed to conspire against domestic stability. It's perfectly possible to meet a member of the opposite sex at 10 am on Monday and be simulating sex with them within the hour: and however consummate a professional you may be, if the task of snogging your opposite number is intensely pleasurable, you can be sure your enjoyment will communicate itself in one form or another.

'Would you mind not squeezing my breasts so hard? You're crushing them,' I was once asked by an actress 20 minutes into rehearsals for a play. You don't get that sort of request on your first day at Boots. Or if you do, perhaps you could put me in touch with the particular outlet.

The advantages of living with another actor are self-evident. Your partner will possess an inherent understanding of the forces bearing down on you both: the euphoria of auditioning, the concomitant disappointment, the periods of depression when you can't get arrested, or, equally vexing, the overnight metamorphosis from the Grim Reaper into Keith Chegwin when you finally get the nod. They'll take it all in their stride, instead of the first bus to Relate.

But while you can expect sympathy and understanding when it's your turn in the karmic toils, they'll expect equal amounts in return, and here's the snag: if there's one thing the acting life doesn't encourage, it's consideration for anyone's situation but your own.

'But enough of me. What did you think of my performance?' may parody the way most actors approach daily existence, but only just. And if one of you is soaring into the stratosphere while the other can't get seen, it can heighten feelings already bubbling below the surface: envy, frustration, and what Stephen Fry described as that most corrosive of emotions: self-pity. It's difficult to force yourself to go along to swanky first night parties and endless awards ceremonies when the only thing you've made in the last year is the bed.

AFFAIRS

There are only three certain things in life for an actor – death, taxes and affairs. Even the ones who claim to be happily married are likely to have weathered all sorts of squalls that won't have made it into the press.

At least when you're working from home the vicissitudes of the daily routine are dissipated. But once you're away on tour or a lengthy TV shoot, a happy and secure home environment is about as much use as a chocolate fireguard. Bundled together in unfamiliar lodgings, miles from anywhere, with money in your pocket and nothing to spend it on but visits to National Trust properties, time and insecurity can make for combustible bedfellows. This is why luvvies are so promiscuous once they're living out of a suitcase – it's nothing personal, we're just huddling together for warmth. And it's all too easy to meld fiction with reality.

The RSC at Stratford-upon-Avon used to be particularly susceptible to domestic strife. Indeed, when I first started out in the 1970s, barely a week went by without news arriving of some poor unfortunate mate who'd been spotted driving back along the M40 at 3 am, tears streaming down their face, having arrived at a Stratford opening night only to uncover some stupendous infidelity.

One friend who was married to one of our country's most eligible leading actors used to have a canny way of forestalling any problems, simply by ensuring she turned up a week or two before press night and hung out with the cast after rehearsals. Having previously checked the cast list for her spouse's most likely dalliance, she'd manufacture a few moments in the snug with the leading candidate, before steering the conversation round to the subject of her husband.

'You know,' she'd say airily, glancing out through the bar windows into the street. 'If I found out he was ever having an affair, I'd kill them both. Can I get you a refill?' She rarely had any trouble.

I'm not advocating a policy of tolerance to serial cheating here, merely advising a proper perspective on the nature of the job spec. Once you've been in the biz for a while you soon realise that the majority of emotional fantasies remain just that. Those members of the cast who are now your partner's closest confidantes will soon be the ones whose names they'll be struggling to recall.

Perhaps my favourite tale about the bracing relationship between actors and their itinerant lifestyle was one told to me recently. Early on in his career, the actor in question managed to tap off with a girl who worked backstage with the resident stage crew at a venue in some tough industrial town that the show was visiting for a week. With things advancing smoothly back at her digs, he thought he'd earn some brownie points by attempting to perform oral sex on her.

He'd no sooner commenced than she suddenly yanked his head up from between her knees.

'Don't you come up here with your fancy Metropolitan ways,' she snarled, 'Just stick it in!'

THE SHOW MUST GO ON

I can't leave any section on live theatre without giving brief consideration to this most famous of showbiz commandments.

The tradition of fulfilling your part, come hell or high water, whatever your mental or physical condition, is still hardwired into the DNA of most jobbing actors, so much so it's something of a sacred mantra. Your house may be on fire, your wife eloping with your best friend, but nonetheless you never miss a performance. It's such an inviolate rule that it even inspired Noël Coward to pen one of his best parodies, the song, 'Why Must the Show Go On?'

> *Why kick up your legs*
> *When draining the dregs*
> *Of sorrow's bitter cup?*
> *Because you have read*
> *Some idiot has said*
> *"The curtain must stay up!"*

It's an oft-heard complaint among middle-aged actors nowadays that the younger generation doesn't possess this same do-or-die attitude. Youngsters (they complain) will take shows off at the drop of a hat, inventing spurious injuries or ailments to cover their absence, ones that an older generation would have shrugged off with an impromptu splint or a tot of whiskey.

Musicals, in particular, are particularly prone to abuse in this regard, and it is noticeable how many phone in sick on Friday lunchtime – or the start of the weekend, to give it its proper title. Saturdays are never a good time to be a company stage manager.

But like all homilies, 'The show must go on,' is a good servant but a lousy master.

I taught myself the hard way during a run of a play called *The Old Masters*, in which I was appearing at the (then) Comedy Theatre in Panton Street. The old masters of the title referred not to the two main actors, Edward Fox and Peter Bowles, but to the relationship between two celebrated art critics on which the drama was based. Written by Simon Gray and directed by Harold Pinter himself, it enjoyed a lengthy and harmonious run in the autumn of 2004.

Apart from a couple of spells of laryngitis, I'd not missed a show through illness or injury in 25 years of acting, a fact I was happy to impart to anyone who asked (and many who didn't). My contribution in this particular show was a small one (a 'cameo' as it's called in the trade), limited to a single undemanding scene about 20 minutes into the action. It's also worth pointing out I also had a perfectly capable understudy.

The run of *The Old Masters* coincided with my aged and increasingly infirm old mum having to go into permanent care in a nursing home in Ipswich, the town in which she'd resided for the best part of two decades. One Friday teatime, as I was preparing to go in for the evening performance, I got a call from my elder brother alerting me to the fact that she'd caught a urinary infection and was unwell. 'Perhaps you should come up on Sunday to see her?' he suggested.

By the start of the matinée the following day the situation had worsened. According to my brother (who was now with her), the infection was taking hold and the visiting doctor had expressed genuine concern about her prognosis. Instead of waiting till Sunday, my brother now suggested I come up at the end of Saturday's evening performance.

It's bewildering to reflect on but despite the worsening bulletins being relayed almost every hour to my dressing room, I clung to the notion of completing my two shows without ever seriously considering my priorities. With hindsight, my mental and psychological rigidity undoubtedly had a lot to do with denial – after all, having lasted for 86 years, she wouldn't go now; not for the sake of four or five hours and a packed Saturday night house.

Thus even so, I lingered. By the end of the matinée the situation was no better, yet even now I sat in a small Chinese restaurant on Wardour Street, toying with some noodles and continually glancing at my watch as if trying to solve some complex metaphysical puzzle. For reasons that still haunt me, I resolved to stay on to do my one small scene in the evening, and then skedaddle for her bedside.

I left the theatre the minute I was through onstage. Yet even now, instead of catching the first train from Liverpool Street, I incomprehensibly decided to go home on the tube, make a flask, and then drive there by car. Thus I didn't actually set off properly till nearly 9 pm.

The journey up the A12 was a nightmare of road works, contraflows and Saturday night traffic jams. Just to top it off, somewhere around Colchester the warning light came up on the dashboard (for the first and only time in the vehicle's history), notifying me of dangerously low oil levels in the engine, an emergency that necessitated a lengthy detour to a late-night garage and a light foot on the accelerator for the remainder of the journey.

I parked the car at Ipswich general infirmary just after 11 pm, a full three hours after leaving the theatre. As I hurried in through the double doors, I spotted my brother and his wife coming towards me along the corridor. His look said it all. Mum had died about three minutes before, around the time I was pulling into the car park. When I went in to see her, she was still warm to the touch.

It's a melancholy tale, demonstrating a lack of nous combined with an inability to face up to circumstances. But if nothing else, it's cured me forever of the unquestioning obedience to showbiz's oldest unwritten rule. I've never again allowed a performance to get in the way whenever real life needs prioritising.

PART FOUR

Get Me a Young Michael Simkins!

MICHAEL
SIMKINS

CDA
Caroline Dawson & Belinda Wright
125 Gloucester Road
London SW7 4TE
020-7373 3323
Fax: 020-7373 1110

Height 6 feet 1 inch   Blue Eyes

Walter Matthau once said, 'To be successful in show business, all you needs is 50 good breaks.'

One of the biggest decisions I may have ever made – though it didn't seem so at the time – was back in 1982, when I'd been acting on the stage for five years but without having had so much as a sniff of a TV gig.

The chance to lose my television virginity came from an unlikely direction. My parents still had their sweetshop in Brighton, and one of their regular customers was a tall, fastidious individual in his early sixties, immaculately dressed and with an air of a master spy about him, who, upon overhearing my dad talking about me, mentioned that he worked in the contracts department at BBC Drama and that he might be able to help.

A week or so later he announced he'd secured a part for me in one of the forthcoming BBC Shakespeares; a huge project in which each of the Bard's 34 plays were being filmed for posterity. By now into its fourth season, the drama currently being prepared was *The Merry Wives of Windsor* starring Richard Griffiths and Prunella Scales. I returned home from the pub that night to find I'd been offered my first telly.

The role in question was a one-line servant – hardly a part at all in fact, requiring me for just a single day – but nonetheless it was mine if I wanted it. If I'd accepted, my TV career might have got a kick-start ten years sooner than it actually did. But I turned it down for a nice part in a play at the Thorndike Theatre, Leatherhead. 'Work breeds work,' runs the old showbiz maxim, and I had nearly ten more years ahead of me before I got my next tilt at overnight national exposure. Had I known it at the time, I suspect my choice might have been different.

Theatre and film (you can include TV and movies in the latter category) may be strands of the same profession, but they're as different as chalk and cheese. While many actors successfully straddle both mediums without apparent effort, the requisite skills are as contrasting as driving a Formula One racing car is to steering a traction engine.

Expertise in one doesn't guarantee proficiency in the other. You can hold 2000 people in the palm of your hand onstage and yet look like an exhibit from Madame Tussauds once you're harpooned on the end of a camera lens, and vice versa. Actors who are household names on the small screen frequently have all the charisma of the government front bench once they're in the glare of the footlights.

But of the two, there's little argument as to which is the more powerful. For while it's easy to overestimate the importance of live performance when you're inside the cultural hothouse of the theatreland, once you get outside the M25 the perspective radically changes.

My in-laws in Grimsby, for instance, are wonderful and cultured folk, who enjoy a night out in the West End on the rare occasions they come to stay, yet they couldn't tell you the first thing about what's happening on Shaftesbury Avenue or at Stratford. But ask them for the latest birth stats in *Call the Midwife*, or the goings-on within the cloistered corridors of *Downton Abbey*, and you'll be up all night.

Most actors hold that being able to flit gaily between the two mediums is tantamount to the perfect career. But unless you're already a 'name', it's not always easy to dovetail the two disciplines successfully, or at all. 'If you wish to succeed in television, you have to start saying "no" to theatre,' was advice given to me by one of Britain's most influential actors' agents, not in some casting session in Soho, but at the Chateau Marmont Hotel in Hollywood during Oscar weekend.

And that's because the two disciplines march to the beat of very different drums. Theatre gigs necessarily tie you up each night to a particular location in a particular town, and are often months in the planning. Much of TV, by contrast, is organised and cast at the last minute. Although TV execs profess themselves happy to work to pre-arranged theatre schedules, in private they're decidedly queasy about the prospect. Given the choice, they'll always prefer to go for the next candidate, the one who doesn't have to leap into a cab at 6 pm.

To illustrate just how kick-bollock-scramble TV casting often is nowadays, a couple of summers ago I arranged to meet with an old mate, now living in rustic isolation in deepest Kent. With Friday afternoon upon us, I reckoned it was a safe bet to start the car, yet just as I was pulling into his farmhouse near Canterbury at 4 pm, my agent rang.

A new comedy spoof was being made by Sky, one that brilliantly lampooned the various hard-boiled detective series of the sort that had kept me in employment over many years. The part on offer was that of a man who reflexively orgasms every time he suffers a shock. The scene involved my character going to the mortuary to identify the dead body of his only daughter.

You get the picture.

What's more, it was a straight offer. 'What do you think?' said my agent. 'Do you feel comfortable about faking an orgasm?' I assured her I'd done little else for years.

'When does the job start?' I asked.

'7 am tomorrow' she replied. 'But you'll have to be at location in Hounslow by 6 to go into costume and make-up. I'll get them to email you the lines for the scene. You weren't planning anything else tonight were you?'

By 4.30 pm, I was trundling back up the M20 as fast as the rush-hour traffic and an overturned lorry near Chatham would allow. I got home at 9, learnt my lines in bed, and by 8 am the next morning I'd already climaxed.

During my three decades in the business, I've appeared in trillions of primetime perennials, usually playing policemen, unsuspecting husbands or medical experts ('If you look here you'll see the cranium has been split by a single blow from a blunt instrument with an unusual serrated point at the end') and in amongst it all I've had some pretty hefty parts.

Jobs include extended spells on both *EastEnders* and *Doctors*, guest appearances in *Midsomer Murders*, *Lewis* and *New Tricks*, a regular in the first series of *Foyle's War*, and even a handful of feature films, such as the cult hit *V for Vendetta*, Mike Leigh's *Topsy-Turvy*, and the Oscar-nominated *The Iron Lady*. The distillation of my experiences forms the basis of this next section: what it's like to film, how to approach an interview, what to expect when you get on set, and even what it's like to pop over to Hollywood for a pilot season.

It may not be able to tell you how to win an Oscar. But it may help you fake your orgasm.

CASTING DIRECTORS

It was Coral Browne who apparently said, 'I could never see what Godfrey Tearle saw in actress Jill Bennett, until I saw her in the Caprice eating corn on the cob...'

Casting is everything. According to film director John Frankenheimer, it's 65% of successful directing, and I suspect he may have underestimated by at least a third.

Casting directors are the crucial middlemen (or more frequently, middlewomen) in any TV project, and unless you're a personal friend of the director (which, as we've seen, brings its own difficulties) they're likely to be your first point of contact for any job. Before they can even begin making recommendations they first have to get inside the director's head, work out his or her vision for the project, and then begin the torturous process of recommending the available actors (200,000) for the available role (1). They wield enormous influence, if little actual power, and they're crucial to your chances of success.

The most common misconception is that their job is to get actors seen for parts. In my experience it's the opposite. Their job is to not get people seen for parts. There are so many thesps sloshing around that finding potential candidates is not a problem. The skill is actually in ensuring that only the most suitable ten or twelve get through the door.

Casting directors come in all shapes and sizes. The elite few only deal with major movie projects, others specialise in TV dramas, while yet others specialise in comedy, adverts, or even children's TV. The good news is that most of them are hard-working, approachable and above all passionate about their job. They want you to succeed, and the best will have been around for many years and will thus have an encyclopedic knowledge of the business.

Things they won't generally tolerate are actors who arrive disinterested (many do), underprepared (many are), or who are downright rude about the script (even if they're right to be).

Their natural habitat is usually a third floor office in Soho, in a building in which they have to share the one available bathroom with myriad other businesses on lower floors, ranging from bucket shop travel agents, to women called Candy specialising in re-caning seats. Here they sit day after day, their ears welded to the phone, eyes red-raw from scanning their laptops, and surrounded from floor to ceiling by box files, tottering piles of unmarked DVDs and casting breakdowns, and with applications and 10 x 8 photos strewn across every available surface. They work to ferociously tight deadlines and strict budgets, yet have to remain enthusiastic and cheery in the face of irascible directors, miserly producers and a torrent of needy actors. No wonder their smiles sometimes seem a tad forced.

Occasionally your interview will take place in a hotel lobby or at the studio (especially if it's at the Beeb) but usually you'll have to go their private office for the initial meeting. There's always a small anteroom or cubicle constructed out of plywood batons in the vicinity, just so the meetings can avoid prying eyes; but most are so jerrybuilt you can hear the occupants changing their minds.

If you arrive before your allotted time you'll have to perch in the main office on a rickety chair (from which you'll have to remove a half hundredweight of A4 sheets before parking your arse) and sit listening to their assistant making enquiries about other actors for other parts in other projects, any of which you'd saw your head off to have a crack at.

Should the casting director appear before your allotted time, they'll rarely make eye contact, no matter how many times they pass back and forth in your eyeline; don't take it to heart. It's not your turn. When it is, they'll do their best to make you feel a million dollars, until, of course, you've finished, after which don't hang around trying to make idle chitchat. They're no longer listening.

Apart from these occasional meetings, the only other time you'll normally meet one will be on the rare occasions your agent brings them along to see you in action in a play. Afterwards it's customary to share a few minutes in each other's company, either in your dressing room or at a nearby boozer, but casting directors are notoriously reticent to talk about the show they've just witnessed, preferring instead to chatter on about their dog, their kids, or some current news event on the front pages of the red tops. Don't think they haven't got an opinion on what they've seen – it's just that having already talked shop for eight hours in their office, the last thing they want is more of the same now.

Or perhaps they thought your show was a stinker. You'll never know, unless you ask.

Don't.

Most actors put their head in their hands and groan whenever they hear stories of 'networking', (effectively flushing out a job by making sure you hang out with powerful people), as it's so unutterably crass a way to expend your energies, but the fact remains that reminding casting directors of your presence, either by design or accident, can often prove startlingly efficacious.

I once attended an opening night at the Noël Coward Theatre, only to run into a casting director in the street at curtain down, someone who'd not rattled my cage for some years. 'Oh, hi', she said with some surprise, 'How lovely to see you. I'd forgotten all about you.' At the time her sentiment seemed a crushing indictment, and thus I was doubly surprised when the following morning she called me in for a 22-part drama series. What's more, I got it.

The moral of which is, always keep your guard up. The moment you leave your front door you're already auditioning.

THE AUDITION PROCESS

To learn or not to learn. That is the question.

The issue of whether or not to memorise your lines before going up for a casting is the only subject of conversation among jobbing actors. Which is why you should never sit next to one at a dinner party.

Here's why. Unless you're a star-turn, you'll normally be offered an interview at only a day or so's notice. You'll be required to go into the office and perform a few selected snatches from the proposed role, samples that will be filmed on a tiny video camera and subsequently reviewed once you've gone home.

The director will probably be in attendance. The producer as well, with luck. The casting director will not only introduce you, but also operate the camera and feed you your cues when you come to perform. If you stick a broom up her arse she'll probably sweep the floor as well.

Once you've agreed to come in for the gig, a couple of desultory sides of dialogue pertaining to your role will be forwarded by email via your agent. Occasionally you may get the entire script. Often you won't get the entire script, or anything more than a tiny section of it; which means you don't have the first flying fuck what your scene's about, who you're supposed to be talking to, or where it fits into the overall story.

Despite the fact that the total screenplay may well run to 160 pages of complex plotline, all you've been sent are a couple of cut-and-paste snatches, and a brief accompanying description of your character's personality traits.

'Mr. Benson is tall, 50–55, with a predilection for pinstripe suits and a strong line in sarcastic humour – he fancies himself but doesn't like to show it.'

This brief *précis* (and it will be brief, make no mistake) may also contain a tantalising glimpse into where your character fits into the arc of the story.

'He knows Paul is lying but is aware of the delicacy of the situation at Lombard. Two nice scenes, with a possibility of returning in series two.'

Sorry? Paul who? What situation? And what is Lombard? A businessman, a corporation, or an area in Northern Italy famous for its heavy industry?

Never mind. Your job is to stop whining and try to convince the powers that be that you're cocky, secretive, a smartarse, know someone's lying, are on cordial terms with Lombard, and doesn't want to blow the fact that you know about Lombard in case you frighten off someone called Paul.

And then you get into the actual interview room and the first thing the director asks is, 'Have you got any questions?'

There are a couple of things you can do to help your cause. If the series is already up and running, you can usually rustle up a clip on YouTube. This will at least give you a feel for the characters and the style of the piece. But even if this isn't an option, you can always do what actors instinctively do when faced with a situation requiring preparation, accuracy, and spot-on precision.

You can wing it.

Your job is to give the best interview you can. But should you learn it? Opinion is sharply divided.

My advice is to follow a middle way. You don't want to remain script-bound, but playing it like a starchy automaton won't do much good either. So familiarise yourself thoroughly but don't be afraid to glance down; and if do you have any decent chunks, at least commit these to memory so you can throw them upwards and outwards, play eye-footsie with the camera, and show what could be in store.

Sometimes the odds are stacked against you from the off. I've been up for hundreds of castings over the years, some for parts I was born to play, but many more for which I should never have been let in through the door. Years ago for instance, I recall going up to take over the part of Joey in series five of the BBC sitcom *Bread* from actor Peter Howitt, who'd decided to leave the show to concentrate on other projects.

You may recall the series was set in working-class Liverpool. Now, I pride myself on many things in my professional life, but replicating an authentic Scouse is not one of them (it's only just behind my Jamaican and Geordie for all-round awfulness). Nevertheless a job is a job, and a sitcom is a sitcom, so I was determined to give it my best shot.

My reading was in front of Robin Nash, producer and creator of the series, and at the time one of the big beasts in BBC Light Ent.

'I can honestly say that was the worst Liverpudlian accent I have ever heard,' was his pronouncement at the end of my reading. 'You haven't got the role.'

'Quite right too,' I replied, after which we shook hands and I left.

The thing is, you'll never know unless you go along and have a shy at the coconut. I once auditioned for a dramatisation of one of the celebrated Catherine Cookson novels being filmed by Carnival Productions, in the full knowledge that the obligatory Geordie accent already rendered it a fruitless journey. But no sooner had I walked in than the director apologised profusely, before explaining she didn't want my part delivered in Geordie after all, but in Standard English.

'Would you mind having a go?' I heard her saying through a mist of grateful tears.

I got the gig and spent three lovely weeks filming in Northumbria.

So let's say you've read for the character (with or without looking at the lines) and are now settling down to a few brief pleasantries before you're booted out. At some point during the interview, the director will ask you if you enjoyed the script. There are three possible answers to this request, and we're going to take a moment here to give you a multiple-choice option.

Option one

'Yes, I did. It made me laugh and it made me cry. In all truth it's a dazzling piece of writing and I think it will do well. Quite frankly it was a privilege to have had the chance to read it...'

Option two

'Well. I think it's got huge potential, but you may have a problem with the central conceit. I'm just not sure it's entirely believable...'

Option three

'I'm afraid I haven't had the chance to read it...'

Which of these do you think is most likely to advance your chances?

The answer is, of course, option one. Just as writers only ever want to hear one response to their words, 'Hail to thee, O Great One; rise and lead thy people,' directors similarly need to have their own belief in the project reinforced and acclaimed. Thus the slightest expression of doubt on your part will kneecap your prospects of success.

In any case, the casting director doesn't want to gain a reputation for bringing in gobby shitehawks who are going to be a ton of trouble and start arguing about the art of scriptwriting, so anything less than unalloyed enthusiasm will scupper your chances with them as well.

Interestingly, it's worth pointing out that the second answer is the very worst of the three. The third – 'I haven't had time to read it yet' – may at least intrigue them. By suggesting you're too rushed off your feet with other projects to even have the time to give it a cursory glance, at least you're suggesting somebody who's in demand. And that's always sexy. It means someone else wants you. Therefore you must be good. Dare they choose someone else?

A final word about casting protocol.

At some point it's a good bet the director will want to talk to you about your CV, which your agent will have forwarded to him for inspection and will now be laying on the table between you. They're not actually all that interested, but it's a good ice-breaker, and in any case, they know that by asking an actor to talk about their career they can sit back and close their eyes for a few minutes.

While you sit there, he or she will have a desultory glance down your list of credits until something catches his eye – it might be a series he loved, or hated; or perhaps the name of some rival director you've worked with. It's impossible to predict which of your many jobs he'll alight on, but you can be sure it won't be the one you hoped to talk about.

'I see you worked on so-and-so,' he'll say. 'I didn't see it. What was it like?'

There's only one response to this charged enquiry. Never diss the aforementioned job. Even if it was a pile of cack, even if it sunk with all hands and nearly bankrupted ITV in the process, your answer is that it was fabulous, everyone got on fabulously, you thought the director was fabulous, and you think it utterly fabulous to have had the experience.

The reason is simple. Even if the director's secretly hoping you'll offer up a hatchet job on some hated rival whose downfall preoccupies his every waking hour, at some point during your response it'll strike him that one day soon you may be in an interview room talking about him.

So. Everything's lovely. He's lovely, the script's lovely, every other script you've ever done has been lovely, and you've loved coming in today. Don't learn your lines but learn your speeches. Thanks so much for seeing me, and goodbye.

Nearly. One final tip.

Don't take the script/sides/lines with you when you leave the room. Instead, leave them on the table and stride confidently out. Taking the script away suggests a degree of arrogance. And in any case, you've got so many other scripts waiting to be read back at home that you simply haven't got room in your recycling bin for even one more...

Have you?

LIGHTS, CAMERA, INACTION...

Not so long ago I was asked if I'd be prepared to take part in a dirty two with a High Court judge. I was happy enough to accept – of course I was, I needed the money – but it led to other things. Before I knew it I was involved in a deep three, during which I was required to go in tighter, much tighter. Soon enough I noticed a blonde and a redhead had appeared. As I recall, the blonde was even covered in gel.

Lest you think I'd finally succumbed to the porn industry, these phrases are all part of the archaic language of filming. Dirty twos, for instance, are when the camera is filming two characters, but with the protagonist's shoulder in the foreground, suggesting the action is being viewed from their point of view (POV). A deep three, as the name implies, is a long shot of a trio of characters in the middle distance, while redheads and blondes are types of lights. Pans, tracking shots, crossing the line, reverse angles, tilts: you could write an entire book explaining the finer points of TV jargon. And many have.

THE CREW

The good news for actors is that you don't really need to know all this. You can get along perfectly well in the medium without being able to tell one end of a camera crew from another. Nevertheless, a TV studio can be a strange and unnerving experience for the rookie.

Quite apart from all the unfamiliar equipment and the jargon, there's the crew themselves. There are normally tens of them scurrying about, laying cables, adjusting stands, holding up strange contraptions to the light. Each individual is clad in the identical garb of film technicians the world over – cargo pants in the winter, baggy shorts in the summer, caterpillar boots, T-shirts and Rohan windcheaters. And finally, belts slung across their spreading midriffs, each compartment stuffed to the gunnels with unfamiliar items whose purpose only they know.

Best boys, dolly grips, and gaffers: each has its own set of highly specific duties, and woe betide anyone who attempts a task beyond their remit. They're working long hours at withering speed, and some of them will have worked together many times. Everyone there is dedicated to the single goal of chiselling out seven to eight minutes of drama per day before home time. That may not seem much, but in the case of single camera filming it's a prodigious quantity. A feature film would happily settle for between two and three minutes, while a big-budget action movies sometimes talk in seconds.

Joining a series that's already in full swing can make you feel helplessly out of your depth; a guest at a party in which everyone else is speaking Arabic. If the crew seems unconcerned with what you're doing in front of the lens, that's because they are unconcerned. Their job is to make it all look right, and what you do once the camera rolls is not their problem. The only people you need to listen to are the director, the cameraman and the boom operator. One directs you, one films you, and one makes sure you can be heard.

The first rule of filming is to make friends with the cameraman. He or she has the ability to make or break your performance. They're relying on you to perform your agreed moves consistently and fluently throughout any number of successive takes; so if you're rising from a chair, or striding in briskly through a set of doors, don't do it once as if you're Alan Sugar, arriving for an episode of *The Apprentice* and the next, as if you're a geriatric struggling for the last digestive at the care home.

Consistency is the name of the game. Do the right thing, make their job easier, and they'll reciprocate by ensuring your performance looks twice as good. And while they may never learn your name, they'll frequently offer a quiet word of thanks once the scene is in the can. Praise such as this can make you feel a million dollars in this alien environment.

THE ACTORS

The friendliness (or otherwise) of your fellow actors can also enhance or destroy your experience. If you're only doing a couple of scenes in one episode you'll be entering a tight-knit world in which the leads have already bonded over many weeks. If they've any manners, they'll do all they can to welcome you on board, introduce you to their colleagues, include you in their chitchat and even fetch you a piece of cake from the tea trolley. At the very least, they should be able to rustle up a polite enquiry as to whether you had a good journey here. Things like this can make a big difference when you're unsure of yourself.

If, on the other hand, they don't even offer any of these common courtesies, they're what we habitués of the filming world refer to by another piece of highly technical jargon: tossers.

I recall one comedy drama series in which I briefly participated. The scene in question, which was to be shot in a swanky new bar in the city of London on a Sunday afternoon, was a relatively simple one, involving a young banker-type trying to chat up the female lead, not knowing that she is, in fact, an angel.

I arrived for my one scene feeling pretty confident. Yet it evaporated like morning mist once it became clear the actress I was working with didn't have the slightest intention of speaking to me throughout the entire three-hour shoot (in fact, she could only just bring herself to look at me during the take).

By the time we got to our close-ups, it was I, not her, who felt invisible, and long before my increasingly dispirited portrayal was captured for posterity, my confidence had shrivelled like male genitalia after a dip in the North Sea.

I'm delighted to report the series bombed and that her career has somewhat stalled as a result. Angels may not exist, but there is, it seems, a God.

THE EQUIPMENT

Because of the complex logistics and financial implications of overrunning on any given project, filming will always continue if it's possible to do so. Even if the location is flooded or one of the lead actors is struck down with flu, there's sure to be a plan B in place to ensure something's shot, even if it bears no relation to the proposed schedule; a system usually known by the term 'weather cover'. The only insuperable problem is on the rare occasions that the camera goes down on you (notice the porno jargon creeping in again).

The only time I've ever heard of a project being stopped in its tracks in such a fashion was an instance related to me by a mate who'd been working on a new drama set in Manchester. Worse still, it occurred on the first day of filming, and to a rookie director.

After the first couple of takes, the sound operator alerted the debutant to the fact that a rogue noise was inundating all the takes and ruining the dialogue. Every time the cameras rolled it started up again; a dull, metallic clinking sound.

Despite everyone's best endeavours, it proved impossible to locate the source of the noise. New magazines of film were slotted into place, every conceivable working part of the camera was squirted with a special air jet to lubricate the working parts, mobile phones were removed, even the air conditioning system in the studio was switched off at the mains. Yet still the sound persisted every time the camera whirred into action. With four hours already lost, the cast was sent for an early lunch while the decision was made to strip the entire camera mechanism.

Eventually the source of the sound was located. It turned out to be the director jingling change in his pocket.

REVERSES

Here's a useful rule of thumb. You can always judge the quality and manners of the other actors by whether they do their 'reverses'.

Let me explain. You're shooting a scene. The director films the master shot of the two of you talking, then moves on to the medium, which still features the two of you, but much tighter. Finally they come to the close-ups.

They'll start by filming the close-up of the other actor (especially if they're the lead), before moving on to the corresponding one of you.

When they film the other actor, protocol dictates that you stand just beside the camera lens and offer up your responses, so your co-star has both an eye-line to focus on, and some genuine emotion to play off. Then it's your turn. For which, of course, the other actor will reciprocate the courtesy. And this is what is called the reverse.

This may be the moment when the other actor finds a reason not to stay. They've got a headache, they've got something in their eye, their feet are cold, they've got a lot of make-up to clear off, their car's waiting, their teenage son needs picking up from school, or they've got an awards ceremony to go to.

And as they're first up tomorrow at 7 am, would anyone mind?

Either way, before you know it they'll be off to their dressing room with little more than a mumbled apology, leaving you to perform your own close-up, the shot which justifies your existence in the project, to the assistant runner, who's 17, has dyslexia, has never read the scene and who doesn't look at you because his eyes are locked on the script. Not that it matters much, because even if he did look at you, he has all the artistic expression of Kim Jong-un.

Proper actors always stay to do their reverse.

PACING YOURSELF

Here's the best bit of advice I can offer up about succeeding in television.

Don't come too soon.

The two greatest dangers any greenhorn actor faces in this strange and exotic world are indolence and catering. Both phenomena play little part in live theatre, where you'll either be working hard or getting on with your own domestic routine back at home.

Not so on television. It's in the nature of TV drama that you spend vast swathes of time simply waiting about to do something. Any casual visitor to a location inevitably summarises the experience by declaring, 'I can't believe there's so much hanging about', but in fact, contrary to the glitzy image pedalled by the media, hanging about is 99% of the job spec.

So be warned. Your big moment may come long after your alarm clock has woken you. Even if you're called at 6 am, it might be 10 or 11 am before you're called to the set. Plenty of time to don your costume, visit the make-up truck, sample the free breakfast, and return for multiple visits throughout the morning to overdose on pastries, muffins and cups of tea.

Even if you're not required till the afternoon, the second AD will suggest you, 'Come in for lunch'. The reason given will be so you can familiarise yourself and say 'hi' to the director, but in reality they simply want you on hand in case they get a spurt on. A plate of roast lamb and some jam roly-poly is a small price to pay for corporate peace of mind.

Be assured, they won't get a spurt on. Everything takes a long time, and actors are the one given in this complex set of logistics. Before you, there's the cameras to position, then the sound, then the lighting, not to mention the laying-down of the runners for the complicated tracking shot.

Ready to go? Not quite. Now we've got to wait for the sun to go behind that big cloud so the shot will match up with the one taken before lunch; then there's a further hiatus while we wait for the overhead flight path into Heathrow to change.

Ready now? Well, nearly. We still need to send the third AD off down the road to stop the traffic and move on those yobbos who are making wanking signs from that multi-storey car park in the distance.

You may be on call for hours, possibly days, before you're actually needed. Sounds nice, doesn't it? Gossip and grub: the lifeblood of the itinerant actor. But both these seeming allies are in fact your silent assassins.

Because what do we do? Well, let's have another bacon bap. Then a doze. Then a wander along to the nearby trailers to have a chat with the other actors, the majority of whom will be equally bored and looking for a bit of banter to pass away the morning. The hours will soon fly by, with plenty of stories and lots of laughs. By which time it's lunch.

Unless you're careful, by the time you're called onto the set you'll have yakked your way to a standstill and in addition have half a hundredweight of calorific, stodgy food washing around in your digestive system.

By the afternoon you'll be fatigued, sluggish, and mainly preoccupied on trying to stifle an overwhelming need to belch or go to the toilet. You'll have bloodshot eyes and a mouth that tastes like Alan Yentob's jockstrap.

The best actors, by contrast, don't waste their resources. Which means that when they get to their close-up at 4.40 pm, they'll nail it. I witnessed this expertise at close hand when I did a spell on the movie *The Iron Lady* with Meryl Streep. The scene involved a complex dinner party (always the most exhausting of set-ups, with its myriad cutaways and continuity nightmares) and Streep's ordeal at the head of the table was compounded by the fact she was playing the former PM in her dotage, a look that required being fitted with intricate hairpieces and complex prosthetics. By the time she waddled onto the set at 8 am she'd already clocked up three hours in the make-up chair.

After introducing herself to the other actors grouped round the table, and apologising in advance for not dropping her accent between takes ('Do excuse me, but if I drop Thatcher's voice I'll never get the bloody thing back'), she then completed a 12-hour day in ferocious heat and underneath layers of padding and latex. Throughout it all she was charming, funny and inclusive, but she didn't waste a drop of energy. Which is why she was still able to act everyone else off the screen at the end of the day. Which is why she ended up winning an Oscar. And in case you were wondering, she also stayed to do her reverses.

SOAPS

For most jobbing actors over the age of 35, getting into a soap opera is the holy grail, and a regular berth in Walford or Weatherfield is your best remaining chance to access the things you once dreamt of: fame, fortune, and an appearance on *Celebrity Big Brother*.

Being on the nation's screens each night not only offers instant celebrity (albeit of a temporary nature) but so much more. You'll attend swanky awards ceremonies, receive lucrative invites to open supermarkets and nightclubs, get asked onto talk shows, be offered freebies to exotic holiday destinations in return for a few hundred well-turned words on your experience, and write your own autobiography (*Michael Simkins – My Hollyoaks Years*). And if you can't manage to write it yourself they'll even arrange for someone else to do it for you. You'll also earn a substantial amount of money.

That's the good news.

The bad news is that you'll be working murderously hard, up to five or six days a week, week in, week out. When you're not filming you'll be trying to learn mind-boggling quantities of lines. You won't be able to stop at a motorway service station for a cuppa without bringing the place to a standstill, or have a discreet meal *à deux* without having an autograph book stuffed in your face every time you lift a spoonful of soup to your chops.

If you go out you'll be snapped outside your local Tesco Metro by some low-life pap, who'll then display your *dishabille* for the delectation of the masses (with the addition of specially-printed fluorescent arrows to accentuate sweat stains, pimples, cellulite or unwashed hair).

Needless to say, if you're snapped snogging somebody outside a nightclub with your hand half way down the back of their jeans, the incident will be marketed as if it's a hanging offence (unless it's with your regular partner, in which case it won't get a mention).

In addition to the long hours and the pressure to deliver, the conditions at work are surprisingly spartan. And with the necessity of getting three or four episodes in the can each and every week, you'll be working whatever the weather and however wretched you're feeling. Soap operas don't stop for anything.

How it's all changed. When I was growing up there was only one, *Corrie*, and it was on only twice a week. Thus the storylines could happily move at the speed of continental drift.

Back then, the burning issue was whether Ena Sharples would go to the corner shop for some sweets, or break open the box of Newberry Fruits given her by Minnie Caldwell at Christmas. A storyline such as this could keep the programme simmering happily for months on end.

On the Monday evening she'd get up from her chair, by Wednesday she'd be in the hall putting her coat on, and eventually, days later, the bell of Florrie Lindley's corner shop would ring and in she'd walk, having taken several episodes to traverse the 15 yards from her front door.

Only then would the nation have the answer to the question that had been occupying our collective conscience for so long

– would Ena plump for a quarter of Nut Brittle or go for the Cough Candy? If anything really terrible happened, such as the night Valerie Barlow electrocuted herself on the steam iron, the entire nation stopped, almost literally.

Nowadays, someone being electrocuted by a steam iron would hardly get you to the first ad break. One moment an entire metro train is crashing down from the viaduct, wiping out a fair proportion of the cast in a single episode, and yet within a couple of days the survivors will all be back in the Rovers Return all talking about the problem of dog mess on the pavements.

People get murdered, suffer miscarriages, fall to their doom from the roofs of apartment blocks, yet no sooner are their vital organs splattered over the concrete than they're bundled into the soap equivalent of Room 101 and never referred to again. And no wonder – for there are new murders, new affairs, new people teetering on apartment blocks.

Which is, of course, why soaps are so addictive.

Because of the close-knit nature of the project, joining the cast of one is akin to standing on a station platform and trying to board a speeding train by hooking the handle of your umbrella to one of the carriage doors. As your shoulder is yanked from its socket, all you can do is to grit your teeth and hope you can cling on until you can get your fingers round the handle and begin scrambling properly aboard.

Once you've managed to do so, you'll find yourself in a Kafkaesque scenario, whereby you're sharing your ride with a load of people whom you know intimately, but none of who have the first idea who you are. Look! – there's Dot Cotton! – there's Gail Platt! – there's lovely Norris from the corner shop! And over there in the corner is that girl who pulls pints in the Woolpack that your mum used to say needed a damned good wash.

These individuals have been in your sitting room most evenings for the past decade or more (in truth you've probably spent more time with them than your own parents). You know them intimately, and now you're working with them. Except of course, it's not them at all. It's June Brown, Helen Worth and Malcolm Hebden.

No wonder it can be an unnerving experience.

In 2013, I did a stint on *EastEnders*. Having never previously been a particular follower of the series I began watching episodes religiously, if only to ensure that when I finally came to filming I didn't aim my lines to the wrong character, or mistake Steve McFadden for the second AD and ask if he'd mind making me a cup of tea.

Until then, I must confess to having retained a certain sniffiness towards soap actors. They were skilful, no doubt about that, but was what they were doing really acting, or, as someone suggested to me recently, merely 'behaviourising?'

Ten weeks in Walford was all it took to realise that in the case of the best of them, there's a quiet type of genius at work. Most soap stars are working fiendishly hard, memorising tracts of scripts (much of it necessarily inconsequential), often at short notice and with sudden changes of dialogue thrust upon them just as the camera is set to roll.

They have to summon up tears and rage on demand, deliver their lines with accuracy, fluency and speed, and make sure they hit their marks while doing so. They also have to negotiate their character through some highly unlikely *volte-faces*, as the scriptwriters heft their character from one fresh crisis to another.

Worse still, the episodes are not filmed in chronological order, so the regulars will be juggling endless storylines and various time frames in their heads. Because of this, soap stars acquire what can only be called a facility for instant acting. To say they can turn it on and off like a tap is to suggest a degree of denigration: but it's a marvellous and powerful thing to witness at close quarters. They can laugh, cry, or, in the case of one actress I worked with, even blush to order – it's seamless, utterly believable, and a master class in economy, precision and verisimilitude.

Never mind Steppenwolf or Lee Strasberg. This is the real method deal.

PAYING THE BILL

The hazards for the unwary newcomer is best illustrated by my first-ever soap gig – on ITV's *The Bill*.

The trailblazer in hard-bitten copper-on-the-beat TV series, this fast-moving chronicle of daily life at Sun Hill Police Station managed exactly 2400 episodes, and in doing so gave parts (and practice) to literally hundreds of actors. Technically speaking it wasn't a soap at all – or at least that's always what the producers claimed – but apart from its stand-alone storylines, it ticked all the boxes for a conventional soap, namely two or three transmissions a week, ongoing narratives, teams of regulars filming episodes concurrently, and with the whole enterprise fuelled by a small army of writers, producers and admin staff. It even had its own permanent studio in south London.

But unlike most soaps, it also required hundreds of actors to fill one-off parts – criminals, victims, shop assistants, solicitors – and thus proved an invaluable nursery slope for the young actor who didn't know a dolly grip from dolly mixture.

'I'm going up for *The Bill*', was the most oft-heard expression among thesps bumping into one another on the street, so much so that the weekly journey on the Northern Line down to the base in Colliers Wood became something of a ritual. I went for so many over the years I could virtually have made the journey blindfold.

Like all soaps, the turnover was furious. In fact, it was arguably the trailblazer in dispensing with the traditional methods of measured camerawork and intricate lighting, in favour of a more fluid, *cinéma-vérité* approach, with cameras crashing through doors, following characters up stairwells and along corridors, almost as if the cameraman had barged in while the actors were still rehearsing. Which at times was pretty much how it was. And terrifying for those not accustomed to it.

Although my debut in *The Bill* was minimal (one line – *'Thank God you've come, he's down there by the water feature and he means business'*), the episode I'd landed was a specially commissioned, big budget two-parter, about a deadly bomb lying concealed in a holdall at the bottom of an escalator in a busy shopping centre, with some disgruntled nutter threatening to blow it and everyone else to kingdom come.

The vital scenes were to be shot at Brent Cross shopping centre, then the biggest purpose-built mall in the UK, and thus it had to be filmed on Sunday when the shopping centre was not open for trading (remember those days?). It also required hundreds of extras/support artistes/background to play terrified shoppers. By 6 pm we had to have it in the can or make do.

At which point enters specialist Bomb Disposal Officer Lance Corporal Michael Simkins.

I arrived at Brent Cross at 7 am on the Sunday morning to be greeted by the customary location filming scenario I was eventually to grow so used to – a squalid car park occupied by a laager of pantechnicons, Winnebagos and catering trucks, and populated by a tiny handful of unit drivers, all leaning on the bonnets of their Mercedes and reminiscing about the old days when they worked for the Kray twins.

Despite the hour, the tarmac underfoot was already slimy with pools of stagnant, soapy washing-up water and various other detritus, much of which it was best to avoid stepping in or examining too thoroughly.

I was delighted to discover I had my own dressing room (known in the business as a 'three-way'), a mobile portakabin divided into three compartments and with my name scrawled on a sheet of paper to denote my momentary status. It was a proud moment. Surely it could only be a small step from here to a personally embossed canvas chair and my own chef.

Filming was already in progress, so having donned my army uniform and matching beret I sat happily in my three-way, surrounded by toast crusts, shirt pins, and old call sheets from previous episodes, falling gently into a migraine inducing stupor, courtesy of a Calor gas heater roaring away in the corner.

I was only rescued from carbon monoxide poisoning by a knock on the door just before 11 am. 'Right then sir,' said the third AD (they always call you sir because it saves them having to remember your name) 'We're ready for you'.

Inside, Brent Cross was like a zoo. Thousands of exhausted extras lounged about, eating sweets and sitting on the floor reading *Puzzler* magazines, while in between them the film crew busied about, lighting the area at the top of the escalator in readiness to shoot my entrance.

Eventually the director, a harassed young woman named Cindy, came across and introduced herself. But if I thought she was about to take me aside for an in-depth discussion about the psychological intricacies of my character, I was to be disabused. Remember, this is soap.

Having placed me at the top of the escalator and discussed the various moves and progressions of the shot with the lighting cameraman (a process known as the line-up) the director stood me down for several more minutes while final checks were made. My brief scene with the regular from Sun Hill was to be only one segment of a long tracking shot filmed on a steadycam (a portable camera strapped to the operator's chest), following the officer as he threaded his way through the shoppers, onto his brief exchange with me, and then on to a concealed balcony from where he'd spend a few moments looking down on the nutter.

With the minutes ticking by and no sign of any actual filming, the second AD trotted up and asked if I'd like a snack, and soon I was munching on one of the most gloriously greasy sausage rolls I'd ever eaten. Catering on soaps is always high on calories and short on nourishment, but having missed breakfast it was just what I needed. If this was what a career in TV was like, I'd finally discovered my life's mission.

I'd just finished my final mouthful and was still trying to find a handy pocket in which to stow the tin-foil wrapping, when I was aware of a commotion nearby. Through a scrum of extras I could make out a policeman shouldering his way towards me through the throng; one I immediately identified as the regular with whom I would share my brief exchange.

He approached me and stuck out his hand. Just as I was about to introduce myself and tell him how much I admired his work, I heard him offer up his first line of our dialogue: and in a split-second I saw that behind him was a cameraman and a boom operator with a microphone on the end of a long pole, focusing on me from over his shoulder. We were already trying a take.

I can't recall whether I gave my correct line in response, but it didn't matter much as my mouth was still full of processed pork. Having delivered an incomprehensible facsimile of my one speech, and in doing so sprayed about a half hundredweight of puff pastry over his tunic, I stood trying not to choke as he swept on past me and back into the crowd.

'Cut!' I heard someone say.

And that was it. Job done. Minutes later I was back in my three-way and hanging up my outfit. I'd just committed to celluloid my first ever appearance on British television and had done so while eating a sausage roll.

It goes without saying that I learnt fast. Never again did I allow myself to be caught unawares, and after a few more gigs I soon acquired the knack. But I never forgot the first rule of soap: you'll always hit the ground running.

Incidentally, there was a curious aftermath to this incident. Despite my bomb disposal officer being one of the most inconsequential roles ever seen on British television, it was eventually to gain a fame and mystique far beyond its merit. It so happened that Thames Television, who made the programme, decided to decorate the walls of the studio corridors down at Colliers Wood with stills from the series. And as luck would have it, out of all 2400 episodes they could have chosen to feature, a huge photograph of me standing in a beret, still with half a cheek full of sausage meat, was chosen as the image for the corridor leading to the staff canteen.

Over the next two decades, more actors and directors saw me in that photo than watched me on the box. It led to a mistaken and entirely spurious reputation for always being in work, and I dread to think how many availability checks I missed out on as a result of this misconception. But at least I was famous – sort of.

IN TOMORROW'S EPISODE...

For most actors, their time in soap will be limited to a few weeks or months, just until their storyline is exhausted. Nevertheless, for those who do become residents, there will come a moment when the thorny issue arises as to whether it's time to leave.

It's likely to prove one of the most difficult decisions you'll ever have to make. Your life will have dramatically changed since you arrived, red-faced and anxious, a decade or so ago. You'll have bought a bigger house, you'll have acquired a taste for luxury holidays (of course you have, you've worked hard for it), you may now have kids, and on those few occasions when you get to meet other jobbing actors out there in the real world, they'll assure you that, 'It's bloody chilly out there.'

It's always bloody chilly out there. Nonetheless what will happen if you decide to leave? Never mind that the rest of Equity is wondering how to get in while you're staring back, wondering if you dare get out; once you've packed your bags and leapt off the apartment block, will you soar into the cosmos or drop like a stone? The problem is, you won't know till you take the leap.

It's all too easy to see a career in soaps as the universal panacea for all the gnawing uncertainty. But many years after my first appearance on *The Bill* (and having returned to play several different characters in the intervening years), I gained a different perspective when I found myself back at Colliers Wood in early 2006, this time playing a businessman whose daughter is caught up in a siege at her local youth club.

On the day of the shoot, I found myself being bussed out to the location with several of the regulars, including one with whom I'd appeared several times. But if I'd been hoping to find that most rare breed of actor, the one who's continually employed, professionally secure, and with a high public profile and an enviable standard of living, I was in for a shock.

Throughout our brief journey he kept up a steady, if unthinking, stream of consciousness about his myriad worries. Would he be asked to stay on for another year? What should be his response? How much more money should he ask for? Was it time to leave and try something else? What storylines did they have in mind? Would he get something really juicy or was he destined to stand behind the front desk for weeks on end? Was he getting stereotyped? Why hadn't he heard from his bloody agent? What was going on out there in the rest of the business?

The individual in question had enjoyed 23 years of consecutive employment, yet despite this he seemed a parody of the itinerant, self-obsessed neurotic actor travelling on the barge and asking the lock-keeper if he could have a word about the billing. Truth to tell, I found his anxiety oddly comforting.

The moral is, whatever and however well you're doing, the daily neurosis that attends the job of acting never goes away.

There's no escape. Whether you're working in Walford or Wal-Mart, you merely swap one set of opportunities and anxieties for another.

WHODUNNITS...

Apart from soaps, the most common form of employment for jobbing actors is the TV murder mystery.

You know the thing I mean. First suspect is murdered before the opening credits. Second suspect is murdered just before the first ad break. Then a hiatus while the detective careers around in a vintage car, knocking up the locals and having desultory drinks in country pubs with his trusty sidekick – followed by a final grisly slaying (normally heralded by a shot of a gloved hand turning a door handle at dead of night) just before the final break. Then finally, the breathless dénouement, where our hero bursts in and bundles the miscreant to the ground just as they're taking aim once more.

Cue police, sirens, lengthy explanation as to why it turned out to be the least likely suspect of the lot, and then the final tracking shot from high up in the trees of car doors slamming shut and police driving away with the villain.

Murder is a dirty word ...
If there's one thing we Brits like, it's a good murder. The more the merrier in fact. Three per episode is the statutory minimum, and hopefully more. God knows what the death toll in the tiny village of Midsomer is like, but I wouldn't want to live there.

I've done time in them all: *Lewis, A Touch of Frost, Above Suspicion*, several Agatha Christies and Barbara Vines, and four series of Lynda La Plante's *Trial and Retribution*; during which I've played everything from the pre-title dead body, through numerous red herrings and villians, right up to the investigating officer.

The best thing about murder mysteries is that they're classy. You'll get decent locations, a read-through before shooting commences (for which you'll get paid extra) and even a personal car to transport you back and forth on your allocated days.

You'll also earn your initial fee several times over. For so popular are they as a genre, that they're repeated regularly for several years, as well as sold widely abroad. Decades later, and just as you're rummaging down the back of the sofa for some loose change to get you through the weekend, the letterbox will rattle and a cheque for a sizeable sum will plop onto our doormat. Murder mysteries may have done for thousands of poor unsuspecting victims, but they've saved countless more impecunious thesps from putting their head in the nearest gas oven.

What are you driving at, Inspector?

Unless you're playing the eponymous hero, the best parts are the ones who manage to stave off early death. If your character is discovered trussed up in a bin bag before the end of the opening credits you'll struggle to make much impact with your role. If, by contrast, you get the murderer whose true identity is only revealed in the final moments, you're laughing all the way to the cast and crew screening.

If cast as a victim, please take best advice and make sure you die in a position that is comfortable. You don't want to have to lay jackknifed, chest-upwards, over a *chaise longue* for hours on end while DCI Barnaby or Jack Frost have to film three pages of dialogue over your inert body. Behind a sofa is the safest bet.

Playing the murderer is, of course, the best of all worlds but it comes with one enormous handicap: memorising the speech explaining just why you had to do away with half the population.

You know the sort of thing – you've been wrestled to the ground just as you're about to plunge the dagger in and now standing in handcuffs and surrounded by burly constables, you've been invited by our hero to explain the reasons for your crazed behaviour over the previous 53 minutes.

'I hated her you see. I always have. She was my wife's first cousin. Dorothy was her real name, Claire was merely the one she'd invented just so she could get into the house and befriend Charles and Mary in order to get at Gabriella's fortune. She'd been Gabriella's confidant when she was married to Arthur, my brother's old tutor. I knew she was trying to blackmail Gabriella, and I wouldn't have it. So I let myself into Peter and Mark's house while they were away for the weekend with Gordon and Harriet, but I hadn't realised Graham was staying there, so when he discovered me I had to kill him too, and then leave his body in the garage owned by Winnie and Lionel so it would look as if Claire had framed them all by coming over while they were out at the golf club with Rufus.'

It goes on like this for several more pages before a long pause, after which the culprit says wearily:

'I don't expect you to understand, Inspector...'

Too right. Whether in the Gorbals or Godalming,

confession speeches are impenetrable, interminable, and almost impossible to learn. In any case the audience will have long ago given up on the convoluted chain of events you're endeavouring to tease open, so you're saddled with the double whammy of having to deliver an un-actable speech in the knowledge that no-one's following it because they're all turning to one another and saying, 'Well who'd have thought...'

You do, however, get some lovely close-ups, and if you ask nicely, the make-up girl may even give you some fake tears. Pure gold for your demo showreel...

YOU KNOW MY METHODS

My favourite summation of the screen actors' craft came from the inimitable James Cagney, when he said, 'Find your mark, look the other fellow in the eye, and tell the truth.'

As in all branches of the profession, the leading protagonists are extremely skilful at their craft and you can learn a lot by studying their methods. I've worked with most of them, and their expertise in bringing each new episode to life is something else. Keep an eye open if you get the chance.

My time as Sergeant Hugh Reid in the very first series of *Foyle's War* gave me the chance to witness a very particular form of genius close-at hand. The actor playing Foyle, Michael Kitchen, already had a prodigious reputation on both stage and screen, and his character as Foyle is famously chewy of disposition, not given to hysterics or wild outbursts of emotion, preferring to leave the baddies to condemn themselves out of their own mouths. At times he hardly seems to speak.

And here was the problem. So adept was Kitchen at being able to summarise the whole content of a speech by a simple glance, that it gave the scriptwriters something of a headache. It soon became apparent that Kitchen could convey the entire sentiments of long speeches with a single sideways grimace of the sort that was to become his character's trademark.

'I can do that speech with a look,' he'd often say; and what's more, he could.

All well and good, but the repercussion was that swathes of the script were being lost. Fortunately, the producers soon adjusted accordingly and the show turned out to be one of the great hits of the genre. But if ever an actor demonstrated the principle that a picture paints a thousand words, Kitchen was the man to do it.

WRAP PARTIES

Wrap parties are impromptu beanos, thrown by the production company at the very end of a filming project, to reward everyone for their monumentally hard work over recent weeks.

They're usually flagged up at short notice, and if possible should be arranged so as to dovetail with the very end of the gig – ideally only an hour or two after it's completed, allowing just enough time for everyone to nip home and freshen up, but not enough time for the whole sense of giddy relief to dissipate.

Usually they'll be thrown at an intimate venue in central London. There'll be a free bar and wall-to-wall margaritas. Custom also dictates that the venue should never be quite large enough to accommodate the guest list, a situation that further intensifies the air of savage hedonism.

A good wrap party should be sweaty, grossly overcrowded, overlaid with screamingly loud music, and populated by people getting rat-arsed on bottles of Mexican lager with wedges of lime stuck in the neck, and all screaming at one another at the tops of their voices.

If you've worked on the project in any capacity you'll receive an invite, even if you only did a single day on it several weeks ago.

And here's the snag. The party is for the poor sods who've endured all eight weeks: the regulars, the drivers and caterers, and above all, the crew and technicians, most of whom will have aged years in the process and who won't have been able to enjoy more than an odd glass of alcohol for some months lest they fail to wake up in time for their next day's call at 5 am.

These are the rightful recipients of such a shindig, the ones who've soaked up so much stress and pressure. But if you've only been a casual participant my advice is to avoid them. I've had some of the loneliest evenings of my life wandering round wrap parties. It may seem a jolly notion to link up with old muckers for an evening with a free tab, but you'll end up searching desperately for anyone whom you recognise and who'll talk to you.

Those who are prepared to talk to you will only be doing so because they've made the similar mistake and are now feeling as lost and dispirited as you are. You'll end up having conversations such as this, at necessarily ear-splitting volume just so you can make yourself heard above the din…

'Who did you say you were?

'Brian.'

'And if you don't mind me asking, what's your part in the project?'

'Pardon?'

'I said, "What's your part the project?"'

'What's my what?'

'Your part. Your role.'

'Oh yes, no, I'm not actually in the series; I drove the vans which contained the rainmaking machine. You know, for when they needed rain.'

'When they needed what?'

'Rain. For rain scenes.'

'Oh rain scenes, yes.'

'That's right, I've got a small special-effects equipment rental business out in Virginia Water.'

'Did you say Virginia Water?'

'That's right.'

'Yes I know Virginia Water. My cousin Madeline lives there. Near Gomshall. Do you know it?'

'Sorry, where?'

'Gomshall, is it called?'

'Oh yes, Gomshall, I know Gomshall. Are you an actor then?'

'Yes I am.'

'So what have I seen you in..?'

Finally you'll get the message and troop off into the night; dismayed and dispirited, and with the sound of 200 crazed celebrants singing, 'Hi, Ho, Silver Lining' following you on the breeze.

THE FUTURE STARTS HERE

I can't finish any section on television without mentioning the nemesis of the modern actor.

I speak, of course, of HD.

HD – or High Definition Television to give it its official, butter-wouldn't-melt-in-the-mouth moniker – is still only in its infancy as I write this: yet the mayhem and destruction it's already wreaking among the ranks of Equity suggests things are only going to get worse.

There's now no hiding place for the lived-in face. Back when I was lad, when moisturiser was unheard of and TV transmissions were in 405 black-and-white, the picture quality of most television dramas was so poor that trying to work out who was who, was an evening's entertainment in itself.

Then came colour and 625. And suddenly the world seemed a wonderful place. Now viewers could enjoy every nuance of an actor's facial expressions, allowing a more textured, thought-driven style of TV acting rather than the thick-cut theatre-based methodology that had hitherto prevailed. And with colour adding yet another dimension to the viewing experience, actors really could dispense with the grand gesture and concentrate on subtlety.

When I watched my first colour broadcast sometime in 1967 – the American sketch show *Rowan & Martin's Laugh-In* – the effect was so garish and dazzling that I had to watch it through splayed fingers. But for actors the camera lens' ability to access both our skin tones and our innermost thoughts was a godsend. *I Claudius, Rumpole of the Bailey, Brideshead Revisited* – no wonder the period came to be known as the Golden Age of television drama.

But now the devil literally is in the detail. Nowadays every single blot and blemish of your fizzog is available for all to see in withering clarity. Anyone with dodgy veneers, ancient fillings or a yellowing tongue can expect to have their most intimate aural blemishes splattered over the nation's sitting rooms in eye-watering detail.

So intrusive has technology become that one leading soap actress of my acquaintance recently admitted to me that she never watches herself in HD. 'If I did I'd no longer be able to act,' she explained ruefully, 'I'd either have to contemplate a head transplant or suicide.'

I soon saw what she meant. My appearance in HD in the spring of 2012 not only marked my debut, but also that of the scar over my right eye I'd got when I fell against the rocker of an armchair aged six, the dimple in my lower right cheek left by a mouth abscess in 2001, and the innermost recesses of my nostrils, which resembled something you'd see David Attenborough hacking his way through in pursuit of his beloved mountain gorillas.

Apart from making the lives of the make-up artist supremely difficult, it's also made the question of whether to turn to artificial aids to prolong your shelf life an impossible dilemma for jobbing thesps. Yet while creases and laughter lines now show up like the contours of an ordnance survey map, an anaesthetised upper lip in HD can make you look as if you've been punched in the mouth or suffered an attack of Bell's palsy.

Luckily for me it's all happened a bit too late to matter. But if you are only just starting out, you'd better be prepared. Floss your teeth, stay off the fags, buy a nose hair trimmer, get plenty of sleep and invest in a good moisturiser.

Either that, or find a firm specialising in cryogenics.

HOORAY FOR HOLLYWOOD

Sooner or later, if you build up a sufficient head of steam in theatre, or gain a sufficiently tasty profile on television, you'll begin to fantasise about having a crack at Hollywood.

For many British actors, a fantasy is all it remains, something to be mulled over during those idle hours in between doing something else. For a few, particularly those who are currently 'hot', the prospect of boarding a plane bound for L.A. proves irresistible. And for the tiny fraction of that number who strike gold, life will never be the same again.

Tinseltown is a city built on tears and disappointment, and its atmosphere is heavy with the thwarted dreams of anyone who ever won third place in their local beauty contest and got on a Greyhound bus. Going up for jobs is a scary business. And that's deliberate. Because the whole industry is designed to remind you each and every day just how astronomically high the stakes are.

If you succeed, the rewards are eye-watering and Hollywood makes you feel like you've solved every problem it's ever had. But fail, and you'll come away with a sense of being no more than the shit on someone's shoe. Each interview, each fresh opportunity, is a blazing lottery ticket.

I once asked an actor friend of mine why he stayed out there, trying to beat the odds, suffering the daily ignominies and disappointments, when he could simply return and resume a perfectly respectable, if unspectacular career back in Britain.

"Do you know anything about football?' he asked me by way of reply.

'Sort of,' I responded.

'Well look at it this way. Hollywood is the acting equivalent of the World Cup. Everything else is the Evo-Stik League, Southern Premier Division…'

Just how utterly different things are over there is best illustrated by an incident that happened to me a year or two back. I got a call from an actor friend of mine, who, having decanted from the UK to forge a career (and a family) over in Hollywood, had been back to see his folks in Aylesbury for New Year. Now it was mid-January, and time to return for pilot season.

His agent back on the West Coast had already lined up a whole string of tasty potential projects, the first of which would be conducting their initial interviews while he was still in the air. Thus he was putting a couple of auditions onto videotape to beam over, so he could be kept in the mix in case they fancied seeing him for a recall once he landed. And he needed my help.

'Simmo,' he explained, 'I'm due to pop into the offices at Spotlight to put something down on tape to send back to LA. Two separate projects, both of which need me to read a couple of scenes. Thing is, I want to do it properly. Rather than speaking my lines into a vacuum I'd love to have a real actor off camera to feed me my responses. Would you have time? There's a free lunch in it if you say yes.'

I was under the cosh at the time with rather more prosaic projects of my own, but I was keen to help, and he'd mentioned the magic words 'free lunch'. In any case, I'd done hundreds of such auditions myself at Spotlight, albeit for domestic castings, so I knew the form. Even with two separate gigs requiring a couple of scenes in each, it shouldn't take more than 40 minutes to pop them on tape if my own experience was anything to go by. I said I could give him an hour.

I was about to learn my first lesson about Hollywood, pilot season, and the difference between 'them' and 'us'. I'd expected to turn up, speak the lines to camera with script in hand, just to offer up a flavour, and go home. Thus when I arrived I was surprised to meet my friend lugging an entire suitcase up the stairs. It was packed with everything you might need to perform a one-man show at Edinburgh. Costumes, hats, miniature lights and lighting stands, even make-up.

It transpired he'd not only hired the room, but the camera, the monitor, mixing equipment and even someone to operate it. It took him nearly half an hour to prepare for the first project, that of a slimy gigolo in the Deep South in some mini-series, taunting his nervous young bride with his tales of sexual conquests. When he finally emerged from the toilet he was clad in skin-tight jeans, his hair slicked back, and with his formidable biceps freshly oiled in a cut-away t-shirt. He'd even brought a straw hat and a sun lounger.

In addition, he'd learnt both scenes dead-letter perfect. Each one took nearly ten minutes to deliver, and after each take he insisted on watching the entire thing back on the playback monitor before attempting it again. Two scenes, three takes on each, with an equal amount of time spent reviewing the takes: nearly two hours gobbled up.

The whole lengthy process was then repeated for the second project – this time a secret agent in a crowded restaurant trying to do a deal with a call from his kidnapped spouse. This one required a complete change of costume and make-up, a repositioning of the lights, and the same endless process of different takes, followed by a review of the footage.

The whole event occupied nearly four hours, after which there was no time left for the free lunch.

'Why have you gone to all this trouble just for an initial interview?' I asked him as I left. 'Matey,' he replied, 'It's what you do. Welcome to Hollywood.'

In Britain we make bicycles, in the States they make cars. This statement may sound like some grand economic pronouncement by the head of the IMF, but in fact it's the way one actor described to me the chasm between the acting business as approached here, and how it is over there. Everything in Hollywood is on a vast scale, with budgets to match. Films and movies are churned out as if on a factory production line, while TV series are in production 24/7. The possibilities are endless. Sadly, so is the queue of actors in contention.

This all means it represents the Mecca for all aspiring thesps. However big you are in the UK, it's in Tinseltown where the real fame and fortune lies. If you're successful, you can end up with the trappings of real success – a house in Beverly Hills, a private jet, a coke habit and a selection of pneumatically-inflated lovelies to serve your every need. Swimming pools, movie stars. In Britain it's show; in Hollywood, it's business.

Consequently, LA attracts thousands of Brits each year to have a tilt at pilot season, the annual feeding frenzy during which the majority of the forthcoming projects are divvied up.

Some arrive with prodigious domestic reputations, forthcoming projects they can employ as calling cards, and with agents and publicists already strewing their path through immigration with palm leaves.

Many more just rent their flat out for a couple of months, book a flight and hope to bunk down in a friend's spare room. For the majority, it's little more than an extended holiday and the chance to sample, albeit largely vicariously, the wonders of La-la land. For the lucky few, it will lead to stardom and riches beyond their imaginings. All you need is iron self-belief, a hide like a rhinoceros, and an ability not only to dream but to self-delude. You also have to be able to manage a convincing American accent.

The snag is, you never know whether you'll be the lucky one. It's a virtual casino, in which, as long as you've got a place at the table, there's always the chance 'red' might come up, When Dionne Warwick sang, 'In a week, maybe two, they'll make you a star', she captured perfectly the mindset which lures you there, and if you're not careful, traps you forever. The weather's beautiful, the food's to die for, and there's always the promise of hitting the jackpot just round the next corner.

As one veteran described it to me recently, the problem for Brits sampling the whole glitzy, depraved carnival, is that it's not easy to return to real life.

'Once you've experienced turning left into first class, it's much harder to go back to turning right into economy', was how he put it.

Having never sampled the former, I'll have to take his word for it.

GETTING THERE

In order to work in the States, you must either have a Green Card, a special O-1 visa, or some powerful friends.

If we exclude the third possibility (if you've got powerful friends you don't need my help) this leaves you with two alternatives. Practically it's only one, as a Green Card isn't possible to begin with, not unless you've already got dual UK/USA nationality or are happy to go through with a sham marriage. So let's have a look at the most likely option to get your foot in the transatlantic door.

An O-1 is a special document which allows you to try your luck stateside without having to go through the grubby and disagreeable business of swearing allegiance to the Stars and Stripes and putting yourself in the firing line if they ever go to war with China.

The visa doesn't allow you to work everywhere – a couple of the major studios remain beyond its remit – but broadly speaking, it allows you up to three years in LA to go up for auditions, accept offers, and get on the payroll. You can subsequently apply for a 12-month extension, as and when the need arises.

To secure a O-1, you will first have to convince the Department of Homeland Security that you are, 'An alien of extraordinary ability' (their words, not mine). What the man with the crew cut wearing the Aviator shades deep in the bowels of the Pentagon needs to be assured of is that you're a truly exceptional talent, whose presence in his country would fill a special and unique niche that no other individual on the planet can ever quite occupy.

In theory, this is a cinch. You simply have to get a number of influential people from your address book to confirm in writing your status as an unparalleled genius and saviour of the free world. If your address book contains the names of Donald Trump, Condoleezza Rice, Julia Roberts, Tom Hanks, Warren Buffett and Hillary Clinton, you're laughing.

If however, the best you can offer are Russell Grant, David Dickinson, Howard from the Halifax adverts and that nice lady who presents *Gardeners' World* on BBC2, the issue is somewhat more complicated.

Never mind. The important thing is to get the letters. You can always hire a lawyer who specialises in such, and who'll help you correlate the necessary paperwork. For which, of course, they'll exact a substantial fee.

The most important consideration is to find some people with headed notepaper. It says much about the quaint old-fashioned way they do things over there that headed notepaper still impresses the man with the crew cut. So you ask your sponsors to offer up (on headed notepaper) 30 or 40 lines as to why the United States is stuffed without you.

About 15 or 16 examples should suffice – fewer if they're genuine big-hitters, more if your trump card is Adrian Chiles. Or you can do what some people do, which is fake them yourself and just get your friends to sign them (*'Hi, I'm Martin Scorsese. Simmo's a genius'*).

But this is only the start of it. In addition you'll be required to accumulate a dossier of awards, reviews, press cuttings, testimonials and old programmes, anything to convince the man with the crew cut of your luminance and integrity. Anything and everything that might buttress your candidature will help. You may not think that winning best newcomer in the *Manchester Evening News* Theatre Awards circa 1988 will improve your chances, but the man in the Pentagon won't have even heard of Manchester, let alone the *Evening News*. All he knows is that someone, somewhere, has given you an award.

The business of bringing together all these disparate elements is a lengthy and complicated one, and you should be prepared for the long haul. If you're successful, you'll be invited to attend the American visa office in central London for a final grilling. They will ask you questions about your life, purpose and aspirations and will almost certainly take a dim view of points on your driving licence or any unpaid parking fines.

You can also apply for your partner to accompany you as what's called, 'a trailing spouse', a role for which I'm already something of a natural.

The other requirement for a O-1 is that you must have some imminent stateside projects for which you're already booked. The reality is you're not booked at all – if you were, you wouldn't need the 0-1 visa in the first place. You know that, your lawyer know that, but the man with the crew cut doesn't.

So to circumvent this problem, you'll have to invent some bogus jobs for which your name is already heavily penciled. 'Uncle Hal' in series two of the all-action pioneer drama *River Deep Mountain High*; the senior consultant in a new 12-part hospital-based teen romance called *Cut & Thrust*; after which you're down to provide the voice of the Giant Grampus in a new kids' animation series, *Trouble in Toytown*. That sort of thing.

Don't worry. The man with the crew cut doesn't watch TV anyway. He's too busy trying to weed out shifty undesirable foreigners who'll invent anything just to get through immigration control to worry about your application. It'll be fine.

The process is lengthy, unwieldy, time-consuming, stressful, and will cost you, from soup to nuts, approximately $5,000. But if that's your poison, then good luck. You've got 36 months to make an impression.

Upon asking another veteran of the process about the difference between a O-1 and full US citizenship, he assured me there's only really one worth mentioning. When you arrive at USA immigration on a O-1, the customs official says, 'Are you planning to work here during your stay?'

When you show them a Green Card, he merely says, 'Welcome home.'

PILOT SEASON

Pilot season lasts from the end of January through to March; during this eight-week orgy of opportunity there'll be hundreds of projects being cast, and tens of thousands of actors vying to get seen for them. At the height of the mayhem you can find yourself going up for several interviews per day. A friend of mine once summed up the experience as akin to being serially date-raped by every low-life sleazebag in Hollywood.

The first thing to know about Los Angeles is that everything takes time. Remember, you're in huge sprawling city with no centre and virtually no public transport (courtesy of the motor industry who made sure all the tram and train lines were torn up and trashed back in the 1930s). If you haven't got a car you're either a bum, or been convicted of DUI (driving under the influence).

Consequently every single living being is dependent on the car in order to get around. A journey from Santa Monica on the coast to a studio at Burbank will take anything from half an hour to three, according to the traffic. Freeway driving, like pilot season itself, is not for those of a nervous disposition, and seasoned veterans assure me the best investments you can make are a reliable car, a satnav and a head on a swivel.

Even when you reach your destination, the parking lot will be the size of Ealing and several blocks away from where you're actually supposed to be; and while there'll be a specially designated area for celebrities, usually right across from the main entrance doors, as one of nearly 50 Joe Blows you'll be directed to 'Parking Structure Z', a bleak compound up to 40 minutes' walk from your appointment. So leave yourself plenty of time.

The pre-read

The idea of the pre-read is to see if the project in question thinks you're even worth a look-at in the first place. Remember, in Hollywood, time is money, and people haven't got time to waste if you're not right for the part. Of course, if you're sufficiently far enough up the acting food chain you may be able to circumvent this doleful pre-op and go straight to surgery. But for most actors, 'sufficiently far up the food chain' is an elastic concept, and invariably refers to those individuals who are just a tiny bit more famous than you.

What happens is this. You go in to the casting director's office and read a scene to them (or rather, perform a scene to them – the notion of not learning your words beforehand is an alien concept in Tinseltown). I've chosen the phrase 'to them' rather than 'with them' with care, for they won't be offering anything back. Instead, they'll sit looking back with the dead eyes of a two-day-old cod; and that's because they're 'assessing you' (their words, not mine).

Within a few sentences they'll either tell you to stop because it's fine and they'll be getting you back to meet the team, or to stop because, 'You're wrong for the part, you're not attractive enough, and the rhythms of your speech are totally incorrect' (as was told to one friend recently). If the answer is the former, you go home and wait for the real torture to commence. If the answer is the latter, you go home and shoot yourself.

Initial interview

Your initial interview will find you pitched against up to 40 or even 50 rivals, all of whom are ideal for the part. Once invited in, your five minutes of fame will be filmed and scrutinised by up to eight individuals, including the producer, director and the 'creative team'. There's no chit-chat: no, 'How was your journey here?', no request for news about your family or whether surf's up on Venice Beach. Instead, a simple, 'Hi. You ready?'

The answer is yes.

Once you're finished, they'll thank you for coming and return you to the parking structure to collect your car and punch in the co-ordinates on your satnav for the next appointment.

Within half an hour you'll know their decision. The news will be broken to you via a call from your agent, your personal manager or even your entertainment lawyer, and will come just as you're negotiating your hired Chevy back out onto the San Bernardino Freeway. It'll be only one of two responses. 'You did great,' or, 'It's not going any further.'

If you did great, things immediately begin to crank up: for before the studio contemplates getting you back for the recall they'll now want to know your 'quote'.

Your 'quote' is the episode fee you would expect to realise, were you ultimately to be selected for the role. This figure will be based on a complex series of statistics involving what you were paid for your last job and the several before that (even if it was back here for the Beeb), but what's really happening here is that the studio wants to negotiate the deal before it gets serious.

Remember, they're looking to tie you down not only for the pilot and an initial series of up to 12 episodes, but for six or seven years after that. In the unlikely event the show is a smasheroo, you'd need never work again. Thus the cards are currently stacked in their favour. You want them more than they want you, so it's in their interests to wrap things up in advance while you're still desperate, but while you're (now) carrying a scintilla of hope.

The studio test

This is the second (or third, depending on your place in the food chain) phase of the casting process. Upon arriving, you'll be handed a 30- or 40-page contract, thrashed out between the studio and your lawyer, and covering everything from the initial pilot fee right through to series seven. In the event of any problems, you'll have to call your lawyer before going into the meeting. There usually aren't any problems. These people are sharp.

Whereas before there were six or seven assessing you, now there'll be ten or twelve; the ones who met you first time around of course, plus the studio executives.

Habitués of studio tests talk of two types of experience. Either the room is 'pretty warm', or it's 'pretty cold'. If it's warm, it probably means the execs have already earmarked you as their favourite. If it's cold, you've only just snuck in and are basically there to make up the numbers. But this doesn't mean you won't get the gig.

'Hi. You ready? Let's go…'

You'll get the result of your studio test just as you're inching your hired Chevy back out onto the San Bernardino Freeway. Once again it'll be your agent or personal manager making the call, and as before, either, 'It went great', or, 'It's not going any further'.

The network test

This is where things start to get really serious. Instead of the bare office that's been the venue for your previous encounters, the network test will probably take place in a tiny screening theatre, an environment that only ratchets up the anticipation. There'll be up to 25 individuals in attendance, not only the creative team and studio execs, but now the network execs from Fox or CBS, who are looking to buy the programme from the studio and who thus have a keen interest in who's going to be on board. Whatever the studio bosses may think, if the network bosses don't like you, you're stuffed.

'Hi. You ready? Let's go…'

By now, you'll be one of only two potential candidates left in the frame. Or maybe three. Sometimes the studio includes what they call 'a ringer', some poor sap who still thinks he has a chance, but who's actually been set up to go in before you in order to make you, their preferred candidate, look good in front of the network chiefs.

The ringer doesn't know that, of course. The ringer thinks he's still in with a shout. Which of course he is. Because the studio execs won't know he's the ringer and perhaps will choose him after all. The ringer might even be you.

The stakes are huge. Even if you only ever get to make the pilot you're going to make a good deal of money, certainly enough to get you through the rest of the year if you take it easy and nurse the clutch of your hired Chevy through a few more tens of thousands of miles. Candidates must leave nothing to chance.

But let's assume the news is good. You've nailed it and you've got the pilot. Now at last you can relax and celebrate.

Except you can't. Because you haven't.

One acquaintance managed to get through all the interviews, studio tests and network tests, signed the 50-page contract, and duly turned up for the read-through. At the end of the morning he was just inching his car out of parking structure when his manager called. The studio hadn't like his read-through. They thought there'd been no chemistry between him and the lead actress. He'd been fired.

Although he got his full pilot fee (around $50,000), the next day he was once again surfing the San Bernardino Freeway.

But let's assume you've made it through the table-read, you've filmed the pilot, which has actually got picked up against all the odds, and you're now well into filming series one. Now, at last, you really have made it.

Except you haven't. Because out here, even when you've made it, you haven't necessarily made it. One of my best mates ended up doing the lead in a huge 12-part TV series for Disney. It represented a enormous break for him, and as if to confirm his burgeoning status, one evening while driving along Sunset Boulevard, and with the first episode about to be transmitted on coast-to-coast TV that very weekend, he saw workmen on a nearby skyscraper unfurling an image of him 40 metres high.

Dual nationality, a beachside apartment, a 12-part series, six of which were already in the can and with the seventh about to commence shooting the following day. And now the final seal of celestial endorsement for any jobbing actor – his mug plastered across a hoarding big enough to be seen from outer space. He'd made it.

The next day he arrived to begin filming episode seven. Around 11 am he noticed a minor commotion on the studio floor, and almost at once the executive producer walked onto the set in the middle of a take.

'Ladies and gentlemen,' he said smoothly, 'as you may know, the viewing figures for the first episode over the weekend haven't been as good as we'd anticipated, and we've taken the decision to pull the rest of the series with immediate effect. Please take a few moments to clear your dressing rooms, do stay for lunch in the restaurant with our compliments, and if you could all be off the lot by 3.30 pm we'd be most grateful.'

The following day he was driving with his wife and family along Sunset Boulevard once again. High up on the wall of the skyscraper, workmen were already tearing down the poster.

When I asked him what the necessary quality is to survive in Hollywood, he smiled ruefully and answered, 'Simmo, you've got to learn to love the word "No".'

AND THE AWARD GOES TO...

It was Lord Byron who described fame as, 'Being known by people of whom you yourself know nothing, and for whom you care as little.'

Nonetheless, if you work hard, remain fit, and enjoy Walter Matthau's 50 good breaks, you too will eventually arrive at the summit of the acting profession, preferably in a stretch limo.

I'm referring of course to the annual Hollywood event synonymous with success in the entertainment industry. Who'd have thought, when you started out all those years ago at the Watermill Theatre Newbury, that one day you'd be sharing the red carpet with the great and the good of Tinseltown? Yet here you are.

'May I see your invitation sir? Thank you, straight along and to the right.'

And now you're standing in a slowly-moving queue, swapping nervous glances with Halle Berry and Steven Spielberg. The doormen are saluting, the walkie-talkies are crackling, the fans are screaming, the police helicopters are hovering, and in less than ten paces (and a couple more security checks) you'll be stepping between the roped-off barriers and into Valhalla.

'Please sir, look this way, can you lift your head up, thank you. Over here now, that's it, could we have a side view, and just one more? And now over here sir please...'

A bank of perhaps a hundred photographers are lined up on one side of the entranceway, some perched on tiny stepladders, those in front using their elbows and camera equipment as defensive weapons with which to maintain their pitch. And all of them have their lenses trained momentarily on you.

'May I see your invitation sir? Thank you, do you have any ID?'

You open the top button of your rented tux to reveal a tiny laminated card on a chain. 'Michael Simkins', it reads. 'VIP. All areas permitted.'

'Thank you Mr. Simkins. Enjoy your evening.'

And there before you in the queue is Antonio Banderas. There's Melanie Griffith, her lips like something out of an Ann Summers' catalogue, and with cheeks the consistency of sugar icing. If you leaned forward you feel you could push your thumb through her pale, luminous cheek, and find yourself tickling her epiglottis.

'Excuse me sir, do you have any mobile phones or recording equipment on you? We operate a strict non-operational policy, so if you could show me they're switched off. Thank you, if you'd like to go straight in...'

And there's Annette Bening. There's Alan Alda and Clint Eastwood. There's Hilary Swank, carrying her Oscar in one hand like it's some novelty doorstop she's picked up in a fire sale at Poundland, wondering whether she can be bothered to cart it home.

'Would you like a glass of champagne, sir?'

I'm speaking, of course, not of the Oscars. They're a relative doddle to get into as long as you know the right people. No, I'm talking about the subsequent shindig, the one that really does redefine the word 'exclusive.' I'm speaking of the *Vanity Fair* post-Oscar-night party.

Of all the various gatherings, the *Vanity Fair* bash is arguably the glitziest of the lot. Since 1984 when the first official one was thrown, the occasion has forged a reputation as the place in which to see and be seen once the gongs have been dished out. And that's because it provides one of the few opportunities for the great and the good of Tinseltown to let their hair down.

And no wonder, for security is ultra-tight. Publicists, personal managers, bodyguards and even agents are discouraged from attending. Cameras are banned, mobile phones confiscated, and anyone even caught scribbling notes in a jotting pad is threatened with expulsion (which is why the men's toilet cubicles are continually occupied). Stars need to know they can relax before they can relax. In any case, Graydon Carter didn't get where he is today by mixing with the hoi polloi.

Gaining admission to this most discriminating of gigs is nearly as hard as acquiring a O-1 visa. Yet in February 2005 I managed it, courtesy of a leading UK national newspaper that sent me over to LA to record my impressions of the event.

I'd already spent the hours in the run-up to the party mixing with the rich and famous, mainly by hanging about in hotel lobbies and cannily timing my use of the lifts. On the day itself, I'd even hitched a ride to the Kodak Theatre (where the Oscars were staged) in a stretch limo with one of the nominees. Sitting in a car the length of my sitting room, surrounded on all sides by identical vehicles all moving at a steady 20 mph, and with cheering crowds and snipers on every rooftop, had been an experience to savour. So this is what fame felt like.

And now, at 11 pm on a sultry West Coast evening, with the statuettes attributed for another year, I was here, at Morton's Restaurant in West Hollywood, for the biggest, premierest party of them all.

The one advantage of being a nobody where everyone else is a somebody is that you become invisible. Nobody knows or cares who you are. Nobody needs you. Nobody has a screenplay to pitch, or a calling card to press into your palm, or a lunch date to propose. Nobody wants to touch the hem of your genius. And because of this, nobody can see you.

I took full advantage of my enforced anonymity. Over the next three or four hours I wandered at will, stopping only to gawp or to refill on bubbly, and spent minutes on end studying the most famous actors on earth from a distance of mere centimeters: yet not once did anyone meet my eye or ask me what the fuck I thought I was staring at.

Sometime towards the end of the evening, with the clock approaching 2 am, I was stumbling uncertainly along a walk-way surrounded by fake greengrocers' display grass, when suddenly I saw a figure tottering towards me. Female, about 5' 6", neatly dressed in a jade-coloured trouser suit, with black heels and salt and pepper hair elegantly coiffured, there was something about her that acted like an electric cattle prod on my senses. But who was she?

She was old – just how old it was impossible to say, due to the staggering quantity of cosmetic surgery. Her original features were in there somewhere, but hidden like an optical illusion.

I crossed my eyes and stared hard. For several moments nothing happened. But just as she was nearly past me, the transformation occurred, the surgery clarified, the creases fell away, and I realised I was looking at Jane Russell: once one of the most glamorous movie stars in the world, as well as lover of Howard Hughes and owner of the most magnificently cantilevered front elevation since the Norman Conquest.

Indeed, she'd once been considered the only woman sufficiently eye-catching to be able to star alongside Marilyn Monroe without ending up being as anonymous as I was now.

Russell's appearance here this evening seemed to represent everything wonderful and insidious about the acting game. In one sense, her very presence was a magnificent example of how showbiz keeps you young and hungry, long after the others have consigned themselves to a life of watching *Countdown*. Here was a woman still strutting her stuff at the age of 83. She may no longer have it, but at least she was trying to find out where she had mislaid it.

Yet her features, and those of so many others around me, also betrayed the crushing pressure that success in showbiz can exact. Of the hundreds whose paths I'd fleetingly crossed since my arrival, there seemed to be barely an individual over 40 who hadn't succumbed to surgical or chemical intervention in order to prolong their career.

It was late, and I was becoming maudlin. Besides, I had an early morning plane to catch. This time tomorrow I'd be back in the London and preparing for an interview for *Emmerdale*. Hollywood would soon become Cricklewood.

Perhaps because of this, I suddenly wanted somebody to recognise me too, here tonight, just once, before it was too late; even if they didn't mean it. But who was I kidding? Unless the Coen brothers had happened to be staying incognito in Harrogate in 1985 and caught my Hans Andersen, it was never going to happen. At least not here. That sort of stunt really does only occur in Hollywood musicals.

I went to the cloakroom, retrieved my coat and mobile phone, and called a cab. And it was while I was waiting in the foyer that I heard it.

'Simmo!'

A woman in her thirties with bright blonde hair was waving at me from between a forest of celebrities. She shimmied over. 'Dorka. Remember me? We worked together on *Castles*.'

Through a sea of fatigue the details came swimming back. Dorka? With a name like hers, how could I forget? We'd worked together on a series back in 1996 or '97. As far as I remembered she'd been head of make-up for a Sunday night drama I'd made for the Beeb, one that had failed to capture the attention of middle England and been subsequently dropped after the initial series.

'What are you doing here?' she asked.

'What are you doing here?' I replied. I felt like I was suddenly in the denouement of my very own rom-com.

It turned out Dorka had subsequently become Clive Owen's personal make-up artist; in fact nowadays he never went anywhere without her, which explained her presence here this evening. (Owen had been nominated earlier in the Best Actor in a Supporting Role category for his performance in the film *Closer*).

After a few brief pleasantries and some chitchat about the whereabouts of mutual acquaintances, Dorka and I wished each other well and parted. She had given me my 15 seconds of fame. I could leave America a contented man.

It's some years now since my one brief glimpse into the secret life of stardom; yet even now, nearly a decade on, whenever I wake in the middle of the night from nightmares of penury, humiliation and driving up the San Bernardino Freeway in the wrong direction, all I have to do is to look across to the hook on the inside of my bedroom door, to where my tiny laminated label still hangs on its chain. Sometimes it catches the streetlight and winks back at me. 'Michael Simkins. VIP,' it says. 'All areas permitted'.

In fact, only recently I was reminiscing with my wife about the event. 'Could you have imagined in your wildest dreams that one day I'd fly to Hollywood, be driven to the Oscars in a limo, and be recognised at the most exclusive showbiz party on earth?' I said dreamily.

Her muffled reply came from somewhere deep within the duvet.

'To be honest darling, I don't think you've ever featured in my wildest dreams...'

PART FIVE

Who Was
Michael Simkins?

MICHAEL
SIMKINS

c/o Spotlight

Height 6 feet 1 inch   Blue Eyes

A couple of married friends of mine, both successful in their own areas of the business, admitted recently they'd just dumped an entire trunkful of old videos and scrapbooks chronicling past performances into a skip marked, 'general waste' at their local civic amenity site.

And with one mighty heave, it was gone – old programmes, back editions of *Plays & Players*, posters, flyers, good luck cards, mementos, and entire sets of past *Spotlight*s, not to mention miles of videotape recordings.

At first it sounded a draconian, not to say capricious act. After all, they've got a teenage son who himself is hoping to go on the stage. This sort of journeyman archive is exactly the sort that is likely to prove irretrievable once it's been cast aside. Yet my friends assured me the sense of relief they felt as the whole clutter disappeared beneath mountains of MDF and soiled toilet bowls was well worth the cost of the petrol.

Their reason was both straightforward and practical. The son will one day inherit all this junk. And that's essentially what it'll become. It's stuff that he won't ever want to watch or rifle through – and in any case there are far better examples of them in action available at the click of a mouse – and leaving this legacy of lumber will give him an insuperable problem once they're quietly tucked up in the care home.

He would be unwilling to do the deed himself for reasons of guilt, yet with no desire to wade through it (and no VHS machine on which to do so) this cornucopia of clobber would have merely transferred from their attic to his, to be passed on in time to his own offspring; who, one suspects, will be somewhat less sentimental.

You don't need to ask where you are in terms of ageing. The actors' directory *Spotlight* will do it for you. Where five decades ago you first toddled in through the category marked 'Juvenile', in the intervening decades you've made a slow, steady progression through the entire book – 'Younger Character', 'Leading & Younger Leading', 'Character'– until finally your agent suggests it's time to move once more. What she means is to tick the box marked 'Old Gits, M to Z' on this year's renewal form. This is your penultimate move. The next is to Obits.

Most actors don't give up the business; the business gives them up. The most common complaint about the acting game is that it's unfair. But in fact it isn't at all – it's merely indifferent. It gives everything to some, and nothing to others, and it's not going to explain why.

And however successful you are, once you turn 60 (and arguably a decade younger than that if you're an actress), it becomes increasingly difficult to maintain your profile or your revenue stream. Unless you're already an established national treasure, the parts become smaller, the opportunities fewer, until you're playing what one elderly actress described to me as, 'sad cardigan' roles.

Georgina Hale, once one of the most ubiquitous faces on British stage and screen in the 1960s and '70s and an individual with a CV to die for, summed it up in an interview she gave in 2002.

'Once I reached 51, my life changed. The parts aren't there. The people you've worked with have retired or died, and there's nothing. Four years ago I tried to change my agent, and 11 agents turned me down. One told me they didn't take actresses over 45 because it was too depressing to talk to them on the telephone. I had periods where I wondered if I'd actually done all these things, or whether it was somebody else...'

But before you reach for the sleeping tablets, don't worry; the future needn't be quite as bleak as you might think. There are still parts around; it's just you have to be realistic and adjust your expectations. Many actors who no longer have the energy or memory for stage work for instance, prolong their shelf life by doing soap, or radio drama. And if all else fails you can always go up for those afternoon TV commercials for Stannah stair lifts and walk-in baths. Good repeat fees too, I'd imagine.

Nonetheless, there comes a time when whatever fame you once enjoyed will be no more than a dream you once had. A top theatrical agent admitted to me the other day that not only had she never heard of the actor Michael Hordern (one of my greatest heroes) but that she also, 'Has trouble watching black-and-white movies'.

Memories are short. Time moves on. There are only so many hours in the day. In any case, fame, as the philosophers are always telling us, is transitory. Even if you do struggle to the top of the heap, you'll eventually be pulled down by age or failing memory. Look at the number of actors and actresses who were once regular guests on the Mavis Nicholson afternoon chat show, all of whom are now nothing more than clues in old *Puzzler* books.

Who's Mavis Nicholson? Exactly.

I recall reading of the death of British star actor Anthony Steel, one of my earliest screen heroes, and a man who specialised in chunky, dependable beefcakes. He was once one of Hollywood's most bankable stars, and had relationships with celebrated beauties Patricia Roc and Anita Ekberg.

Yet he ended up living alone and unloved in a bedsit in Denham aged 80, before finally ending his days in the quiet seclusion of Denville Hall, the home for retired actors in leafy Buckinghamshire. As for the incomparable Terry-Thomas, I need hardly recount his doleful demise, one that was only remedied when a number of stars that had once worshipped at his shrine clubbed together to ensure him a decent dotage.

The story of an old friend, an actor called Barry, has always stayed with me. An actor of saturnine good looks with a deep chocolatey voice just made for Ferrero Rocher ads, Barry enjoyed a steady if unspectacular career in regional theatre and TV for nearly 50 years.

Just before he died, he told me of an occasion when he'd been summoned to a major regional company to be interviewed for a part. The newly-installed artistic director talked at him for half an hour, waxing long and lyrical about the part, the play, the company, the theatre and the city, and its socio-geographical positioning in the culture of the wider community. At the end he finally drew breath and turned his attention to his interviewee.

'Now then,' he said, 'Is there anything you'd like to ask before we finish? Are you familiar with the building? Have you ever seen anything onstage here?' 'As a matter of fact,' replied Barry, 'I've done 53 separate plays here...'

I SAY, YOU FELLOWS...

Here's a tale about getting old and how to deal with it.

Some years ago a national newspaper asked me to do a feature on the actor who once played Billy Bunter.

If you're under 40, not only will the name Gerald Campion have little resonance, but you'll probably be scratching your head to identify the name of Billy Bunter. Yet for over half a century following his creation in 1908, the original 'fat owl of the Remove', as he was always known, was the pre-eminent figure in children's literature. Never mind Enid Blyton or JK Rowling, the adventures of Frank Richards's greedy schoolboy with the straining waistcoat and check trousers sold in quantities these two other titans of children's literature could only have dreamt of.

Once television came along, it was only a matter of time before someone at the BBC decided to commit the nation's greediest schoolboy to celluloid, and it was a portly jobbing actor already in his early thirties, Gerald Campion, who was selected for the role and whom I subsequently watched spellbound every week on my parents' black-and-white TV.

Campion had already carved a decent career playing unctuous loafers in films like, *Carry on Sergeant* and *School For Scoundrels* but at the time of his being offered the job he'd partly forsaken acting to run Gerry's Club, the legendary drinking den where both the famous and infamous of British celebrity culture in the 1960s gathered to party. Here, at all times of the day or night, you could find everybody who was anybody in '60s showbiz, from racing drivers and hell-raising thesps to East End gangsters and dissolute politicians. Gerry's Club was the biggest and louchest of them all: and Gerald Campion was its presiding genius.

The role of Bunter was to transform Campion's life, and make him one of the most instantly recognisable faces on TV. Campion was Bunter and Bunter was Campion, and his weekly screen adventures made him a star. Yet now, 40 years on, he'd more or less disappeared from public view.

I eventually tracked him down to a house in the French countryside just outside Agen in Aquitaine, where, aged 81, he now lived with his second wife Susan. Campion not only offered to meet, but also invited me down to his home for the weekend.

He met me off the train late on a sunny Saturday afternoon in early April. Seeing him at the end of the platform was like stepping back 50 years – the cap may have been replaced by a functional trilby, and the food-encrusted blazer by a natty windcheater, but the figure before me was still the unmistakable icon of my recollection.

That night we sat in his lounge, sampling one of the two or three most delicious meals I've ever eaten while we chatted about the old days. Campion proved as scurrilous a companion as I could have wished for. After several bottles of wine he eventually nipped into his bedroom and returned with the visitors' book from the original club, a huge faded ink-stained ledger covered in brick dust which he'd personally saved from the demolition ball upon hearing that the building was about to be gutted and turned into flats.

God knows how much it would have got in any auction of theatrical memorabilia, but even as an autograph book it was worth its weight in gold. Graham Hill jostled with Tony Hancock, Stanley Baker and Richard Burton with Shirley

Bassey and Ron Grainer, while on every page were inscribed the monikers of once-famous names, nearly all of them now half-buried in time; including, I noted wryly, Glyn Owen.

Campion seemed to have the goods on nearly all of them – "Her? Gay as a cricket', 'He was a filthy drunk!' 'That one lost several million in a blackmail scandal!' 'He liked having his arse whipped by tarts.' 'He was a notorious swinger of course – tried it on with us once but I told him to fuck off.' Once an actor...

The following morning Campion played for me a TV recording of one of the few remaining Bunter episodes preserved for posterity. As we sat watching, his wife stood behind his armchair, one hand stroking his hair tenderly. Occasionally she'd lean forward and kiss the top of his head.

Campion loved the celebrity status Bunter afforded him, yet once it had run its course he largely turned his back on the profession in favour of his other love, cooking, an art form in which he became equally celebrated.

When I asked if he thought Bunter would ever be made again he squealed with laughter.

'Of course not. Dawn French was approached a few years ago, and there was even talk of Elton John playing him, but can you imagine – watching him in school uniform being thrashed on his rump or larking around in dormitories with teenage boys? There'd be an outcry!'

Watching Campion watching himself that morning was my abiding memory of my time there. Once one of the most famous faces in the country, he now enjoyed his occasional brief glimpse back in time, but was no longer enmeshed in it. Here, it seemed, was that rarest of creatures: an actor who fully understood the vagaries of the greasy pole of showbiz, and who'd got out in style rather than clung on at all costs. If I've ever seen contentment personified, it was watching him with his head being stroked in that lounge that sunny morning in France.

On my return I sent in the piece as requested. The editor declared himself delighted, yet weeks passed without any sign of publication. I soon fell into a regular weekly pattern of phoning for an update, and each time I received the same answer, 'We're looking for a hook. Be patient.' Occasionally I'd relay the news back to Gerald, who responded, not with impatient pleas for recognition, but with tips on how to cook the perfect roast chicken and recipes for Lancashire hotpot.

One Wednesday morning I made my customary call to the paper. The answer was the same. Be patient. We're looking for a hook. I'd no sooner put the phone down than it rang again. This time it was a member of Campion's extended family, phoning to tell me Gerald had died suddenly that morning of a heart attack.

I called the editor. This time the response was less polite. 'For Christ's sake,' he responded, 'You only phoned an hour ago. I told you it'll be published when we can find a reason.'

'He died this morning,' I said.

'It'll be in tomorrow,' he answered.

The invaluable lesson I learnt from Campion was one of perspective. Once it all becomes too much, get rid. Hold onto the few things that really matter, and junk the rest. There will come a time when nobody is much interested in your back catalogue simply because they can't remember it. Keep looking forward if you can. Rather than clench your fist, relax and let it go.

Whatever you do, try not to turn into an 'In my day...' actor. Nobody will want to listen. It's gone. In fact, in all but a few cases, it went the moment the curtain fell or the episode was transmitted. And a jolly good thing too.

In any case, you can always rely on your partner to remind you of the reality of your situation. Only recently I walked into our bedroom naked and asked my wife Julia how she thought I was bearing up to the vagaries of *anno domini*.

'I don't know what you're wearing, but it needs ironing,' she replied.

SEVEN UP

It's been 38 years since I stumbled out of the front doors of RADA. At the age of 56 I'm now happily married, have a car, a lovely house in North London and sufficient savings in the bank to allow myself a comfortable old age, as long as the Eurozone doesn't go belly up and I make sure I peg it by the time I'm 60.

So much about the business has changed in that time. Membership of Equity is no longer mandatory, rep has all but disappeared, and the three terrestrial channels that once dominated the market have been joined by hundreds of competitors. Even the behemoth of cable broadcasting, Sky, is finally stirring itself to produce quality drama.

Much, however, still remains the same. The West End, NT and RSC still sit at the peak of the theatre world; fringe is as popular as ever (and just as badly paid) and the UK still has an embryonic film industry, mostly churning out high spec costume dramas or forgettable modern comedies.

I thought it might be an idea to wrap things up by giving a brief résumé of the various fortunes of the 20 other individuals who, along with me, were disgorged on that hot, steamy summer's night.

In 2003, I was asked by the *Telegraph* to write a feature on, 'What happened to my class of 1978?' The notion was that I'd track down each individual, get their story, and correlate the results into an article: the sum of which would shine an entertaining and illuminating light on the business, and perhaps provide a few pointers for anyone thinking of setting out on the same career path today.

You may recall me mentioning the teacher back at RADA who'd assured us all those years ago that within five years, half would have given up the business, and that by 2000 there'd hardly be a man left standing. Now at last I had the chance to bench test his breezy prediction.

But how? Unless they'd decided to exclude me from their plans and had been carousing in secret, my term-mates had not had a reunion since the night we left. And 38 years is a long time.

At least I knew where to begin. Of the 21 of us, I could reach a handful merely by picking up the phone or opening my address book. They would lead me to a handful of others, while a quick search on the internet would unearth a few more. But there was still a substantial minority whose whereabouts remained an utter mystery. If the article were to work, this is where I'd have to concentrate my fire. In the meantime, I started with the ones whose fates I already knew, and work outwards from there.

One of our number had died within months of graduating from a serious illness she'd bravely concealed throughout her studies. Of the remaining 19, Timothy Spall, the outstanding student during my time there, was deservedly a household name. What wasn't generally known was that he and I had sworn a pact in the final days of our course, promising each other that if we didn't make it as actors, we'd open a wet fish shop in Pevensey Bay. Thankfully, neither of us ever had to call in the bet, though I've come far closer to phoning him than he has to phoning me.

Apart from me, only one other graduate was still earning a conventional living from the business. Three more former students whom I contacted declined to take part in the interview, for reasons that were tantalisingly left hanging in the air (although each admitted acting was no more than a distant dream they'd once had).

Of the remaining 15, one was still acting and directing in school and community projects in South London. Another, a preternaturally camp young thing from Liverpool at a time when Larry Grayson was still ploughing a somewhat solitary furrow, ended up being stooge for Rod Hull & Emu, followed soon afterwards by a year in *The Mousetrap*. He was now happily teaching art speech and drama at a provincial college; as was another female student from Glasgow, though she divided her time between acting, mothering, and running a bail hostel.

Another had crossed the divide and become a leading agent for a decade, before giving up. Yet another was now running a fashionable restaurant on London's South Bank.

As regards the Americans in my term, one who freely described himself in his contribution as, 'A spoiled brat from the Midwest', had returned to the States where he'd ended up as, 'A roving film professor'. His fellow American, Paul, meanwhile, was an artistic director of a small regional venue in New Hampshire, and was the living definition of contentment.

Of the remaining students, one had retrained as a solicitor, another had joined the SAS, while a third had spent a spell in prison for unspecified criminal activities.

My friend Michelle still occasionally acted but was now far better known as mother-in-chief of virtually the whole acting profession, in her role as proprietor of the *Maison Bertaux* tea rooms in Soho, the favourite gathering point for actors in central London, and an establishment she ran with all the bohemian élan she brought to her occasional stage roles.

Hamish from Edinburgh bobbed along for a number of years, before realising that he didn't want to spend his life being other people, a realisation, 'Nearly as shocking as hearing I'd got into drama school in the first place'. He was now working for the Scottish Tourist Board.

That left three, of which there was no trace. I rang my contact at the newspaper and announced we'd have to go to press without them.

'What do you know about them?' she asked.

'Nothing', I explained. 'They've vanished off the face of the earth.'

'Nevertheless,' she persisted. I heard the click of a ballpoint down the line.

I dutifully gave their full names, and the places they'd originally hailed from – Dublin, Boston and Hemel Hempstead. Beyond that I could offer nothing. And in case she was wondering, RADA couldn't help. I'd already asked.

She rang back an hour later.

'One is running the House of Bamboo Chinese restaurant on Wembley High Street, another is looking after her second husband's ailing mother in Iowa. A third is now a mental health nurse, living in Catford,' she said. 'I'll email you their telephone numbers.'

'How on earth have you found that out?' I asked, open-mouthed.

'Please don't ask,' she replied. 'Let me know how you get on.'

I rang all three, who thankfully were so gobsmacked to hear my voice after so long that they utterly failed to ask me the one question I'd have been hard-pushed to answer. Their stories, too, were included in the finished piece. One of them even turned up for a reunion photo shoot outside the old RADA portico on Gower Street, the same one from which we'd scattered to the four winds all those years ago.

So there we have it. 21 actors. Of whom, one is dead, one's a star, two more are earning a decent living, three or four others are hanging on, six or seven more are teaching, one's fresh out of jail, one's a soldier, one's working in the tourist industry, and three others don't want to talk about it. Which pretty much tallies with my tutor's prediction.

So what's my distillation of all this? After nearly four decades of 'keeping a large number of people from coughing', do I have one final nugget of advice to pass on?

'It's not fair and don't be late,' perhaps?

Not exactly.

Remember: when I asked a leading national organisation to discover the whereabouts of three people who'd disappeared off the face of the earth, it took less time to track them down than it would to have read a Shakespearean sonnet.

My conclusion?

Whatever you end up doing – always pay your tax.

ACKNOWLEGDEMENTS

My sincere thanks to everyone who by accident or design, has helped in the compilation of this book. You know who you are.

A very special thank you to Andrew Goodfellow, Liz Marvin and James Gill. Thanks also to Lloyd Owen, Simon Paisley-Day, Rufus Wright, Gareth Armstrong, Alison Skilbeck, Angus King, Stephen Greif, Ric Bacon, Michael David Smith, Patrick Marlowe, Robert Daws, David Pullan, Jenny Gayner, Edward Kemp, Patricia Myers, Emma Basilico, Nathan Lee, Jim Barclay, Graham Seed, Jonathan Cake, Simon Holmes, Emily Bruni, Tim Wallers, Clive Hayward, Peter Woodward, Alex Hanson, Richard Lumsden and Belinda Wright: and most of all to my wife Julia, without whom the last 25 years would have been a lot less fun.